J

His Time in Hell

His Time in Hell

A Texas Marine in France:

The World War I Memoir of Warren R. Jackson

George B. Clark, editor

★
PRESIDIO

Published by Presidio Press, Inc.
505 B San Marin Drive, Suite 160
Novato, CA 94945-1340

Library of Congress Cataloging-in-Publication Data

Jackson, Warren R.
    His time in hell : a Texas marine in France : the World War I
  memoir of Warren R. Jackson / George B. Clark, editor.
     p. cm.
  ISBN 0-89141-751-6
    1. Jackson, Warren R.   2. World War, 1914–1918—Personal
narratives, American.   3. United States. Marine Corps—
Biography.   4. World War, 1914–1918—Campaigns—France.
I. Clark, George B. (George Bransfield) II. Title.
D570.9 .W26 2001
940.4'1273—dc21

                          2001034641

Printed in the United States of America

Contents

Dedicated To
Thomas F. Rowe
Gunnery Sergeant, USMC
World War I
1 June 1902–16 January 1999

Requiescat in pace

Preface

Words placed in "[*italics*]" are added as brief annotations or corrections. Those in "[plain text]" are words that he meant to add but didn't. Mostly what you will read are his own words in his own style, which is all right. I have changed a few spelling mistakes. Words that are normally capitalized, like *Marine,* are corrected to reflect current usage. Otherwise, it is nearly pure Jackson.

Sometimes the words he used may not be interpreted easily by the current generation. The vernacular was somewhat different then. The common phrase "over the top" or "we went over" means simply going on the attack. It is derived from those who went from trenches up and out into No Man's Land. Except for their time at the Verdun sector, the 2d Division was never in real trenches. Men killed in battle were "bumped off" or "rubbed out." They then "went west," meaning, I suppose, back to the United States. H. L. Mencken (*The American Language: Supplement II,* page 594) was unable to discover the origin of "bumped off," but noted, "It was used by British soldiers in World War I." I have looked in vain for definitions of other words used such as "bunch" for his own buddies. He used that term very often, so it must have then been in common usage. Occasionally, he used a then common piece of slang, "crepe-hanger," as a modest form of abuse. It describes a person who has nothing good to say about anything. Usually he, whoever the target, was the ultimate pessimist. Also the word "slum," which meant then, and perhaps now, a not-too-appetizing stew. Probably the reader can interpret the meaning of most words from his tone. Generally, his language remains current.

It is obvious that he had a good memory or used a set of notes or a diary he'd kept while in the Corps. In one instance he admits using letters home as the basis for at least a part of his manuscript. It was written, so it seems, about ten years after the fact. The date on the title page, 1930, could have meant anything, including the date he presented it to his family, friends, or whomsoever. And, the reader will note, Jackson had a sense of humor, especially when describing his troublesome periods.

Among the things that remained with him from "his time in hell," two stand out: the horrors of being subjected to shellfire on a regular basis; and, possibly most important—at the time, at least—going hungry. Ten years or more after the fact, and those two things were what he remembered the most. One can read the obvious fear in his words that I warrant was still in his mind, about the shelling that began at Verdun—fear that, he makes it plain, persisted through nearly every engagement. Hunger pangs were never satisfied by the AEF. A man had to go and take care of himself; otherwise, it appears, he would literally have been starved most of the time. In fact, Jackson goes so far as to castigate the members of the company "kitchen" for cowardice when they did not bring food forward to the fighting line. The logistics of food supply was still a disaster as late as the winter of 1918/1919, when the war had, at least technically, ceased. The terrible situation had no reason for persisting, but it obviously did and for a rather lengthy period into 1919.

He names names, and just a decade after the end of the war is not reluctant to note by name those who failed to pass his litmus test. The possibility of being sued for libel seemed not to enter his mind. He was angry at some of them for being cowards or worse, incapable of fulfilling their obligations though accepting the rank and privileges that went with them.

The copy I worked from was very kindly provided by Mr. Peter Meyer of Burlington, North Carolina. He was a Marine, as was his grandfather to whom I have dedicated this edited version. I also wish to thank Ms. Barbara Mason of Sam Houston State University for trying hard to make life a bit easier in pinning down the very elusive Warren R. Jackson, almost an ethereal figure for me.

Introduction

This is an extremely valuable memoir of a World War I Marine, notwithstanding his use of the word "soldier." Many of the veteran Marines used that term because they were frequently addressed as "soldiers" and, in fact, were soldiers. After all, technically, Marines are soldiers of the sea. He enlisted 10 June 1917 at, I believe, Houston, Texas. This manuscript provides many details about enlisted service during that period—many more than others that I've read. In addition, the reader will find that Jackson's normal human strengths and weaknesses shine through on every page. He wasn't always in the forefront of battle—he occasionally "fell behind," and it is quite evident that at times Warren R. Jackson, Serial #122672, like so many other men, was afraid.* Sensibly so. He did not come out of the war as a hero. Unless you are willing to accept that a man who was awarded two Silver Star citations and a Croix de Guerre was a hero. Rather he became a survivor, and there weren't too many of those in his position as an infantryman in the 4th Marine Brigade.

His service was entirely with the 95th Company, 1st Battalion, 6th Marines, and he managed to last out the entire war, from Verdun to the Meuse River campaign and through the occupation of Germany. He even managed to escape the terrible influenza epidemic. If what he says is close to the truth, he might have been the only Marine in the company to have stayed the entire route, from beginning to end. He became a corporal, so he must have done some-

* I believe his middle name was Richard.

thing right, though he claims he tried hard to have that promotion rescinded. Jackson writes as a self-deprecating, nonheroic type. Based upon his promotions and the fact that he was often selected for roles requiring intelligence and fortitude, I believe otherwise. He writes his story well, though there are occasions when the structure of his sentences leaves a lot to be desired.

From his first days at Paris Island (it wasn't to become "Parris Island" until 1919) until he states, "Home at last!" this massive description of what it was like to be a Marine in the war will hold you enthralled. Warren Jackson was an intelligent man and well able, unlike so many other men of his time, to elucidate clearly what had happened to him ten years before. Fortunately, it was not so long a period to forget and yet soon enough to have some obviously strong emotional experiences he wanted to tell about. He underwent various "seasonings" that differed somewhat from what happened in the next "Great War."

I have been unable to learn much about Jackson or his descendants, if any, nor actually for sure where he originated from. His original title page shows that he listed Huntsville, Texas, as the place of origin of the manuscript. Many phone calls to historical societies in that city, advertisements in the local newspaper, and even several calls to men named Jackson leave me with no more information than I now have about him. And, unfortunately, that is practically nothing. He may have originally come to Huntsville from Leming, Texas, to go to the Sam Houston Normal Institute. It is also possible that he lived in Batesville, Texas, at some point, both being south and east of San Antonio. That is based upon evidence provided by archivist Ms. Barbara Mason of Sam Houston State University. Later, I believe he taught in the school system at Hull, Texas, near Beaumont. He most certainly returned to the school after the war. He was listed as a "sophomore" as late as 1922. His friends, Ball, Palmer, and Otey were also students at the same school.

He indicates that he had a friend named Lucy living in Huntsville and he stopped there on his way home to Houston. But nothing more is said about that city or Lucy. He indicates being at a "university" but doesn't say which, though I was inclined originally to pick the University of Texas at Austin, because he gave them a copy of the manuscript. Checking with their alumni office brought forth nothing; they have no record of his ever having been a student there. Interestingly enough, they did record a Warren R. Jackson, but he was a much younger man who went on to obtain an advanced degree and eventually became a doctor.

Read the following and I'm sure you will agree with me that this will rank among the few really "telling tales" of that period. The closest match may be that stirring tale told by Elton E. Mackin that was published by Presidio Press in 1993 as *Suddenly We Didn't Want to Die.* Mackin and Jackson were two of a kind. Both did their duty as best they could, yet suffered mightily from the aftereffects.

George B. Clark
Pike, New Hampshire

List of Military Personnel

Alexander, Pvt. Earl F. 95th Co. Enlisted 13 June 1917.

Ansel, Pvt. Paul J. 95th Co. Enlisted 11 June 1917. WIA.

Ashwood, GySgt. Forest J. 95th Co. Enlisted 13 June 1917. Was also in the 75th Co. WIA twice. (3) SS, (2) CdG. Later a second lieutenant.

Bacon, Cpl. Hollis P. 95th Co. Enlisted 10 June 1917. WIA twice.

Ball, Pvt. Albert M. 75th Co. Enlisted 10 June 1917. WIA.

Bannister, Pvt. Preston. 95th Co. Enlisted 10 June 1917. WIA.

Barker, Maj. Frederick A. CO 1/6. NC, (4) SS, CdG.

Barker, HA1st Leonard H. 95th Co. NC, (3) SS, CdG.

Bell, GySgt. George H. 95th Co. Enlisted 11 March 1918.

Bergeman, Pvt. William C. 95th Co. Enlisted 11 June 1917.

Berry, Pvt. Joseph L. 76th Co. Enlisted 10 June 1917. Later with the Chief Paymaster in Paris.

Black, Capt. William B. 95th Co. KIA 12 September 1918. Home was in Philadelphia, Pennsylvania.

Bundy, Maj. Gen. Omar. CG 2d Division.

Burrows, Pvt. Harry. 95th Co. Enlisted 10 June 1917.

Campbell, Sgt. William D. 95th Co. Enlisted 10 June 1917. WIA. SS.

Caskey, Pvt. Charles A. 95th Co. Enlisted 3 June 1917. WIA.

Cauldwell, Capt. Oscar R. 95th Co. WIA. Later a major.

Conroy, Sgt. William. 95th Co. Enlisted 27 July 1914. WIA.

Daly, 1st Sgt. Daniel. 73d Co. Enlisted 1898 [?]. WIA. DSC, NC, SS, MM, CdG. Had also previously earned two MOH in China and Haiti.

Dickman, Maj. Gen. Joseph T., CG, III Army.

Dowel, GySgt. James M. 95th Co. Enlisted 13 June 1917.

Farrant, Sgt. Oliver C. 95th Co. Enlisted 27 August 1914. DSC, NC, (2) SS, CdG. DOW on 22 July1918. Home was in Dorchester, Massachusetts.

Ferris, Cpl. William C. 95th Co. Enlisted 26 May 1917. KIA 4 June 1918.

Finck, Pvt. James M. 95th Co. Enlisted 13 June 1917. WIA.

Foley, Cpl. John. 95th Co. Enlisted 11 June 1917.

Gargan, 2d Lt. Joseph F. 95th Co. Also with the 74th Co. WIA. Later a captain.

Haugen, Pvt. Nils H. 75th Co. Enlisted 17 April 1918.

Hickey, 1st Sgt. John. 95th Co. Enlisted 10 May 1916. WIA.

Hindman, Sgt. Thomas J. 95th Co. Enlisted 24 May 1917. KIA on 19 July 1918. Home was Nashville, Tennessee.

Howard, Pvt. Penn H. 95th Co. Enlisted 30 December 1917. (2) SS.

Hughes, Maj. John A. Commander of 1/6, Verdun through Soissons. NC, (3) SS, CdG.

Hunt, Pvt. Clayton E. 95th Co. Enlisted 12 June 1917. WIA.

Isham, Pvt. Edward. 95th Co. Enlisted 22 August 1916.

Jackson, Cpl. Norman R. 74th Co. Enlisted 29 April 1917. DOW on 15 April 1918. Home was Bonne Terre, Missouri.

Johnson, Pvt. "Chick." 95th Co. Enlisted 22 April 1917. There were three men named Johnson in the 95th Co. Because of varied circumstances I'm guessing it was Carl L. Twice WIA.

Kearns, Capt. John. 95th Co. He DOW on 20 July 1918. Home was Helena, Montana.

Kochis, Pvt. John. 95th Co. Enlisted 10 June 1917. KIA on 19 July 1918. Home was Barberton, OH.

Krieger, Pvt. Edward L. 95th Co. Enlisted 11 June 1917. DOW on 16 June 1918. Home was Buffalo, NY.

Larou, Cpl. Olin F. 95th Co. Enlisted 12 June 1917.

Lejeune, Maj. Gen. John A. Commanding General, 2d Division.

Lynch, Cpl. Cornelius S. 95th Co. Enlisted 13 February 1915. (4) SS. Later a first sergeant, a Marine gunner, then a second lieutenant.

Maher, Sgt. Joseph F. 95th Co. Enlisted 10 June 1917. SS. DOW 16 September 1918. Home was Chester, Pennsylvania.

Masica, Cpl. Alexander W. 95th Co. Enlisted 24 May 1917.

Mastin, Sgt. Roland G. 95th Co. Enlisted 10 June 1917. KIA 1 November 1918. Home was Stotesbury, Missouri.

McClure, Capt. Clarence M. 95th Co. Former enlisted Marine.

McKelvey, Pvt. David O. 95th Co. Enlisted 11 June 1917. WIA.

McWilliam, Pvt. John A. 95th Co. Enlisted 11 June 1917. WIA. SS and CdG with Palm.

Mills, 2d Lt. Morgan R., Jr. 95th Co. Gassed. SS and CdG with Palm.

Morrison, [?] Can find no listing of that name in the company. Perhaps it should have been Cpl. Alfred L. Morris, 95th Co. Enlisted 25 May 1917. WIA.

Moss, nothing else known.

Muck, Pvt. Clarence R. 95th Co. Enlisted 11 June 1917. WIA.

Otey, Pvt. Laurence B. 78th Co. Enlisted 8 June 1917. Gassed.

Osterhout, Pvt. Edward C. 95th Co. Enlisted 9 May 1917. WIA.

Overton, Capt. Macon C. 76th Co. (2) DSC, NC, (3) SS, (3) CdG. KIA 1 November 1918. Home was Ensley, Alabama. Former enlisted Marine.

Owrey, Cpl. Charles. 95th Co. Enlisted 11 June 1917. WIA.s

Palmer, Pvt. Jesse A. 74th Co. Enlisted 10 June 1917. Gassed & KIA 19 July 1918. Home was Huntsville, Texas.

Parker, Sgt. Porter R. 95th Co. Enlisted 10 June 1917. WIA.

Piggott, Pvt. Raymond W. 95th Co. Enlisted 12 June 1917. KIA 19 July 1918. Home was in Long Bottom, Ohio.

Pope, Pvt. James C. Enlisted 11 June 1917. WIA.

Popham, 1st Lt. John N., Jr. 95th Co. WIA.

Powell, Pvt. John H. 95th Co. Enlisted 10 June 1917.

Quattlander, Pvt. Paul J. 95th Co. Enlisted 25 May 1917. DOW 20 July 1918. Home was Birmingham, Alabama.

Rheinheimer, Sgt. Charles J. 95th Co. Enlisted 5 August 1917.

Riha, [?] Joe. 95th Co.

Robertson, Sgt. Alex W. 95th Co. Enlisted 24 May 1917. WIA. Later second lieutenant while in Germany.

Rosenow, Pvt. Theodore. 95th Co. Enlisted 11 June 1917. KIA 19 July 1918. Home was Menasha, Wisconsin.

Sandusky, Pvt. John. 83d Co. Enlisted 9 June 1917.

Schmidt, Trumpeter Frederick W. Jr. 95th Co. Enlisted 26 June 1917.

Schuette, Pvt. William F. 95th Co. Enlisted 9 June 1917.

Schuler, Pvt. Lloyd. 95th Co. Enlisted 9 June 1917. DOW. Home was The Bronx, New York.

Shepard, Pvt. Andrew L. S. 95th Co. Enlisted 10 June 1917. WIA.

Shepherd, Pvt. Royal H. C. 95th Co. Enlisted 10 June 1917. WIA. DSC, NC, SS.

Slaughter, Pvt. Charles C. 95th Co. Enlisted 14 May 1917.

Small, Pvt. Eddie E. 95th Co. Enlisted 10 June 1917. DOW on 14 June 1918. SS. Home was in Toledo, Ohio.

Smith, 1st Lt. Clarence W. 95th Co. KIA on 13 June 1918. SS, CdG. Home was Washington, D.C.

Speake, Sgt. William L. 95th Co. Enlisted 26 May 1915. DOW 12 September 1918. Home was Bowie, Texas.

Spindler, Cpl. Leslie. 95th Co. Enlisted 10 June 1917. Silver Star.

Stanners, GySgt. James E. 95th Co. Enlisted 11 November 1913. Promoted to second lieutenant.

Stavely, Pvt. William A. 95th Co. Enlisted 11 June 1917. KIA 19 July 1918. Home was Chicago, Illinois.

Stowell, Maj. George A. 75th Co. Formerly CO 76th Co. CO of "minor" battalion at early part of the Meuse River campaign. Later CO 1/6. (2) SS, CdG.

Summerall, Maj. Gen. Charles P., USA, CG V Army Corps.

Summerlin, GySgt. Wilbur. 95th Co. Enlisted 10 June 1917. Later promoted to second lieutenant and served in the 74th Co. (4) SS, (2) CdG.

Taylor, GySgt. George A. 95th Co. Enlisted 24 May 1917.

Timmer, Cpl. Peter. 95th Co. Enlisted 11 June 1917. WIA. SS.

Toth, Cpl. Charles L. 95th Co. Enlisted 4 March 1914. KIA 7 April 1918. Home was originally in Ujpest, Hungary.

Washburn, Sgt. Harry J. 95th Co. Enlisted 4 June 1917. WIA. Later a second lieutenant.

Wasser, Pvt. Simon S. 95th Co. Enlisted 11 June 1917.

Weinberger, Pvt. Adolph, Jr. 95th Co. Enlisted 9 June 1917. WIA. SS, (2) CdG.

Whalen, Sgt. Joseph G. 95th Co. Enlisted 12 June 1917. WIA. SS. Later a second lieutenant.

Wheeler, 2d Lt. Frederick C. 95th Co. Later with the 75th Co. as a
1st lt. WIA twice. DSC, NC, (3)SS.
Wolf, Cpl. Benjamin. 95th Co. Enlisted 2 June 1917. WIA.
Wright, Pvt. Burt A. 95th Co. Enlisted 22 February 1918. WIA.

1: At Paris Island

It was June 1917. The train sped to the southeast, a train carrying boys—most of them were hardly more than boys—to a U.S. camp.

At one of the occasional stops Small, a big, husky fellow bubbling over with energy and good spirits, could stand the hours of sitting no longer. Beside one of the coaches he was soon turning flips and doing numerous stunts.

He had repeated this performance for possibly the third time, when a shrill feminine voice, belonging to Wilbur Summerlin, came from somewhere down the train:

"Fireman, fireman, save my child! Fireman, oh, *fireman,* save my *child!*"

And such a voice—who could have a voice like that! The speaker's head protruded from a window; the voice belonged to a *man.* Could such a sissy be going to a training camp? He was.

"Fireman, fireman, *save* my *child!*"[1]

Small, big as he was, was as nimble as a kitten, and heads craned out of every window enjoying his performance. But the show was soon over. Our entertainer had looked as though he could face man or beast without flinching, but that voice, that shrill, mocking, unrelenting flow of sarcasm, was too much. The big "fireman" was nonplussed and we saw nothing more of him during the journey.

Just before dusk the portion of our journey by rail came to an end. We had reached the Atlantic. Into some small boats we got, and headed for an island a mile or more distant. It was growing dark as we approached. Light could now be seen streaming from the windows of several two-story buildings and cheery voices emanated from here and there.

But our boats were not headed that way, it soon developed. It was quite dark when we pulled up to some sort of dock at another part of the island. Upon landing, we scrambled laboriously over a lumber pile. Beyond us a few dimly lighted shacks were scattered about, and we proceeded in that direction.

On short notice we were hurried into a line, for what purpose we did not know. When I got to the head of the line, a cheap knife, fork, spoon, tin cup, and tin plate were pitched at me, with an unceremonious caution to "hold on to 'em—if you lose 'em in four years, you're out o' luck!" Such implements as those? And where did he get the *four-year* stuff? We had enlisted for the duration of the war, we *thought*.

A ration of coffee, and some sort of stew and bread, were served us, and then I found myself following the man ahead into a long shack in which, by flickering lights, we were to eat our supper on a table running down the center, the length of the shack. A bench was on opposite sides of the table, on which we were to sit while enjoying our meal.

I have said that we were served stew. So had others been served before us. And such a waste of stew. Stew on the benches, stew on the table, and enough stew left in place to float it. And the swarm of flies—I had not suspected there were so many flies in the world.

The meal over, and for the most part uneaten, we were ordered to another part of the camp, into a "bunkhouse" filled with row upon row of cots, and here each man took a bed.

There was no use in making the initiation into military life too gradual, and on that night in June it began for that group. Before we had gotten to bed, a self-important soldier appeared and proceeded to set forth certain laws of the Marines, which *altered not*. And woe be to the transgressor! In unmistakable terms the man told us there was a line around the bunkhouse, which was the "deadline," and the man who attempted to cross that line would be shot by armed guards who patrolled about "the quarters" all night. That was plain enough. No exploring for us that night.

And such was the first night in a recruit camp, at Paris Island, South Carolina. We were ousted early the next morning, and specific directions and orders were given as to "making up the bunks and sweeping down the deck." Nor were these orders given in such a way that any of us wanted to argue the question.

Outside the bunkhouse men could be seen moving aimlessly about. And such looking men! To all appearances the entire wardrobe of some of those men consisted of only one pair of greasy pants. No hat, shirt, underwear, socks, or shoes. Others wore only underwear or pajamas. And nearly everyone to be seen was sunburned and disgustingly dirty.

For breakfast we had navy beans, dry and hard as grains of coffee. While we partook of this delicacy, we were given a pleasant surprise, when Laurence Otey walked up. He had left Huntsville before several others of us, and had arrived on the Island some days before. He proceeded to give us some of the "inside dope." We would remain in the camp where we then were until our "papers" came from Washington. This might be two or three days or that many weeks. After this would come our second physical examination, and those who passed it would be sworn in, receive uniforms, and "go over the fence." Meanwhile, we would carry lumber and sand, peel potatoes, and do anything else we might be called upon to do. But strategy must be resorted to avoid too many "working parties."

After breakfast there came a voice out of the crowd, almost in thundering tones:

"EV-ER-Y BO-DY who came in last night or the night before, right over this way."

Such a voice—the man could be heard a mile. And it was only through him that a man could be reached for any purpose, to be examined, sworn in, and so forth.

The second physical examination came for a group of us, and this by an expert who went over us with searching eyes, and from head to foot. He wasn't satisfied with a mere looking-over either. He proceeded to dig some. Two of us had the pain and humiliation of having an ear dug into. The result of the excavation in my case was the discovery and extraction of a large body of foreign matter.

In the eye examination, one of the boys who had come from Houston with us was unable to see, at least he did not call out the letters when told to do so. It was obvious that the examiner strongly suspected the fellow of deception. I had none too much confidence in my eyes, though for no good reason, and was disturbed over the result should I be unable to make out some of the letters I was supposed to read. When I found my fears were unfounded and I passed the test without difficulty, it was a great relief.

It was on Sunday morning, 10 June, that my name was called out to be sworn in. When the time came for signing up, I did not so much as read what I placed my signature on. There was only one thing for all of us to do, and we did it. During previous days we had been thoroughly impressed with tales of men who did not like what they had seen of the Island and had refused to sign up. And they were all but tarred and feathered before being "kicked off" the Island.

The oath on entering the service was taken by several at a time, each man with a hand on the Bible. The oath stipulated that those taking it would be obedient to their country and so forth for *four years. Four years!* When all of us had left for the recruit camp, the understanding was that we would enter the Marines for the duration of the war. Now we signed the paper—and were afraid not to sign—for four years. The one who administered the oath told us that while it read "for this period," we would be discharged when the war was over. This wasn't much consolation, when we had signed for the regular peacetime enlistment, in the navy and Marine Corps, of four years. And this matter was a source of no little worry and discussion among the bunch for a long while to come. But we were at last in.

Back home the glaring posters had read "First to Fight!" "First on Land and Sea," "France in 90 Days," and the like, and now we were a part of it. Every man in that group wanted to fight, or thought he did.

We were now in an organization older than the United States Government itself. It had been in every major engagement in which America had been involved since the War of the Revolution, and had served in scores of minor engagements. On battlefields the Marines had fought side by side with soldiers, or, it might be said, as soldiers. They had seen action "from the halls of Montezuma, to the shores of Tripoli." Detachments of Marines had served as landing parties for battleships. The Marines had been entrusted with a multitude of other duties, from guard duty on naval vessels and manning the lighter artillery to guarding the mail.

No sooner were we sworn in than we were ushered hastily into a room where we were issued clothing. Each garment was pitched at us with "If it's too little, bring it back. If it's too big, keep it." Men could have gone through the place for a thousand years without finding it necessary once to return any clothing on that score. The issue consisted of a campaign hat, two OD shirts, two pairs of khaki pants, a pair of tan shoes, socks, and underwear, all of which seemed designed for Goliath or one of his larger brothers. Notwithstanding the misfits, we were very enthusiastic over getting into the clean new uniforms and away from that part of the Island.

Three of us who had been to school together, Jesse Palmer, Albert Ball, and I, were fortunate enough to be placed in the same company, 10th Company D. We had moved some hundreds of yards away, where we now occupied tents.

It is quite impossible for one who has not seen and experienced rigid military discipline to understand what we were to experience. It was to be a new life and in a new world. It is no exaggeration to say that the potentates of old expected no more severe discipline than was expected of us. The men now over us were bent on making Marines of us or killing us. There were times when we doubted that we could come up to the standard set. We were in a new realm, with even a language that was strange. A meal was no longer breakfast or dinner, but chow. A bed was a bunk and was in a bunkhouse, bedtime was taps, a suit of clothes was a uniform, and so on.

The days were full and, as we were in the open most of the time, chow time found us ravenously hungry. But some of the food we were to receive was as bad as the discipline was severe. The bread we found at the mess hall was covered with mold, and the sausages that appeared on the table at each meal were often actually putrefying. One noon when we went into the mess hall, the very odor of the food nauseated us. It was either eat what was before us or go hungry, but we could not eat that. Some days afterward a number of inspectors, said to be from Washington, spent some time with us, and afterward the chow was slightly improved.

About this time a Springfield rifle was issued to each man, and shortly afterward we moved to another camp about a quarter of a mile away. I think it was not until this time that we received our future sovereigns, two corporals and a black-haired, dark-skinned man with a deep scar on his cheek, who was to be our sergeant. His small, piercing black eyes caused us to be concerned.

And here we learned our first lessons about drill and many other things in connection with military life. And we thought we learned, too, that there was a lot of hell mixed up in it.

While we were in this new position, Albert Ball had a violent attack of ptomaine. About the same time two men were said to have died of ptomaine in another camp on the Island. It was a wonder that more did not die.

Under stress of wartime conditions and the subsequent rush, we were to go through a course of training to learn in a few weeks what before the war had taken several months. Everything was done under high pressure, and we were made to feel that the world would literally come to an end if we did not do things when they were supposed to be done, and do them right. Among the first painful obstacles that beset our path was the learning of the twelve General Orders and the insignia of the army and navy. One afternoon we stopped drilling long enough to go under some shady trees to be examined as to our knowledge of General Orders and insignia. Everyone was asked a question or two. Jesse was asked something that not one of us knew and was made an example of by being forced to double-time around the drill field while the rest of us sat and watched. In addition to this punishment, his sin of not knowing something or other resulted in his further having to stand in front of his tent that night on the company street and study the unknown parts by lantern. Jesse was one of the brightest fellows I had ever known, but it was just his misfortune to be picked on. Nor was this the last debt Jesse was to pay for having volunteered for the Marines.

We were to go on guard. As stated, we had studied our General Orders and, in further preparation for duty on guard, we were told how to walk post correctly, the proper way to salute, and a multitude of other details that must be learned to avoid committing some fatal mistake.

When the evening came for us to go on guard, it so happened that I was placed on post number ten, the most important of the guard, as it guarded the entrance to the camp. I was provided with a lantern, and during the two hours on watch I was to inspect all the passes of men entering and leaving camp. My watch was from eight until ten, and I was armed with a stick or club. In case anyone approached I was to call out sharply:

"HALT. WHO GOES THERE?"

"FRIEND."

"ADVANCE, FRIEND, TO BE RECOGNIZED."

When the person came within two or three paces of me, I halted him again, and when I had satisfied myself that it was all right, I let him go on.

In addition to inspecting passes, I had a patrol of several hundred yards, and at the end of my beat I met another sentry. In case I should hear anyone going to and from camp, I hurried down to the place where my lantern hung on a tree to examine the pass. Should any difficulty arise, I was to call out loudly: "Corporal of the Guard, post number ten."

If it was a long way from the guardhouse, it was the duty of the man on the beat next to mine to repeat what I had said, and so on until the call was received at the guardhouse, and the corporal on duty that watch went to the post.

Soon after I went on post, experienced soldiers who had the pass privilege started leaving camp. However, they did not go by until I had carefully examined the passes. There was a movie over at the Old Barracks, and as all were in a hurry to get away, they were much annoyed at my looking over the passes as I did. I suspected that someone would be sent along there purposely to find whether I was doing what I should do and in the right way, someone who would be glad to catch me napping. I exercised special care to keep this thing from happening.

When my watch was half up a rainstorm came, and the rain fell and the wind blew! I was soaked to the skin in a few seconds. Then I took cramps, and my stomach did cramp! I had never been in greater misery in my life. Under such circumstances I should have called the Corporal of the Guard for someone to relieve me. But call for relief was unthinkable. I would undoubtedly be disgraced to call for relief on this, my first watch. I might even land in the brig. That was enough. None of my ancestors could have had greater mortal fear of being cast into a dungeon than was the dread we had of being put into the brig.

In the midst of the rainfall—and my cramps—the men who had left camp were returning. They were in even a greater hurry than when leaving camp earlier in the evening, but for the second time I inspected their passes.

The rain finally stopped, and by this time my cramps had left as quickly as they had come. Then the corporal of the guard came around and asked me if I was *wet!* Nothing between my OD shirt and heaven with it raining as it had, and then for that corporal to come along and ask if I was wet!

After four days in this part of the Quarantine Camp, we rolled our possessions in a blanket, tied the two ends together, flung the roll over our shoulder, and then went for a hike of several miles to the Maneuvering Grounds.

From a military point of view, the ten days ahead of us must have been well spent. Drilling about five hours or more in the morning, that much or more in the broiling sun in the afternoon—these things did not cause me to meditate on serving out the full thirty years in the Marine Corps.

Upon the slightest mistake made by one of the men, Sergeant Bunch cursed furiously. However, I learned later that he was not nearly so proficient in this art as other sergeants on the Island. The use of physical violence by sergeants was not uncommon in some of the companies, and this, very frequently, against some harmless offender, who often would be so badly frightened that had he known how to do correctly in the first place what he was supposed to do, he would have been sure to get it wrong under those circumstances.

After swearing at the man for a while, it was not uncommon for the sergeant to call the man out of the ranks and force him to run until his tongue hung out, while the other men looked on, wondering whose turn would be next. Returning the man to his position, he would probably swear at him some more, and if the sergeant got tired he would probably then turn the man over to one of the corporals, who in turn swore at him a while "to put a little discipline in him." Once or twice, Sergeant Bunch told me to "wipe a smile off my face," but that was as far as the correction went. Also the smile.

Nor was drill our only pastime. Many hours were spent in carrying buckets of oyster shells from the beach a mile or more away. At other times we were engaged in "policing" about the camp, that is, cleaning up the place. At the beach several of us took our first salt-water bath, and on one occasion I came very near getting too far out.

Our supper came about five o'clock, and afterward about two more hours' drill. One evening we were returning from an unusually hard day's drill. As we did, a conspicuous man in the front rank— a man who had not outlived the penuriousness many of his race are noted for—spied one lone dime on the ground, and for the dime he dived. Along with the usual curses and threats, Sergeant Bunch returned us to the drill field, where we enjoyed doing cadence for an endless period. This cadence was the bringing down briskly or stamping, on command, of the left foot on every fourth count or step. This was most painful when there were tired, sore feet. Added to this kind of thing, there was double time until dark. All this because only one man of the more than fifty in the company had angered the sergeant.

After ten days at the Maneuvering Grounds, we marched to the New Barracks, which was to be another step in our training. Instead of tents for quarters, we now occupied bunkhouses. The food was an improvement over what we had had, and our treatment in general was more humane.

In the camp was a good canteen, though men frequently had to wait for hours for their turn to buy. It was the common thing during the rush to buy, when a group of men had for hours waited their turn, for a corporal—lord of the Island—to push ostentatiously ahead to buy what he wanted. A YMCA furnished no little recreation for the men on an island with practically no white civilians and unable to leave. The name of our company had been changed for some reason. It was now the 51st Company.[2]

As the kitchen had no regular mess force in addition to the first and second cooks, volunteers were called for each day to wash dishes and serve meals. Those who volunteered for this work were not only excused from drill that day but had pretty much of a free hand with the food. One day when my stomach had even more than the usual emptiness, I went to the kitchen.

While there, indiscreetly I did some lifting that I should have asked for aid in doing, and thereby gave myself a severe strain. Although I did not seem to begin to get over the strain for months, I refrained from going to see the doctor. I feared he might be unable to locate the trouble, and thus automatically classify me with several men at the "sick bay" who were suspected of feigning craziness and what not in order to get a medical discharge.

While at the New Barracks we made our first trip to the rifle range and there fired the Springfield the first time. The days of practice there were indeed a novel experience. With the aid of skilled riflemen, several of whom held, or had held, world's records, we learned to adjust the leather slings for shooting. We learned to set the sights for the various distances, how to hold the rifle when shooting to obtain the best results, how to place cartridge clips in the magazine, and so on. We learned that there was a proper way to get down and to lie down when shooting from the prone position, how to use the sandbag rest, and a host of other things that experience had taught experts with a gun.[3]

The men fired in relays from two hundred, three hundred, and five hundred yards slow and rapid fire, and six hundred yards slow fire. When the time came for a group to fire, the one in charge of the line would call at the top of his voice:

"Ready on the right? Ready on the left? Ready on the firing line. Commence fir-ing!"

Then so many rifles firing at once set up a terrific din. There was a given period in which a man was to fire his ten shots. If the fellow got excited or was unnecessarily fast, of course his marksmanship was lowered—but on the other hand, if he fired too slowly there would not be enough time to shoot all ten cartridges, and this ran his score down. When the time expired, there came the voice again above the rattle of the guns:

"Cease fir-ing!"

And then came the report from the "butts" of the results. At the more usual slow fire, the target was a black spot or bull's-eye, surrounded by several circles. If the man was fortunate enough to hit the bull's-eye every time, he made 50. This was, however, most unusual. If he hit within the first circle, but did not hit the bull's-eye, the score for the shot was four instead of five, within the next circle was three, and so on. If, due to any cause, the man failed to hit the target at all, a white flag was waved in front of the target by one of the two men in the ditch under that particular target.[4]

We took turns serving in the butts. While there was a minimum of danger there, it was very exciting for the beginner to be down in the ditch behind and below the target while steel balls from one of the highest-powered rifles in the world sped bullets overhead. At intervals the targets were drawn down and patches put over the holes.

The first days on the rifle range were for practice, and then came the exciting days we "shot for record." If a man scored 250 or more he was to receive an expert rifleman's badge. This was most coveted. Should his score be from 238 to 250, he received a sharpshooter's badge and was still in the class with good riflemen. From 202 to 238 was the score for marksman, into which class perhaps eighty percent of the remainder of the Marines fell. There were dark rumors that if a man's score fell below 202 he would be forced to remain in the kitchen, or do other work, foreign to fighting. I missed rock bottom by a narrow margin. This was doubtless due in part to my having a sty on one eye when I shot, as at a later date I made a score considerably above the average.

With life in the recruit camp, we were indeed in a new world with new values. A man was not known by what he possessed or had done in civilian life. The question was what could he do and what did he do *then*. And this new world was one of caste and was to remain so. The man who had just come from civilian life and was new in things military did not need to tell it for the fact to be known. To a recruit of even a few weeks, the man's newness and lack of military training and ways—these were as obvious as his two legs. If a tender, unbronzed skin did not tell the tale, a host of other undeniable facts did, from the way he walked to the way his hat sat upon his head.

We could not but look with scorn on the new man—certainly without admiration, to say the least. On the other hand, the man who had been in the service even a few weeks seemed in a class apart, vastly superior to us. In my deluded imagination, and I think it was so with most of the others, these older men in the service had attained and experienced what would never be ours. Nor was this kind of veneration to diminish with passing months.

After four or five weeks at the New Barracks we went to the Old Barracks. It was of this place that we had read back home, before we enlisted. Here was the old and permanent camp with brick barracks, where men had trained before the war. However, we were not quartered in the barracks proper, but in nearby tents. And it was fortunate for us that we were in the tents, as the barracks were said to be alive with bedbugs.

At the Old Barracks I spent my second time on guard. While our first guard was more for training than anything else, the circumstances now were altered. And we were thoroughly impressed with the necessity of being on the alert. On Paris Island was a naval prison, and I "caught" the prison guard. During the four two-hour periods I was on guard, my post was just inside the prison. Prisoners went out under guard during the day for various purposes. It was my duty to unlock the iron door and to check the prisoners in and out. I searched all incoming prisoners to see that none carried weapons of any kind, and I was careful to do the job right, though one or more of the prisoners protested that this was foolish. At certain periods the men were allowed to smoke, at the end of which time I was to see that they did not smoke.

It had been rumored that if a man let a prisoner escape, he had to serve out the sentence of the man he had let get away. While doubtless there was no truth in this, the possibility of such a catastrophe greatly stimulated our watchfulness. The grave responsibility that seemed to be mine bore heavily upon me, and it was with great relief that I went off the guard the last time.

Only once during the weeks in the recruit camp did I get off the Island, this to go one day to Port Royal with some working detail. It seemed like getting out of jail. About this time a number of men were picked from the bunch to go on ship duty. Some of the largest and best-appearing men were taken, and it was considered something of an honor to be chosen for this work. Doubtless many of those who went wished later they were still with us.[5]

At the Old Barracks I worked again in the mess hall for a day or two, though I think I was assigned to the work this time. Since coming to the Island we had eaten in our mess kits only, and now at the Old Barracks it seemed most strange to go to the mess hall and eat out of plates again. There was a canteen, too, in this camp, where a fellow did not have to fight for everything he bought. Plenty of sweets, cigarettes, and so forth for the fellow with the money to buy. And there was a gymnasium with picture shows and other indications of civilization. In fact, we seemed to be returning to the world.

These last days on the Island had been very different. The severity of discipline during earlier weeks is almost unbelievable. Men who in civilian life were fearless and intelligent now exercised meticulous care to do what the sergeants and corporals ordered. One further example to illustrate: I think we had been on the Island only about two weeks. The company at the time marched in two sections, one some yards in advance of the other. The company was marching through oozy marshland, bordering the coast. Squads right about, or a similar command, had been given, but those of us in the leading section had failed to hear. We stepped into the water fouled by a nearby latrine. No order to the contrary meant just one thing, to go ahead, and we went. We were almost to our waists in that unenviable of places when orders to the rear were heard.

The day had finally come for us to leave Paris Island, and a glorious August day it was that we departed, hoping it would be forever.

Notes

1 Taken from an anonymous piece of lampooning doggerel first heard in 1875 when firemen were always volunteers and "saving" women and children from fires. In the 1930s Joe E. Brown appeared in a movie entitled *Fireman, Save My Child.* Brown being in it, it was a comedy of course.

2 This is rather strange. The "real" 51st Company had been formed nearly two months before as a part of the 2d Battalion, 5th Marines and was then on its way overseas.

3 He means "rifle." The word "gun" is generally for nonrifled barrels.

4 Then commonly known as "Maggie's drawers."

5 I'm not sure exactly what he meant by this. Certainly being a seagoing Marine meant a cleaner existence and better food. Although admittedly, there was the "spit and polish" that the Marine infantry didn't have to bother with.

2: To Quantico and Then to France

Upon arriving at Port Royal, we were met with the pleasant surprise of sleepers waiting on the tracks for us. A few hours running and the train stopped for lunch, and what a meal was brought to the coaches for us!

A night on the train and we got off at Quantico, Virginia. Here, companies were reorganized for wartime strength of 250 men each. Charlie Slaughter, whom I had gone to school with at Huntsville, and I were put into the 95th Company. Jesse Palmer was in the 74th, and Albert Ball in the 75th. All of these companies with a machine-gun company, composed the 1st Battalion. Four second lieutenants and a captain were assigned to the 95th: Capt. Oscar R. Cauldwell and 2d Lts. Frederick C. Wheeler, Joseph F. Gargan, Clarence W. Smith, and Morgan R. Mills Jr. I was in the 4th Platoon, under Mills, who had trained at VMI. Among the noncommissioned officers who were assigned to the 95th Company at this time were GySgts. James E. Stanners and John Hickey, and Cpls. Charles L. Toth and Cornelius S. Lynch. Stanners and Toth had just come from thirty-three months on ship and were assigned to the 4th Platoon.

No sooner were we in camp than we began to explore. The all-important question was what kind of place were we in. What kind of treatment did the men there get, what was the chow like, how many hours drill, what liberty, if any, and so on. One of the first sights that greeted us in Quantico was a road or a street down the middle of the camp, a road with glaring and painful signs of having recently been worked, with more labor in sight. But I was relieved on learning that outside labor and not the Marines did the work on the roads.

The chow was said to be a great improvement over what we had at Paris Island, and while we were told the drill was hard, it ceased at four in the afternoon and we could spend the remainder of the day as we liked.

Until now we had been under navy regulations. Henceforth, we were to be a part of the army and under army regulations. This involved changing the way of doing a good many things, manual of arms, bayonet exercises, and so forth. The changes seemed very hard, and like starting all over again—but we soon became accustomed to the new ways.

The first three hours every morning we spent in close order drill, skirmishing, bayonet exercises, bomb throwing (without bombs!), and instruction in various other things it was felt we needed to know.

Before going in at noon came battalion drill, under Maj. John A. Hughes. And a soldier among soldiers he was. A wound he had received in the leg at Vera Cruz three years before was still being dressed, but the observer would never have suspected this to see his tall, stately figure, vibrant with energy, stepping across the drill field.[1]

With his eagle eye nothing seemed to escape him! Though there were about a thousand of us marching before him, let one man far down at the center hold his rifle out of line, and there came the ringing command from the major: "Number three in the rank of the Fourth Platoon of the Ninety-fifth Company, pull down the butt of his rifle!" Or such and such a man "get in step!"

I do not now recall hearing of any punishment meted out by the major, but there was something in his voice and manner that made a fellow want to be on the alert. Wherever the trembling offender might be, Major Hughes saw, and the dressing down he got made him wish he were in another world, even though the temperature there might be above normal. Nor did men in the ranks bear the whole brunt of the major's onslaughts. Lieutenants, and doubtless captains, trembled under his biting sarcasm. Sarcasm it seemed then, but we were later to see Major Hughes in a different light.

Just before going in at noon we drilled to the music of the newly formed band.

After the day's drill the men were marched to the Potomac River, possibly a half mile distant, where we washed clothes and bathed.

This done, we were free to go to the little town of Quantico, a stone's throw from camp, or spend the evening as we saw fit. On Paris Island failure to be in the bunkhouse on call at any time, day or night, when the whims of a sergeant might want a fellow, resulted in a scorching reprimand or worse. Here it was very different—we were on our own until taps.

We felt like lords to have the privilege—and it was a privilege to get away from camp for a while—of even going into the small, dirty restaurants at Quantico and order what a fellow wanted without a threatening sergeant standing over, making one feel that his liberty, if not his very life, was at stake.

There was a Y in camp, and many boys congregated there to read or listen to the playing of the piano or Victrola. Religious services were held Sundays. And, too, there was a French class, though I made the mistake of not joining it. Never a day in the service without rumors. Encyclopedias would not hold the rumors that were passed in any one organization during the war. There was talk that we would be sent to Cuba.[2] The dope was stronger that we would soon be sent to France.

With the first day of September 1917 came payday. And for the men who could get a blouse to wear, there was leave to Washington, about thirty miles north. Each man had been issued a blouse at Paris Island, but they had been ruined when we shot on the range. And there were none too many blouses then in camp, so that fabulous prices were paid to obtain one. It was not until almost train time that I succeeded in getting one of these coveted garments and *buttons*. The crowded train left at four in the afternoon, with most of us on our first leave.

An hour later we were in the Capital City, and I could not have been more bewildered on the Amazon than when I got to that city. However, I followed the crowd, and with two other fellows I got a room before night.

And how grand it was to get up in the morning when one got ready, instead of by the bugle call, and to go where a fellow wanted to go and when he wanted to. And a man had to pinch himself when he went to an honest-to-goodness restaurant—it seemed most unreal to order a meal of one's own choosing.

I had wanted to go up into the Washington Monument, but went there at the wrong hour. But I visited the zoo, the Congressional Library, and went up into the Capitol. It was Sunday afternoon, I think, that I went up, to find at the top a man sprawled unconscious in the middle of the floor, a bottle beside him.

Early in September we learned definitely, if anything in the service is definite, that the organization was soon to leave for France. Heavy seabags were issued, as well as new clothing. A representative [of an organization unknown] passed out pocket testaments to all.[3]

Early one morning we splattered through mud and water to the train, on the first lap of our journey. After a day's ride we pulled into Philadelphia, and after several hours waiting we marched alongside what seemed to me a gigantic ship, with lights streaming from every porthole. It was the USS *Henderson,* and about nine o'clock that night we boarded her. Of course, to all of us not used to ships, it was strange.

The next morning the ship drew anchor and was slowly moving out. Two or three planes flew over, the first I had ever seen. The companies assembled on deck and stood at attention while the boat pulled out of the Philadelphia Navy Yard.[4] Before night I experienced a dizzy sensation. In fact, my stomach was beginning to feel as though it would cause less annoyance could I get rid of it entirely—so I thought, as I lay on a hammock holder looking out a porthole at the waves. How sickening those waves looked!

The *Henderson* drew into New York Harbor not far from the Statue of Liberty, and the anchor creaked down. The next thing, of course, was how long would we be there, and would any leave be granted to New York City. Days passed and we remained in the harbor, with no liberty except for some Red Cross nurses and several naval officers. One rumor had it that we were not allowed leave because spies in the city might learn that our ship was soon to depart for France, and the information might be passed on to submarines. Another rumor was that no leave was being granted because on a previous stay of the *Henderson* in the harbor, men were allowed to go into New York and some failed to return.

For a time I found our stay in the harbor most interesting. It was a novel sight to see ships of every description lying at anchor about us or plowing to and fro. However, these sights soon became commonplace and life on the boat became monotonous. There was not a book to read, and there was little else to occupy us. Had there been sufficient room the officers would doubtless have had us drilling, but this was a physical impossibility—though the companies did assemble and go through the manual of arms. But why were we kept on the boat so long?

About nine o'clock of the night of the twenty-fourth of September, the big engines began turning over. Soon we were slowly but surely moving out. Only a few men were on deck, most of them having gone below and turned in. I remained above after taps, watching the lights of the city and to take a farewell look at Old Liberty.

Much rejoicing was heard among the bunch the next morning when they were told that we were at sea. Little time was lost to get up on deck to view the boundless waters. Yet where did we find ourselves but in the identical spot where we had spent the past six days, a short distance from the Statue! That night the ship moved out again, this time in earnest.

The next morning I waked with that dizzy sensation again. Nor did I want any breakfast, though most of the fellows seemed to relish their meal. As the hours passed the sickening feeling increased, and the farther the ship got out, the more thankful I became that I had not decided to be a *sailor*. While we were on the water, several hours daily were spent in an attempt to drill, on a rocking boat, but with negligible results. A guard and a submarine watch were posted.

During the day, when we were not being called out for a working detail or for a multitude of other things, I would try to lie down. But of all the places in the world to lie down undisturbed, I would put the transport last. The Genius of Evasion could not have found on that ship a place that was not scrubbed down, brushed down, or downed some other way every hour of the day. Nor could a fellow play the part of an innocent bystander and remain tranquilly in one place, or in a half-dozen places, without a painful and never-ending greeting of "Move along; you can't stand here!" A million dollars for a place to lie down and never see another ocean or sailor!

Every man was supposed to have his own hammock to sleep in, with his name on it; but there were not enough hammocks to go 'round. The result was that just before taps, when the order was given to get the hammocks, there was a rush. It was a case of first there, first served, last there, sleep on the deck.

At hammock time the lower deck was always thick with cigarette smoke. The rocking of the boat, with that dense tobacco smoke, gave my stomach anything but a happy feeling. Repeatedly I braced up and said I would just not mind the smoke. But one whiff and I would almost lose my Adam's apple, to say nothing of other organs farther down.

At night the air was bad below, even with the ventilators turned on. So a night's sleep was not to be looked forward to with pleasure. When I think of the feeling I had when I waked in the night, with the boat swaying our hammocks back and forth, and the never-ending drone of the engines and ventilators, even now these thoughts make something inside want to rise.

A number of times, when the weather permitted, a number of us who had been to school together slept on the upper deck—Albert Ball, Jesse Palmer, Charlie Slaughter, and I. And there was talk of home and what we would do when we got back. Jesse was the most optimistic of the group. We enjoyed hearing him tell of his experiences while teaching school, of the fine country dinners "Professor Palmer" had been invited to, and the good times enjoyed generally. But before we were very far at sea, the descriptions of chicken dinners—or any other kind of dinners—had quite lost their appeal for me. Other fellows began to feel somewhat as I did.

We were a few days out when a strong wind blew up, and the hatches had to be closed in order to keep the water from going down into the ship. The boat rocked and pitched, and men were sick who had escaped sickness before. I went below and flopped on the deck. Of all the places in existence to live, the sea came last! When I finally got up (I don't know what could have moved me to get up, since the scrubbing got no attention with such heavy sea) I was so dazed and sick that, drunk-man fashion, I deliberately left lying on the deck a much prized fountain pen that had been given me the preceding Christmas.

Two days passed without my drinking one cup of water. More days passed without eating. The principle had been instilled into me in years past that sick folks should not eat. Though I might doubt that the sun would rise the next morning, I did not doubt that I was sick. However, it was not a mere, puny principle alone that restrained me from indulging. The very odor of food halfway across the ship was terribly sickening. Sunday night I had eaten on the boat. I did not so much as touch one bite of food of any description until the next Friday night. This meal consisted of two prunes, and it was only by persuasion that I ate them.

Once while going across I was scheduled to go on guard. If Pershing himself had issued a special order that Private Jackson should go on guard, it would have just been another order disobeyed. The prolonged misery was greatly increased by our entering the danger zone, which occasioned an increasing number of abandon-ship calls. These alarms, or drills, always came at the most unheard of hours; and if a fellow had been dying of four diseases he would have been forced to get out on deck with the rest. As I look back now, it seems that I got to the point that I doubted that I would *ever* get over that hopeless seasickness, and it was difficult to believe, too, that my stomach would *ever* be itself again.

I had wondered why several who slept near where I did had seemingly not taken off their shoes once while crossing the water. But I learned later that this was for preparedness in case of a submarine attack. Perhaps I did not visualize the consequences, but nothing worried me less than the possibility of such an occurrence. In fact, I even imagined that I wanted a submarine to stick its nose up and give us a "smell of powder."

After twelve days of attempted drill, scrubbing deck, and seasickness, one fine day land was sighted. How eagerly we looked for a nearer view of France! Although miles away, queer looking houses were visible on the distant slopes. As the ship neared land she turned up the coast. Birds of every description flew about in the clear atmosphere and boats, large and small, plowed the waters in every direction.

It must have been nearly dusk when the *Henderson* pulled into the harbor at St. Nazaire. After dark she drew into dock, while a crowd of curious French gathered for a look at us. While there were about sixty-five thousand American troops in France, American soldiers were still something of a novelty. This notwithstanding the fact that some Marines had been stationed in the town for several months.[5]

And how we did itch to get off that boat! But it was not until noon of the next day, 6 October, that we went down the gangplank and were on French soil! It seemed like a dream.

When we landed, one of the first persons I saw was looking at us from a balcony of a dilapidated two-story house across the street. The man was consumptive looking and red haired. While such ignorance seems almost unbelievable, I wondered if most Frenchmen were red haired.

Arms were stacked on the cobbled street, and we were then put to work unloading certain equipment from the boat. A little after dark the four companies that composed the 1st Battalion were lined up, took arms, and were marched to the center of the town. The ancient houses were, of course, in marked contrast to what we had known in the States. And the streets had a lively odor and were poorly lighted. Soon we had marched through the town and were on a country road.

When we had gone some distance a rank odor struck our nostrils. Someone we met on the road told us we smelled the bodies of some hundreds of German prisoners who had recently been shot because of an insurrection. Right then we decided it was an awful war.

Bunkhouses appeared ahead and, though the oilpapered windowpanes permitted no view of the inside, we longed to get in one of those wooden shacks and have a bunk at last that did not rock twenty-four hours of the day. Once the column stopped for a few moments opposite the bunkhouse door, and inside we saw men going to bed—with only some straw in a tick between them and the ground. This took some joy out of us, but we might be more fortunate than they.

We turned aside from the road into one of the streets between bunkhouses, and each platoon of the 95th Company was assigned a house. The nearest approach to furniture in the house was hooks on the walls. The order was given to fall out for straw for the beds. We were probably told that we could not expect things in France that we enjoyed in the States, but this sleeping on the ground so soon after arrival took considerable spirit out of us.

Before daylight reveille was blown, and with it came to me weird and unpleasant sensations. Not only the bugle of our own organization, but bugles at various distances could be heard. Soon after, first call sergeants—and others who aspired to be sergeants—began a continuous harassing "outside." Many a fellow's nap was unfinished as the covers were urgently removed from him those cold, dreary mornings. And it was hard, too, on the poor fellow who had taken his capacity the night before of cognac, *vin rouge, vin blanc,* and even heavier drinks.

When we were all out of the bunkhouses, or supposed to be out, the platoons lined up in semidarkness, when roll was called or squad leaders' reports were made. And any tardy offender got a sound dressing-down that was not likely to be misunderstood for Sunday School talk. The check was probably followed by company exercises or physical drill.

A few minutes later breakfast followed, and a very scanty meal it was! The men lined up for seconds and thirds; and even when the thirds were forthcoming, the whole filled a small part of the cavity. It is surprising how we could have kept healthy and strong when we finished the meals so hungry.

On drill days we had but a short time after breakfast to get ourselves, equipment, and barracks in shape for the inevitable inspection. And then it took all of our time with a rush. Drill call and there must be no delay in getting in ranks. I think that an hour or two of drill each day would not be disliked by most soldiers, but hour after hour of it, on almost an empty stomach, amid constant threats that if we did not do about five hundred percent better the Germans would kill the last of us in the first attack—this kind of thing added none to the joy of living. Most of the morning was consumed in platoons drilling separately. Then shortly before noon came company and battalion drill. Several more hours of this in the afternoon and a small percent of the men were allowed to go on liberty.

As much work had to be done in preparation for the coming of the great army America expected to send to France, and since few stevedores had been sent to France at that time, a good many days we were sent to the docks and warehouses instead of drilling.

While at this work we were often surrounded by an army of French children, crying ceaselessly for *"Un sou, un sou, monsieur."* If a fellow was indiscreet enough to produce a coin, he was immediately besieged by a mob of wooden-shod individuals, who seemed to us to have as little reason as money. A "finis" would never suffice. When everything had been done to get rid of such a horde, still came the voices in relentless monotones, *"Un sou, un sou, un sou,"* repeating each time as though it had been the first. Perhaps we, too, soon grew calloused to the cries of these children, many of whom were doubtless orphans, or worse.

And there were always a number of peddlers about: old men, old women, and girls selling English walnuts, dried fruits, very inferior candies, and cookies that did not deserve the name.

Several days we worked in the enormous commissary, which could hardly have held less than a million dollars' worth of food supplies. And it was there I got my first government food that was not a part of regular rations. One day while we were at the commissary, someone slipped a piece of hardtack to me. No cake I have ever eaten on this side of the Atlantic tasted one-tenth so good as did that hardtack that October day in St. Nazaire. Later I got a box of hardtack of my own. We also got some sugar that had been spilled. On second thought, we may have helped to spill it. We were told that a few days before some German prisoners, who were nearby working in the warehouse, had been digging into the stacks of sugar stacked high, which resulted in the whole caving in and killing seven of them. This tale we were inclined to believe, but it was probably told with the idea of making the sugar go further.

It is difficult to understand, with such supplies already in France, why we should have had so little to eat. And very, very few of the boys had any money with which they might supplement the food furnished by buying food themselves. We had not been paid since the first of September, when nearly all the bunch went on that first leave to Washington. Now almost two months had passed since we had received a cent. Most of the boys could not even buy shoe polish, and this must be provided, regardless, as unshined shoes at inspection meant trouble. The result was that some of the officers took money from their own pockets for this purpose. While it was only October there were indeed cold days, when dreary, damp, and penetrating winds blew off the water into the warehouses where we worked, mov-

ing stoves, water pipe, and everything else in the way of heavy supplies the army might have need of.

One afternoon several walked away from work, and Joe Berry returned a little before dark, drunk. In civilian life Joe had been a pro-
fessional comedian and doubtless a good one. Since the first days
at Paris Island, he had furnished much entertainment for the boys
with his ability to dance and tell witty stories. But it was a very different Joe that came back to the warehouse with the French liquor
in him.

As it was time to return to camp, the company was lined up and
a check made. Lieutenant Clarence W. Smith went down the front
rank of eighty or more men, inspecting all to see who showed signs
of having been drinking on duty. The lieutenant passed all the front
rank without a pause. About a third of the way down the rear rank
he stopped abruptly in front of me, with *"You've* been drinking,
haven't you?"* This for my habitually red nose. [*Jackson added but
crossed out the following:* Notwithstanding the fact that I was one of the
few, if not the only, man in the company who never drank, I might
have gone to the guardhouse had Sergeant Stanners not come to my
rescue by telling Lieutenant Smith that he knew I had not taken a
drink because I had been near him all afternoon. The fellows
thought this was a fine joke on me, and many months afterward I
not infrequently was reminded of it.][6]

In addition to the inspections preceding drill on drill days, there
was the Sunday-morning inspection of barracks, equipment, yes, and
men. When the company did not make a good appearance, Captain
Cauldwell caught it from the inspecting officer. The reprimand was
passed along to the lieutenants, through the noncoms to the privates.
Since Mr. Private was at the bottom, it was impossible for him to pass
the buck any farther.

Eddie Small, to whom we all were informally introduced back on
the way to Paris Island, was my squad leader. The big husky that he
was, though uneducated, he had fine native ability and seemed to
be one of those born leaders of men. Before inspection Eddie was
very much on the alert to have his squad policed perfectly.

Number one in the front rank of our squad was Preston Bannister, a fellow I never quite understood. He seemingly would say any-

thing to get an argument going. A very level-headed fellow, who I believe was also in the front rank, was Krieger, from the state of New York. A third man was a tall penny-squeezing fellow named McKelvey, who hailed from Texas. And there was Billie Schuette, a short, broad-shouldered man, who had been employed in a Chicago post office. When I doped off in ranks, which occurrence may have been quite frequent at this time, Billie seemed to derive special pleasure in calling me down. Another member of the squad, and one of the most intelligent men in the company, was Campbell, who had been a teacher in New Orleans. He spoke French like a native, and soon after our arrival in France he was pressed into service as an interpreter. Campbell had a very gentle, quiet nature, and certain of his mannerisms made him sometimes appear effeminate to me. I was surprised that none of the boys ever attempted to tease him on this account. On the other hand, he was always respected. At least a part of the time in our 5th Squad was another fellow from Chicago—"Chick" Johnson. Chick was of a most amiable sort, easygoing and never excitable. His disposition often resulted in his bad appearance at inspection, which probably brought on extra duty frequently. Another man in the squad was a half-brother of Chick's, Jack McWilliams, who was somewhat the same type of man. They had a certain natural refinement and doubtless came from a good home.

As has been said, after receiving our 1 September pay at Quantico, we went a long while before getting any more money. And surely pocketbooks were empty. Probably the lack of money was most felt by the boys having nothing with which to purchase tobacco. I think some was passed out, but if so, the infrequency and quality were such that the cigarettes were soon gone. How many times did men seem crazed for "just a drag." It was not uncommon for the third or fourth man to smoke from the same cigarette. "Just a drag, please."

And then payday did finally come, and I remember that twenty-fifth day of October almost as though it were yesterday. The money did not arrive until after dark. And it was French money, so it scarcely seemed that we were actually receiving what we had so long looked forward to. Those new five-franc notes handed us were more suggestive of baking-powder coupons, valued at a quarter cent each, than hard cash.

Most of the bunch went that night on liberty to St. Nazaire. And what was there in that land to amuse a man in uniform? He could not speak the language of the people. Had the opportunity been his to go to the theater, he would understand not a word that was spoken. In the restaurants fabulous prices were charged for food, most of which was not prepared, either, by the famous French cooks.

What could a fellow do for diversion? The question was answered as it has been perhaps in every war, by soldiers in a foreign land— wine, women, and song. Nor did the boys fail to talk freely and openly of visits to disorderly districts. Many were the conversations, with unending talk and remarks about this woman and that, who were at these places.

At taps many had not returned, and drunks who had gotten in could be quieted only with difficulty, if at all. After being paid, drunken men returned long after they were supposed to return, and a considerable number failed to return during the night at all. Far into the night someone would run into your bunk and mutter something unintelligible or swear vehemently. A vomit would be heard— perhaps from some boy who had had nothing of American drink, much less French.

Within a short time after we were paid, the battalion brig had sixty-odd men in it, and our squad leader, Eddie Small, was among those locked up. Most of those in the brig got out within a few days without heavy fines being imposed upon them, though our captain had a reputation among other companies of using with great and frequent pleasure the weapon of court-martial. And what a sad-looking bunch it was that went out to drill after such a night. Equipment was in bad condition, and there were faces that said "*Never* again."

A considerable part of the hours off duty were spent at the Y across the drill field. The place was crowded every night with soldiers and Marines, diverting themselves by talking and singing, while some wrote letters home. A short time after we reached St. Nazaire an order was issued in the company that only two letters of two pages each could be written each week. This limitation was probably to avoid giving the officers too many letters to censor. The latter part of October I wrote two letters, which I now have, and I was not unsuccessful in my effort to give the brighter side of things. While the Y gave stationery away, there was much complaint that exorbitant prices were charged for candy and other articles sold there.

About a month in St. Nazaire, and the company was divided for a time, two platoons going to Brest and the other two to Le Havre. Captain Cauldwell told us that after a time in these cities we would spend a period on intensive training, and then to the front. Two platoons boarded either second- or third-class French coaches en route to Le Havre. I have ridden in conveyances varying from a rowboat and a springless freight wagon to an airplane. All were to be preferred to a two- or three-day ride in those cars, crowded as they were.

Entering the coach from the side, one found a compartment with seats facing one another. About ten men were assigned to each of these, and where all the packs and rifles were placed I don't know. There was not even room to sit and for feet and legs. But there was always a hat rack, and there would be more room below if one of the bunch took the rack for the night.

It was either on this trip to Le Havre or on a journey a few weeks afterward that when straws were drawn I got the hat rack. By a severe strain of the imagination, one might think a little sleep could be had when in that rack, if it had not been for that supporting bar. With that thing gouging into my back all night, for the life of me I don't see how I stayed up there, only I did.

During these train trips in France, strict orders were given that the men should not get off the train for any cause. However, when we stopped for a time near whole carloads of apples, orders were forgotten. The rations consisted of hardtack, tomatoes, and corned beef. I am sure that this savory combination was invented by a German spy.[7]

And fellows could not sit forever. There was scuffling—I don't know how there was space for it, and such trips were not always made without sacrificing windowpanes and other things that were not wholly unbreakable.

We arrived at Le Havre and, sometime in the night, were hustled into cone-shaped tents with floors, about ten men crowded into a tent. The next morning we found that we were in a large British rest camp, though the British were housed in wooden barracks. A short distance from our tents was a British canteen, well supplied with all kinds of articles a soldier might want, including weak beer. These Britishers would bring their cups for this beverage and often drank until far in the night, as they sang their strange, weird songs. I won't forget the refrain from one of these, which went, "We'll go over the top, we'll go over the top, we'll go over the top in the morning."

It was with no little curiosity that we looked at our first British soldiers, or Limeys as we called the Englishmen proper. And there were the Scotch with their picturesque kilts, the Canadians, and the husky, fighting Australians. They returned our gaze, as most of them had not seen an American in uniform. And how interesting it was to talk with a soldier about the part of the world he hailed from, as well as to hear of experiences in the trenches.

Some of these fellows were very hard to understand; they seemed to talk very fast and with a sort of nervous and uneven jerk as they spoke. On one occasion a Limey, after talking several minutes, wound up with a question directed to me. I know that I had not been able to catch three words the man had said. And the fellow was supposed to be talking the English language. The companion of the man I understood without difficulty.

The first days in this camp we ate with the British, in their huge mess hall. Meal tickets had been issued, and we stayed in an endless line for a long while, when finally we got our "blawdy" rations, which consisted for the most part of a big piece of bread and the abiding English drink of "tay." This food we carried into the mess hall and ate it sitting on a bench beside one of the numberless rows of tables.

I spoke previously of the "blawdy" rations. It seemed the British were death on the word "blawdy." I remember talking with a mature man one night, a soldier who seemed sensible and unaffected, who used that word four times in one sentence. He was telling me of having taken a blawdy horse down to the blawdy water, and after the fellow had gotten his blawdy full he took him back to the blawdy stables—or something on that order. I suppose we appeared as strange to the British as they did to us; I hope not more so.

There were many things in this camp of interest to us. We saw our first dirigible balloon there. It was a novel sight to see the British do some drilling occasionally. And they put life into their movements.

Just outside the camp was a British Y, which could be found crowded at all hours. In a segregated room there I enjoyed reading from time to time. One book that interested me particularly was a volume on Dr. Moody's life and work.

The Marines spent about half the days on camp guard, and with the damp, cold weather this was usually anything but pleasant. It was my good fortune to get the "downtown guard," as I believe it was called. Six men and two corporals took turns doing guard duty at an army headquarters down in the main part of the city. This resulted in a guard going on every other day. We were taken down and brought back in a truck, packs rolled.

Although during these guard days when off duty we stayed most of the time in a dark room in the attic, the place was a palace compared to the leaky tents out in the camp. We could wander about the town of Le Havre as we liked, and the city was two or three times as large as St. Nazaire and more interesting. Its wide, clean streets were incomparably more attractive in appearance than those of St. Nazaire. But one of the greatest advantages of the downtown guard was getting away from our notorious and never-to-be-forgotten First Sergeant Hickey.

We stood four-hour watches, at the entrance to the headquarters, and our principal duty seemed to consist of saluting an almost endless stream of officers, ranging in rank from a lieutenant to a major general. When relieved from a turn of twenty-four hours on guard, we returned to camp each day just in time to miss the much detested, if not dreaded, Hickey inspections. But for his twenty-odd years in the Marines, Hickey's mentality would not have ranked him as a second-class private.[8] Nevertheless, he was very decided in his tastes. The men he liked he was very friendly toward. But woe to the private who won the dislike of this gentleman—brooms and dishrags were to cling to his fingers. I failed to state that while we were crossing on the boat, Hickey won the appropriate title of "Get-a-Broom" Hickey. No sooner would a fellow on that boat get settled, to think that maybe he would have some quiet and peace at last, then here would come the restless and unavoidable Hickey, looking for a *working detail*. It must be admitted that our friend liked to see work in progress, that is, he liked to oversee it.

When we received the first pay in France I deprived myself unnecessarily by sending a large part of my money back to pay a debt in the States. The result was that at this time my pocketbook was in a sad state of dilapidation. And this resulted in a narrow escape from the talons of the aforementioned Hickey. One night when I went alone on liberty to Le Havre, I did not so much as have money for return streetcar fare. Naturally, there was no alternative but to walk back, and back I started. After going a mile or more I began to wonder if I was on the wrong street. As I went farther, my doubt and apprehension increased. I have an indistinct recollection of meeting two Australians and asking them the way. And then it developed that I did not know definitely the name or number of the camp where I was quartered. I thought it was number two, but I was far from sure. What would happen if Hickey checked up and found me gone! And worse, what would be the result should I not find my way back that night at all?

It was like returning home after being away twenty years, when I finally reached camp, to find that the beloved "Top" had not made the check for the night.

While quartered in these tents, half a dozen or more to a tent, in a British rest camp, I had my twenty-first birthday. The day before I was twenty-one I was a private in the Marine Corps, subject to orders. The day after I was twenty-one I was Private Jackson, status unchanged, so the birthday passed without any unusual pulsations.

After about a month at Le Havre we took a train for Brest, still on the coast and some miles to the south. The details of such trips in France I do not remember clearly. I have only a confused recollection of sleeplessness, hardtack, tomatoes, corned beef, a crowded and bumpy train.

Upon arriving at Brest, we were met at the station by men from the two platoons of the 95th, who had gone there some weeks before. And we doubtless besieged these men with numberless questions as to the quarters, chow, liberty, drill, guard, time of reveille, and so on. We boarded army trucks, and we wound our way up the one endless street of Brest, the Rue de Siam. We turned to the left into open country, and within a few minutes came within a quadrangle formed by a dozen large stone barracks, built by Napoleon, and known as the Napoleon or Pontanezan Barracks.[9]

One of the first things that caught our attention was the spaciousness of the drill grounds within the walls. Surely a lot of drill was in store for us. Be that as it might, instead of the leaky tents we now had the large and roomy stone barracks, equipped with hot and cold showers.

While we were at Brest our time was divided between drill and guard duty on the docks. Guard details went from Pontanezan to guard three days at a time. We were not struck with so much guard duty at a stretch, but during these days we could spend the hours off guard as we chose; while back at Pontanezan there were the detested drill inspections, with the usual red tape to contribute to the pain of life in the Marines.

I made several of these three-day trips to Brest. One of these times I was on number-one post, near the guardhouse, again I was at the gate, another time at the docks proper, in the warehouse and commissary once or twice, and I had the post inside the camp at least once. When on the post in the camp, I was fortunate enough to have access to the kitchen. Certainly while in the U.S. service I tried to make friends with the cooks. At times during the night I won't forget how I got sweetened coffee, bread with plenty of oleo on it, with probably other rarities.

Far the most coveted of the posts was the one in the guardhouse. Among other advantages was an abundant supply of eats. And the boys did not hesitate when on the post to allow no opportunity to pass. At the end of the three-day period, the man leaving the post frequently did not hesitate to carry part of the "post" with him, in the form of raisins, condensed milk, chocolates, and cigarettes. At first I refrained from indulging in any of these delicacies, partially, perhaps, from fear of getting into trouble, but mainly on the principle of the thing. But late I gave way to the temptation to enjoy some of the canned chocolates and raisins.

But it was a shame the way the stores were sometimes carried away. Once when we returned to Pontanezan, one of the boys had something like half a dozen cans of jam in his pack, with no telling what else.

When we were removed from the guard to leave Brest, the information came from what we considered a reliable source that the commanding army colonel was much upset that the Marines were leaving him, as they were the only ones he could trust in that commissary.

Drill out at Pontanezan ended about three in the afternoon, and liberty followed for those who wanted it. When I went on liberty I spent most of the time in the American YMCA, where the time could be whiled away playing checkers, writing home, and where, too, a cup of hot cocoa could be enjoyed. It was a great diversion to spend the evening there.

I often amused myself by simply going up and down the main street, gazing at passersby, and looking in the shop windows. Sometimes I tried to talk with the shopkeepers, but I did not know enough French to get much satisfaction from this. And, too, the odors that greeted a fellow along the streets were a constant reminder of the absence of sanitation and the widespread poverty.

On one of my first trips from Pontanezan to Brest, I was indiscreet enough to give a hungry-looking French boy *"un sou."* Before I had time to take in the situation I was besieged by an unrelenting mob of perhaps twenty. Nor would they be daunted by my "finis," but the number increased even while I was trying to rid myself of the original half dozen. Every one pressed after me with the ceaseless cry of *"un sou"* in a never-ending monotone, and their spirits showed that they were not novices at the game. The purpose of these urchins was to worry the gold-pocketed American until in despair he threw more money at them. I don't know how I would have gotten out of this situation but for a streetcar that came along, which I boarded.

Christmas Day came with a grand beginning. We enjoyed the almost unheard-of pleasure of hearing no reveille, and the consequent luxury of getting out of bed when we chose. The officers opened their hearts and purses so that a large quantity of eggnog was made for the men. But something went wrong in the making and there was disappointment.

With seemingly little other means of spending the money, on payday most of the boys went to nameless places, and this, with drinking of *vin rouge, vin blanc,* cognac, and triple-x, made noisy quarters when normally the bunch were all asleep. I do not forget with what difficulty the giant sergeant, Buck Ashwood, restored quiet at night. His supply of good common sense and Herculean frame and strength were more to be praised, however, than his educational advantages. Again and again could his voice be heard, "Pipe down, men, taps is went."

And physical persuasion was often necessary to get some drunk to bed, perhaps some fellow who hadn't known the taste of anything stronger than coffee before the war began. Vomiting before going to bed, and vomiting after going to bed, were followed the next morning with the inevitable lack of preparation for drill and inspection. Dirty rifles, dirty packs, unshined shoes, and faces that said, "Never again!"

Sergeant Hickey was at this time at the height of his power and notoriety. It seemed that a man of Hickey's mentality and temperament could reach the zenith of his earthly joy only when he was punishing some prisoner, who had been unfortunate enough by the commission of some petty offense to fall into Hickey's care and keeping for a few days, more or less.

Woe to the man who came in too late from liberty. Worse still for the man who stayed out all night; for let him fall into the hands of the illustrious First Sergeant Hickey and the said sergeant did not forego the opportunity of doing a complete and lasting job of punishing. And Hickey did not believe in doing things halfway.

However, Hickey came near defeating his purpose in causing the unfortunate fellow to be more careful the next time and thus deprive the sergeant the bliss of overseeing that individual's private affairs for a few days. One of the most impressive, and without doubt the most effective, of the schemes Hickey concocted was to make the prisoner carry a heavy sandbag on his back for several hours daily. And the unique sergeant of the Marines had a most unusual drill for the object of his prey. At intervals during the day the voice of Hickey resounded throughout the camp, as some man in the brig, with a heavy sandbag strapped on his back, trotted laboriously through the door in and out of the guardhouse—this by the commands of a much-satisfied Irish sergeant. "Inside outside inside! Outside!" Perhaps the prisoner didn't have enough strength or the ambition to move with sufficient speed and alacrity, and louder and more vigorous commands urged the man on:

"Inside! Outside! Inside!)utside!—On the DOU-BLE, there—IN-SIDE! OUT-SIDE!–" many, many times.

Another of Hickey's victims while we were at Brest was Bugler Schmidt, a man who had spent a number of years in the Marines, and who could blow a bugle with rare skill. Truth to tell, Schmidt's ability to dress up and make a hit with some dame downtown far exceeded his energy and promptness in performing duties in quarters. And Schmidt's laziness brought a sad and almost irreparable misfortune.

It was the middle of winter. When a man on guard came to Schmidty to wake him to blow first call, why should a bugler go to the trouble to dress and go out in the cold wind, and walk about the barracks blowing his bugle? A solution soon came to the resourceful mind of Schmidt. He simply stuck the end of the bugle out the window and blew, and then got back in the nice warm bed. Result! Men in the more distant barracks did not hear first call, and there must be a reason why.

To this heinous crime Sergeant Hickey was the equal. As indicated, Schmidt was very much a dandy, and certainly among his most cherished treasures was a long and flowing pompadour. When Schmidt went on liberty the careful grooming of the pomp did not escape his meticulous care. Every hair must be in its place. Alas, alas, the flowing locks were no more. In the clutches of Hickey, and that pompadour was clipped, if not shaved. Ordinarily, Schmidt was equal to any occasion—if he had the stimulus to act—but now with the hair gone he was much abashed. Like the fox who lost his tail, it was hard for Schmidt to face the bunch with locks shorn.

And men whispered darkly, or spoke openly—if we ever got to the front, something would surely happen to Hickey. So many times did I hear such threats made that I began to feel actually sorry for Hickey. Poor fellow, he would be shot down by one of our own men.

There was an American hospital at Brest, and when a death occurred, a funeral "party" of Marines afforded the military burial. At the burying, taps was blown, with our friend Schmidt usually the one chosen for the occasion. And the way he could blow taps! After hearing it at so many of these funerals I never afterward got over the weird, melancholy feeling when I heard taps.

• • •

It must have been late in January that we again boarded second- or third-class coaches. We did not know our destination, but it was understood that a period of intensive training was in store for us before going to the front. The train we rode also pulled a string of boxcars. However, instead of the freight cars being placed near the engine, as would be done in America, they were in the rear. And then something happened, though the how and why we never knew. The brakes went on—and the freight cars at the end of the train kept coming, as though they were going to push us through the engine.

The car I was in stopped almost as abruptly as if it had struck a mountain. There had been voices from those half drunk with French wine, and with the crash these changed to cries of men pinned in the wreckage. Several of the cars jumped the track, coming to rest to the right of it. To the left was a precipice. Some of the men were almost frenzied at the accident, and feeling the engineer was responsible, these fellows wanted to "go get him." To relieve the situation it was necessary to saw and chop some of the coaches almost in two. No one was killed, and only one man seriously enough injured to have to go to a hospital. I recall that a Springfield rifle in one of the compartments where men were was so bent that it made a sharp V. There was nothing to do but camp beside the track until another train could come for us.

On a hill some hundreds of yards away were the picturesque ruins of a castle. It was not difficult to connect with it knights, ladies, and medieval romance. I did not go for a closer view of the castle; probably orders had been issued against our getting that far from camp. Part of the night I was on guard, and later someone waked me to say a train was waiting for us to board it to proceed on our journey. We reached the end of the rail part of our trip in the night, though we did not detrain until morning.

It was a cold, frosty morning that we took our packs and rifles from the cars in preparation for the hike ahead of us, though we, as usual, were quite in the dark as to where, when, or how we would go. However, the officers must have thoroughly impressed us with the hardships that would be our lot in our new abode; I did not expect so much as a tent over our heads. [This was on 28 January 1918.]

We were in northeastern France, in the Vosges Mountains, and soon that line of men was worming its way along the winding road toward our destination. The line of march led through the village of Damblain, a town that was larger and more pretentious than we had expected in that part of the world. Along the road we met supply wagons, drawn by the abiding army mules, the wagons driven by Marines who had arrived in this area days or weeks before us. And upon meeting these Marines we doubtless overwhelmed them with the usual, yet all-important, questions as to what kind of a place would we have to stay, the quantity and quality of the chow, the amount of drill, liberty, and so forth.

Something like a two-mile hike from the station brought us to our new home, the typical French village of Champigneulle. This hamlet was composed of rudely constructed houses, with barnyard manure carefully stacked in front of the houses. And there were narrow, muddy streets, with here and there a dirty ill-clad wooden-shod woman or child, or a bent and bewhiskered old man. The young men were away, many to never return.[10]

About a dozen of us were quartered in a small, two-roomed, mud-and-rock shanty, which had a big crack across one wall. In one of the rooms was the big Buck Ashwood. He could not have weighed less than two hundred fifty, and his voice, mouth, and stomach capacity were not out of proportion to his great frame. And, too, there was Billie Schuette, of whom I believe I have spoken. His voice gave way when the immediate prospect of going to the front faced us. Another under that roof was Corporal Powell, a fine fellow from Philadelphia. In the room where I was billeted the bunks were double decked to allow more floor room. I fell heir to an upper. In the upper bunk across the room from mine was John Kochis, who I think was of Slavic origin. The extreme ignorance of this fellow caused him to be the butt of more than his share of jokes. Krieger, a level-headed fellow from Buffalo, was in the room, and in the room with Ashwood were Burrows, a lad from Ohio, and McKelvey, a lo-ng talking boy from Texas. The bunk under mine was occupied by Owrey, a big fellow from Ohio. Owrey was of German extraction, though thoroughly American. I well remember how bloodthirsty he and one or two others were to get to the front. One would have thought single-handed he'd put a whole enemy regiment to flight. My bunk was swung to rafters by heavy wires, and when I got into it at night I caused dust and plaster to fall on Owrey below. He frequently half jokingly threatened to throw me out if I didn't manage to get into my berth without causing a rain of undesirables to drop below.

It didn't take us long to learn that our time in Champigneulle was not to be spent in the capacity of gentlemen of leisure. They were indeed hard days. Long before day came the blow of the bugle, its notes pensive and forbidden. How plainly I can hear it now, perhaps being blown from a distant part of the camp, maybe almost inaudible, blowing again and again.

But there was no time for idle reflection. Heavy, stiff shoes, cold and wet from the day before, must be put on hurriedly. All was rush and hubbub. There followed the splashing through the miry streets or hurrying laboriously through the heavy mud. Being late at roll call was not greeted with "That's all Johnny"—far from it. After roll call (which might be followed by setting-up exercises) came the almost feverish rush to get quarters clean before breakfast, with cleaning of clothing, packs, and rifles, and shaving in water that may have had the ice first broken off the top.

Then came the lining up with the mess kits for a scanty breakfast of greasy bacon—perhaps with the cold grease already congealed on it—bread, and coffee that was usually unsweetened. And drill began at scheduled time, regardless of how long breakfast might have been delayed. It was not unusual for a rough voice to be calling, "Shake it up and get your packs on" before our turn came to be served the delicacies mentioned.

In past months we had trained very hard at times, but when it rained we stayed in. Not so now. It mattered not one whit whether it poured down, snowed, or sleeted; we went. It seemed to be a war we were preparing for. Yet on arrival at the drill field there followed what the men regarded as worse than senseless for wartime soldiers. The inspection of men, clothes, and equipment was looked on, under the circumstances, as little short of absurd, and painfully so. In the four or five hours drill that followed during the morning, it appeared that some officers—higher up or lower down, as the case might be—were forgetful of the fact that we were preparing to fight and not parade in Washington, at least not in the immediate future. However, in addition to the close order drill came bayonet exercises by the command: "Long point! Short point! JAB!" Our hands often grew numb with cold, pressed against the cold steel butt plate of the rifle. I had not recovered from the strain I received at Paris Island, and the days were most trying. Much of the drill field was spongy and even marshy, which of course added to the discomfort. At one end of the field were bundles of sticks and twigs suspended from poles, and we used these to represent the enemy in bayonet exercises. There were also some practice trenches where we had our first bomb [hand-grenade] throwing. In this, careful and specific directions were given in the manner of removing the safety pin without danger to the man throwing the bomb, and also the way to throw it so there would be a minimum chance of missing the enemy trench.

These hand bombs, as they were called, were roughly egg shaped and almost the size of a man's fist. There was a lever running down one side of the bomb. When the pin was removed, the bomb fired within a few seconds. However, if a man followed instructions and held the bomb firmly, the lever also in his grip, the pin might be removed and the bomb not explode if held until doomsday, so long as the lever was held down. However, to put it mildly, the ordeal was trying to whoever was instructed to pull the pin and then *hold* that bomb in his hand some seconds for the order to throw it.

One or more times while at the drill field one-pounders were placed a few hundred yards back of us and fired over our heads into the woods beyond. Those one-pounders sounded loud and ominous, and we doubtless felt a little relieved when this part of the play was over. There were hours when we practiced on the semaphore signal system, with flags or, more often, simply with our arms.

While at Champigneulle we were issued gas masks, and instruction and practice in the use of them was taken most seriously. Stories were told to us how, upon the approach of gas, through carelessness or ignorance, sometimes hundreds—if not whole regiments—would fall before the deadly gas as though they had been one man. There was practice, practice, practice in putting on those masks. That mask must be gotten on in five seconds or the erstwhile soldier would be a corpse.

Some days we went on marches over the surrounding country instead of going to the drill field, and on those days reveille was even earlier than usual. Lunch was carried with us in the shape of bread and hash, or corned beef, and cold coffee. If the day was spent on one of the periodical battalion or regimental maneuvers, part of the time was spent in standing in the cold, which was almost unbearable at times, and the rest of the time we were running our legs off and perhaps being sworn at because we didn't run faster.

The worst suffering from exposure that I was ever subjected to was on one of these marches. For eight or ten miles we hiked through the coldest rain I ever experienced. Icicles hung from the fences, and the cheap cloth raincoats admitted the icy rain as though they had been sieves. For hours we suffered. Would the officer who led the column *never* turn back! It was actually a surprise when he finally did.

One of the most unpleasant trips during these weeks was to a system of trenches twelve or fifteen miles away. This was spoken of as a divisional maneuver, though I'm not sure that the infantry [3d Brigade] and artillery [2d Artillery Brigade] participated. Most of the night was spent testing our ability in using the gas masks and so forth. The purpose of the higher-ups was to reproduce, as nearly as possible, the conditions actually at the front. It was certainly bad enough, and some of the more credulous and unsophisticated of us even suspected that we might actually be at the front. The road on which we returned the next day must have been unusually hard, as the men were almost lame before the end of the march. I was fortunate in missing the blisters most of the fellows got on the soles of their feet. However, it is the literal truth when I say that so sore were my feet that I feared to take off my socks lest all the skin on the bottom of my feet should come off.

The morale of the bunch was far from the best at this time. One of the things that helped most to bring this condition about was the fact that a lot of the boys were ragged and the rest fast getting into the same condition. And by ragged I do not mean a little worn. It was felt that now we were no longer in the navy and subject to navy regulations, but a part of the army, and higher officials in the army were taking advantage of the situation. However, there was probably no such thought. We had worn our Marine uniforms until this time, but before we left Champigneulle these were discarded for new army clothes.[11] We had had no new tents since we left Paris Island, and now each man was issued a shelter half and some tent poles. I believe it was then, too, that we got our helmets and overseas caps, laying aside the campaign hats.

Sunday afternoons we were privileged to spend as we chose. We could while away the hours around the bunkhouse, and not infrequently we tramped to one of the nearby villages. Among those was Chaumont-la-Ville, where there was a YMCA. My sweet tooth caused me to seek this place out quite often. In fact, I well remember trudging through the snow one night to a village possibly a mile and a half away for the sole purpose of getting some chocolates. I don't recall whether I got the chocolates.

About all that could be bought to eat in Champigneulle were eggs and dried fruits. The little café sold wines at what were regarded as very unfair prices; but though a soldier may complain at what he has to pay, he nevertheless buys as long as he has the money. However, sweet milk could be bought sometimes as cheap as four cents a quart. Perhaps the stables from which the milk came were too unsanitary for germs to live.

NOTE: During the night in the trenches, so severe was the weather, and the men so wholly unprotected, that two of the boys died. This, we were told, resulted in the doctor issuing orders that the marches that had been planned weekly to these practice trenches should be discontinued.

On one of these hikes we were returning late in the day when one or more of the men became so drunk that several of us, along with an officer, had to see that all got in. A hospital corpsman had drunk something very strong and treacherous. All persuasions were in vain. When the company had passed on, the fellow was in the middle of the road, with his back down in the mud and snow, while he kicked his feet in the air like a spoiled child. The fellow seemed to have lost all his senses, with the devil acting for him. When we had gotten him up and down the road some distance, he darted from us into the heels of army mules in a stable. We did not expect to see the drunk man come out of that, but he seemed to have the proverbial drunk man's luck.

On another occasion I brought with me back to the billet from a neighboring village a boy who would not have gotten back that night without assistance. He was a very likable sort of a chap, big and husky, having excelled in college athletics. Perhaps he had not known the taste of drink until the war.

Washington's Birthday was a real holiday for us, with no drill. I can picture myself now, enjoying the luxurious idleness of lying in my bunk instead of being out in the mud and snow. And the snow sometimes got deeper than most of us Southern boys were used to. On the second of March we started early on a hike. It began snowing hard, the biggest and thickest flakes falling I ever saw. Surely we would not continue on in that storm! And the column turned back toward Champigneulle. But we went through the village and kept going. An hour or more later found us deployed on a hilltop. Spurred on by the heated commands of Major Hughes, I tried to run along a fence where walking was next to impossible. Snowdrifts came almost to our hips.

Notes

1 Johnny "The Hard" Hughes gained that nickname because he allowed his wounded leg, which had a fractured bone and was said to have pierced the skin, to go unattended for many hours, nay, days, and consequently he had real trouble with his leg for many years after. See Clark, *Devil Dogs*, for more details about his being severely gassed at Belleau Wood and being medically discharged because of that.

2 There had been continual American interference in Cuban affairs since the island was "freed" from Spanish rule in 1898. In February of 1917 political turbulence was so violent in Cuba it was decided that more Marines should land. Some remained until February 1922.

3 His battalion, the 1st, would precede 2/6 and 3/6 by many months. They would perform services in France like those performed by the 5th Marines after they arrived.

4 This was the first but not the last time he would refer to an ocean-going ship as a "boat."

5 The 5th Marines, the earliest Marines to arrive, had been designated by the AEF as a working force. Consequently, they had spent many months on the docks, unloading ships and performing other non-Marine-type exercises. Much of the force had been at St. Nazaire during those trying months.

6 Evidently Berry threatened Stanners upon his return. He was assigned to the Office, Chief Paymaster, in Paris.

7 The term "German spy" was used humorously to accuse comrades or unknowns of nefarious deeds impinging on a soldier's comfort and happiness. Everything wrong was caused by a German spy.

8 Jackson is most likely wrong with his claim of "twenty-odd years." My records indicate that Hickey joined up a year before war was declared, but that was possibly a reenlistment.

9 This was later to be the major barracks for arriving and later departing members of the AEF. Smedley Butler would gain additional fame and both an Army and Navy Distinguished Service Medal for his efficient management of this camp.

10 The village of Damblain, spelled without the "e" is east of Chaumont. I can find no town named Champigneulle in that vicinity. The nearest is just north of Nancy.

11 For most Marines this was an unhappy period never to be forgotten. The truth to the whole matter was that AEF had proclaimed that they would not be able to provide transportation for a separate store for Marine usage. And Marine Headquarters accepted the fact that when uniforms and equipment wore out, it was to be replaced from regular army quartermaster stock. This was one of the conditions that Pershing had insisted be accepted by the Marine Corps to allow Marine participation in France. It made sense and should be accepted as such by modern-day Marines and their historians.

3: At Verdun

SYNOPSIS

This would be the first time that the 4th Brigade would be in combat since their arrival in France. It would also be the only time they would be in trenches and participate in actions using that kind of cover. The balance of the war would find them on their feet and moving. The war as fought by these Americans would alter the course of the war. The French and British and Germans would also spend much less time underground. Oh, sure, occasionally they would dig holes for immediate protection, sometimes calling them trenches, but generally these would not be permanent as had been the case for nearly four years of war. The tactic was costly in manpower but it ended the stalemated war.

The 4th Brigade, led by the 5th Marine Regiment, would begin arriving at the Verdun Front [actually it was called the Toulon Sector] on 16–17 March 1918. While there, the brigade would not function as such. The 6th Marine Regiment maintained a position quite separate from their sister regiment. They were each in separate parts of the front.

The 1st Battalion, 6th Regiment, of Marines arrived at Lommes on 18 March and marched eighteen kilometers to Sommedieue, where they were stationed in reserve behind a portion of the French X Army Corps. On the night of 22 April the battalion relieved the French at Haudiomont in the front line. By 15 May the entire 6th Regiment had been relieved and pulled entirely out of the line.

The day approached when we should leave for the front. From Champigneulle, frequently on a still morning, long before daylight, the distant sound of the guns was barely audible, like the gentle pat-

45

ter of raindrops on the roof. It gave a fellow a queer feeling, but we little imagined what it all was like. The day before our departure all was astir in preparation for the great event. Many of the treasures that the boys had picked up here and there had to be left behind. They "weren't *uniform.*" Warm woolen sweaters, painstakingly knitted by some fond mother or sister, if not by some unknown, must be left behind with some of the other treasures.

During the preceding weeks the chow had been characteristically poor in quality and small in quantity. There were nine successive meals when our mess sergeant served us army stew, more popularly known as "slum." Long before this time our most detested mess sergeant had received the fitting appellation of "Slum Jim." The night before leaving there was a celebration in which everybody could take part. I think it was "Slum Jim" who had traded a large quantity of flour, which had been issued to the company to be cooked into bread, to the French for wine.

The next afternoon as we were lined up ready to leave, Krieger had a quantity of the wine in his canteen. Furthermore, there was a lot in his stomach. Krieger was usually very sensible and not given to boasting, but I heard him say that he never "got so much in him" but that he had complete control of his faculties. He was too far along to realize that it would get him in bad if the canteens were inspected and his found with French drink in it. I made haste to rinse his canteen in a drinking trough behind us. But it was a very wobbly Marine I marched behind, which in itself was no easy thing to do, as we made our way to the railroad station.

The days of the second- and third-class coaches were past, and it was here that we were initiated in the long-to-be-remembered French side-door Pullman. On the sides of the coaches—though we had seen it before—were the large lettered words, "8 Chevaux, 40 Hommes." Eight horses or forty men. But then and thereafter, the one who was doing the counting seemed always to be in error, as nearer sixty than forty had the pleasure of riding in these boxcars. With two men where there was hardly room for one, the inevitable result was a troubled night with bumped heads, cramped legs, with air that savored of Limburger, though no cheese was there. I waked several times in the night to find someone's foot or leg hard pressed against my head.

And in that crowded place, where else was there to put it! A pack might lose its moorings on the wall, or suspend from the ceiling, and tumble heavily upon some unlucky fellow. And following such an accident there would follow a volley of oaths at the pack and its owner, with some extra cussing for the Marine Corps, the French, and the war in general.

The next morning I had an eye out for shell holes and destruction. It seemed not to have occurred to me that should shells fall along that track, by the law of chance they would sooner or later tear up the track and the rail stations.

The sun was high above us when we detrained at a bleak spot. The sky soon engaged our attention. Far above us, perhaps a mile or more, there came out of nowhere little white puffs of smoke. After each new puff appeared, a faint, dull thud came to our ears. Anti-aircraft guns were firing from hidden spots here and yonder at German planes that had come to make observations. So high were the planes that it was not till after very careful looking that one could just now and then be seen, as its wings turned so that the sun could strike them in the right manner. It was indeed a strange sight.

However, we already felt very strange and out of place. In the case of at least two of us, Bill Piggott and myself, the condition had gotten beyond mere strangeness—there was something wrong, and the trouble was with two stomachs. While the outfit hurried to the wood to get out of view of the enemy planes, Bill and I got sicker. But it was no time or place to stop and be sick.

We were soon hiking along a hot, dusty road, and the farther we went the hotter and dustier was the road. On and on with few rests and the pack straps cutting into our shoulders mercilessly. Many men dropped out of line to rest and finish the hike at their leisure. French supply wagons of every description passed us. Here and there was a French camp just away from the road. Soon our way led along a valley with a beautiful evergreen wood to our right above us. But the charm of the grove was forgotten when, famished as we were, a cold bubbling spring greeted us at the roadside. Under those circumstances necessities were luxuries.

About night we arrived at the village of Sommedieue, wedged between two hills and with a little stream running through it. The

last civilian had long since left the village, and until we arrived
French soldiers were the sole occupants. During the afternoon we
passed through several towns that had suffered heavily from bombing. While Sommedieue was nearer the front, it had suffered less
from air attacks and shellfire. However, there were few houses in
the village that did not bear scars, many houses were roofless, and
others mere shells. Sick as I was, I spent little time reflecting on the
destruction in the place. We were assigned a billet and I pitched
upon the floor unceremoniously, relieved that at last I could lie
down.

At eleven o'clock we were waked by an "aeroplane-overhead"
alarm. This meant to take to an *abri* or wine cellar, and we did not
have to be told twice to get into one of them. The possibility of a
mammoth bomb being dropped at any moment certainly gave im-
petus to our movements. It was long, though, before we were back
in the billets again. Early the next morning I was out to see the sights
of the village. We were emerging into a new world.

We had been in Sommedieue only a few days when the first shell
passed over the town. Another struck on the side of the hill back of
our billet. The orders had been given that, in the event of a shelling,
our one duty was to get to the cellar. That order needed no penalty
to ensure the expeditious observation of it. If procrastination had
been one of my besetting sins, upon this occasion and numerous like
situations in days to come, I ever bore in mind the motto of the organization of which I had been a member: "Do it now!" Needless to
say, when that first shell fell, there was among us a singleness of purpose—the cellar was then the one lovely spot in that part of the
world.

A dud dropped a few yards from the *abri* where we had gone and
several of the fellows, contrary to orders, went to examine the thing.
Not for me. This was a time for safety first. Perhaps not more than
a half-dozen shells fell in the course of a few more minutes, and the
scare was over. It was said that a horse was killed in another part of
town.

Of about nine days at Sommedieue, the first few we spent in glorious idleness. It had been drill, drill, drill, in the weeks before, with
hardly a moment our own. The luxury of loafing was enjoyed by all.

My billet was along the left of the long main street leading through the town, and all day a constant stream of French wagons and carts passed back and forth going to and from the front. The sight was so new I could watch them hours at a time. The drivers were usually middle aged or older. How plainly I can see them now, with their black moustaches and many with beards. The language and gestures of these veterans in driving the big, slowly moving horses was most interesting.

We were about five miles from the front line, and with the occasional firing of the guns along the front plainly to be heard, I was curious to see what it all looked like. Two of us set out over the hill to see the show. After walking several miles we reached a vantage spot, and only a forest met our view, stretching many miles ahead to our right and left. Our curiosity unsatisfied, we turned back. We had perhaps made a mistake of not taking the most direct route to the front, but this was not our greatest mistake. In our ignorance we thought we would see an array of men and big guns, like pictures we had seen of previous wars.

In the village were a few English soldiers who were on detached service with the French. How interesting it was to hear them tell of the battles they had been in. In Sommedieue there were also some 5th Marines, who also had our deep respect. They were older in the service than we were by several months and, the fall before, had been to the "third-line trenches." By virtue of their experience we were hopelessly and everlastingly inferior to them. An impassable gulf lay between them and us.[1]

Across the little stream from our billets was the Foyer du Soldat, a sort of French Y, in a two-story building. The place was crowded every night by the French and a few Americans. I enjoyed hearing the French talk (though maybe I should say *watching* them talk, since when a Frenchman loses both arms he automatically becomes dumb). It was hard to make one another [French and Americans] understand, and besides a lot of the time both sides failed; but there seemed to be a lot of fun in making the effort, though few ideas were exchanged. Milkless, and I think sugarless, cocoa could be bought at an almost nominal sum, and a Frenchman is never in a better mood to talk than when he is drinking. However, he suffers a great handicap in giving voice to his thoughts in not having full use of both hands to embellish his statements.

There were several clear days, and German observation planes were often overhead. The main purpose seemed to be to get pictures of troop movements. To prevent this, antiaircraft guns in the surrounding woods fired upon them to keep them in the air as high as possible. And in this effort these gunners could not have been wholly unsuccessful. The planes were indeed kept at dizzy heights. So high would they be that one could look almost directly at them without being able to see them for minutes. All the while the antiaircrafts were peppering away. The shells would explode, but so high that seconds afterward there came a soft, dull thud. In the wake of each explosion was a roundish puff, like a miniature lump of cotton or a miniature snowball.

The order not to expose the upturned face for aerial pictures was flagrantly disregarded. With keenest interest we watched the one-sided battle between the guns and the planes. Again and again it seemed that a plane had been hit, but we were deceived by the distance. I afterward heard that it was estimated that for every thirty-five thousand shells fired at the planes, only one plane was brought down. The guns nevertheless served the purpose of keeping the enemy observers sufficiently high that the most accurate and telling pictures could not be taken.

But it would have been untrue to the traditions of the Marines for us to go many days without drill. Forthwith, we drilled on the side of the hill out from the village. We had drilled in a good many places and under varying conditions, but we had not suffered the inconvenience, if not hardship, of drilling on a steep and rocky hillside. However, this was because of the imminence of enemy planes. The hill was capped by a wood, and on the approach of a plane it was regarded as important that we scurry to cover under the trees, before old Heinie got a look at us.

One day when I returned to the billet some of the fellows told me that I was to go with a wood detail, for the company kitchen, and that we were to get the wood in No Man's Land. It seems incredible that I should have believed them even for a moment, but in those days the gullibility of all—though I'll admit that some may have been worse than others—was almost unbelievable. I put at least some faith in what I had been told, and, as well as I remember, my emotions were a mixture of uneasiness and anticipation at seeing what things at the front looked like. The wagon and driver came by for me the next morning and we went in the opposite direction from the front for the wood. And I suppose we got the wood; I don't remember. There does stand out in my memory a huge American commissary in a village we stopped in. Canned fruit, cakes, candy, and everything else good to eat were there for the fellow with the money to buy them. There was also a Y in this little town of Dieue, where we enjoyed the treatment given by the young lady in charge.

Early one morning we left Sommedieue to hike through mud and water to the front. In an isolated spot in the forest we stayed in a bunkhouse for two days before proceeding. Late in the day we rolled packs and were on our way again. I was going to say that this was one of the hardest hikes we ever made, but there were so many of "one of the hardest hikes" that maybe I should not begin to recount them yet. Dark was coming on. At intervals along the side of the road were artillery pieces, I think the first we had seen. Dim lights were visible here and there, where some lucky fellows were getting ready to go to bed. Later, the glare from the lights came from shallow holes. We passed through the remains of a village, the ragged walls naked and ghostly. From somewhere out to the right in the darkness came sounds of heavy explosions. These, with the hollow rattle of French wagons hurrying over the rocky road, brought a vague fear of impending disaster. On and on we went. The straps of our heavy packs now cut mercilessly into our shoulders, and we began to have something of a feeling of "Let come what will."

It was probably about midnight that we left the road and wagon train to our right to enter the end of a shallow ditch or trench. Single file we moved along, our rifles slung over our shoulders and the gas masks at alert on our chests. The trench got deeper with an occasional turn to the right or left. Now it was about waist deep. Every moment I expected to get the order to halt for the night and provide for ourselves with some sort of shelter by digging into the side of the muddy trench. A fine prospect for a place to sleep that night! I kept an eye open for a hole that someone before us had dug, but

I must have come to the conclusion that those who preceded us had slept in the middle of the exposed and muddy trench.

After following the trench in the inky darkness for several hundred yards, through a low, flat area, the line made a turn to the left up a hill. Steps had been cut into the slope and up and up we went, with no relief from the ton of lead on our backs. The sides of the trench grew higher. A few feet we walked on a ladderlike "duck" board and then another step higher to another level.

After an age we appeared to be near the top of the hill. The column left the trench to follow a path on the surface of the hill, and there was a rest at last. For some minutes there were great explosions about us and in the valley below. We knew not whether they were occasioned by the firing of our own guns, or the bursting of enemy shells. I wondered if any moment might not be my last. In fact, there was only one thing I was sure of then—that I did not occupy the most enviable spot in the world.

A few minutes' rest and we were on our way and soon in a trench again. After a maze of turns we came to a dimly lighted opening at the left of the trench. A steep flight of stairs led to what appeared to be a *room* below! And forty feet down was an oblong room, running parallel to the trench above. The place was roughly boxcar shaped. With a low ceiling the room was about four feet wide by fifty or sixty feet long.[2] Running the length of the room, and on the side opposite where we entered, was a double-tiered row of bunks nailed to the floor and wall. These consisted of a board frame with some improvised wire nailed to them for springs. I think there was not even a makeshift of a mattress, but it had been a glorious surprise to find this room below, protected from the weather and shells.

There was smoke in the room, but I think never in my life did I welcome plain, ordinary smoke, which came from the fire in the small stove in one end of the room. The French, whom we were relieving, had built the fire, but where they got the wood, or how, we never learned.

At the opposite end of the dugout from the stairway by which we entered was a second entrance by the stairs. Thereafter, at the head of these stairs, a sentry was on duty each night. In case the guard saw a green flare go up anywhere that meant gas, or if he heard the cry of gas, smelled it himself, of if for any reason whatsoever the man standing watch thought there might be gas anywhere on our sector, he was to wake all those sleeping below with the greatest possible haste by crying, "GAS!" The sleepyheads—and there were always among us some fortunate fellows who could sleep regardless of the circumstances—had to be roused by more vigorous means. It was not uncommon for a man to be waked by someone hurriedly placing his mask on him.

As has been stated, detailed information had been given us as to the horrors of gas and known means of combating it. When the gas alarm was given, or gas came over *without* warning, woe to the man who did not get his mask on in those precious God-given five seconds! Our first "gas attack" I do not remember, but a host of general impressions filled my memory of what followed some of those early gas alarms. Far in the night, when a fellow was in a deep sleep, maybe dreaming of feather beds and chocolates "back in the Good Old U.S.," a sudden cry electrified the air.

"G-A-S—G-A-S!"

This followed by muffled cries of "Gas, gas!" from men with their masks already on, and passing the cry along to be sure all waked. And when the alarm was heard we were *to hold our breath,* and get on the mask in minimum time, pulling the elastic straps back over the head, inserting the rubber mouthpiece through which a fellow was to try to breathe, adjusting the almost unbearable nosepiece, and feeling the mask to make sure it fitted closely about the face and under the chin. And "speed" was the watchword. A number of times it happened that after the men had worn their masks for some minutes, the startling discovery was made that some fellow was still sleeping! I want to laugh now when I picture the startled face, with bulging eyes, and the feverish haste of the late waker in putting on his mask.

I doubt if there was a night that we were not waked at least once with the gas alarm. And the orders were to keep on the mask until an officer said to take it off. If this command had been strictly adhered to, some of the personnel of the AEF would be wearing a gas mask today. It was a "court-martial" offense to take off the mask before an order, but I never knew of a man's being punished for disobeying the order. At times during the war I kept on my gas mask for an hour or more, and on another front I wore the mask for about three hours. The discomfort was so great when kept on for very long that it was a common thing for a man to remove the mask in sheer desperation, little knowing, and sometimes not caring much, what the consequences might be. I can see the fellows after the alarm had been given. Some were so foolish as to try to sleep with the mask on their faces and the pinching nosepiece squeezing the nose. Others attempted to talk, but this was almost as hopeless as sleeping. A mouthful of mush and a person could have talked about as well. All looked like as many owls, as they sat on their bunks, the eyepieces growing misty, or groped about looking for something that would likely not be found.

Nor were the gas alarms confined to the night. There were a number of Frenchmen on the hill for various purposes, for the most part to advise their younger brothers in the delightful art of killing. These veterans were much amused at the frequency with which gas alarms were given and the consequent placing on of the masks. An American might be standing by one of the veteran French when the cry was heard, and of course the American's mask went on without delay. Meanwhile, the Frenchman swung his arms in disapproval, with *"Pas gaz."* ["No gas."]

Our officers had been misinformed, and this misinformation had been passed on to very credulous men. Earlier in the war, when a gentle wind blew toward the enemy trench, and with other conditions suitable, sometimes great containers of gas were turned loose to pass over the trenches beyond, and if the men were caught unawares, or unprepared, they went down to a terrible death. However, if the system of gassing was in use at all at this time, the method was infrequently used. Instead, shells were thrown over and contained only enough explosives to break the shell and release the liquid, which immediately formed a gas. This gas, being heavier than air, was not quick to drift away, unless taken by the wind. The mistake we made was failing to realize that even if a gas shell burst several hundred yards away, only a miracle would make it destructive to those so far distant.

But these facts dawned on us only gradually. A man goes on guard at the front for the first time, and because he sees a green flare go up half a mile or more away, everybody in his vicinity is waked to put on the mask. On the other hand, no such flare may go up, but a shell falls that sounds like a gas shell is supposed to sound. The guard goes to thinking. The more he meditates, the more he is inclined to feel that a deadly gas attack has come to snuff out the lives of all it was his duty to protect. The result is a cry of gas, and the green flare is shot up, so that miles along the front men may be waked because one private on watch imagines a gas shell fell. But a few days after our arrival on the hill we began to realize that there was a lot of bunk in the gas "attacks" and we acted accordingly.

Our first impressions of our dugout were by far the best. A leak developed near my bunk, if not on the edge of it. Most of the day, not to mention the night, the dugout was very dark. Lights were never in greater demand than then. Someone was continually stumbling around in the dark looking for something that he seldom found. It was Bennie Wolf, I think, who paid five francs for a used candle, and he would have had no trouble selling it for several times that amount. Almost a dollar he paid, when back home he could have purchased two or three like it for one nickel. About noon, a thin faint ray of light fell by my bunk, coming down the stairway, but it was very dim and soon was gone.

It was while on that hill, several miles from the historic town of Verdun, that we learned that the world was made of mud and *was* mud. We thought we had seen and been in mud before, but not so. Mud, mud, mud! Everything everywhere was covered with mud. There was mud on our hands, mud on our helmets, mud on our faces, mud on our uniforms, and mud on our shoes. It was impossible to get away from or to forget that abiding, clinging, sticky mud. Possibly fifty yards down the trench were a couple of French soldiers on an observation post, and they were almost spotless. We could not understand it. However, they had had several years practice in learning how to dodge the mud. By this time most of us had concluded it was "an awful war" and weren't indisposed to our part in it coming to an end.

The French soldiers referred to had a telescope and could look far over into enemy territory. Often when we had leisure during the day—and the only thing there was more of than leisure was the omnipresent, sticky, sloppy mud—we went down to parley with these men. As intimated before, we were not averse to information as to when the war would end. We got the idea that, as veteran French, these fellows would know something about it—an answer that came quickly and spontaneously, and in the most matter-of-fact manner.

"Dix ans."

Ten more years of that war. If not reassuring, the reply was at least impressive. And this probably gave a fair index to the attitude of the average Frenchman. For nearly four years they had been in it. They'd had war, war—nothing but war. Under such circumstances it was easy to imagine that the war would last until the end of time.

The all-important question here, as it had been for the past eight or nine months, was something to eat. Our troubles in the past had for the most part ended when, or if, the cooks got the rations to cook. Now the big problem was getting the food up to the line to the men after it was cooked. The 95th Company kitchen was over the hill, nearly a mile away, in a shack half above- and half below ground.

Before daylight each morning a chow detail was called out. What a *glorious* feeling it was to spend half the night digging in the rocks on some new trenches, and then after a very few hours' sleep to hear someone call down into the dugout from the trench above:

"Jack! Jack! *Jackson!* Chow detail."

By home standards my bunk, which consisted of a blanket or two on some chicken wire, would not have been considered overly inviting. But when big Buck Ashwood's voice said to come out, that bunk was heaven then. And out into the darkness went the reluctant and more than likely grumbling unlucky ones of the ration detail.

The meal consisted of Marine-regulation war coffee—there was a lot of speculation as to the kind of bark, or acorn, or weed used in making the coffee—punk, and stew. Be it said, however, that "stew" was a misnomer and, to say the least, a most dignified appellation to attach to the sumptuous combination of water, potatoes, dirt, and meat that had probably seen many, many moons while in cold storage. And our beloved mess sergeant, "Slum Jim," regarded table salt as a kind of unnecessary luxury. However, at times he put a little salt into what he—shall I say, "cooked"?

The coffee and slum were put in large cans for carrying, while the roundish flat loaves of French bread had a string run through them, like so many buttons on a thread. And there was little danger of the string cutting through the bread and letting the loaves fall. The texture of French war bread was such that those loaves could undergo a variety of abuses not ordinarily expected of bread and the loaves remained quite unimpaired.

And then the ordeal began, for getting that chow back to the dugout was a struggle. The cans of slum and coffee were suspended from the middle of a specially made pole, a man at each end. And it was a task for two men to carry a swinging can through a narrow trench, thick with mud on both sides. Up a step here, a duckboard missing from the bottom of the trench there, abrupt turns in the trench where it was almost impossible for the two men to maneuver that long pole and the can of slum or coffee so that the turn could be made without a disaster. Sometimes the men would leave the trench to carry the rations on the more exposed surface, but a shell would hit somewhere around and they quickly sought the trench again.

When the chow finally got to the company, it was usually at the entrance of Buck's dugout that the bunch lined up with the mess kits to be served. Buck and "Happy" Summerlin, whom we met back near Atlanta and surprised most of us greatly by becoming a sergeant, gave out the chow. And while it was a big job for half a dozen men to bring in the rations, 250 hungry men certainly made short work of it. A thin slice or two of bread and hardly enough slum to cover the bottom of the mess pan was a slim showing for a meal. And there was always a clamor for seconds, but few were so fortunate as to get any. Since Buck was the biggest, he had the biggest stomach, and there were many complaints of the chow he took for himself to fill that stomach.

Several nights while we were quartered in this dugout, working parties were sent to dig reserve trenches. On at least one occasion I went along with possibly two dozen others who had been drafted into the work. Those who had dug before us had at least gotten down into the rock, and it was almost solid rock. Down would a pick come through the pitch darkness, with frequently nothing more than possible sparks to show for the effort. A light of some kind would have greatly facilitated the digging—if those rocks could be gotten around—but a light of any kind would have been a bold invitation to the Germans to start shelling that spot. The men regarded the effort as virtually wasted, and it is not unjust to say that they spared as much effort as circumstances would allow.

One night while we were digging, the report came that the Germans were making a raid and had broken through the line. We immediately picked up our rifles, which we carried with us at all times, and dropped back to the main trench a few yards away to wait for the raiders should they come our way. Maybe I was a little slow in moving to the rear. At any rate, just as I was about to drop into the trench Bill Bergeman mistook me for a German and had his gun leveled on me ready to shoot. I recognized him in time to holler at him and save myself from getting a load of the thirty-thirty [sic] rifle.

There was evidence of "cold feet." I spoke of Billie Schuette contracting a very weak voice while were back at Champigneulle. He now lost his voice entirely and spoke only in whispers. Several of the men were so sure that Billie was faking that they told him so. Then Schuette made a great show of anger. In case of a gas attack, or any other kind of attack for that matter, there was no good in having a man on guard who couldn't or wouldn't talk, so Schuette was sent back to a base hospital. Months afterward the report came in that he'd admitted playing voiceless to get out of the war.

One night we were hurried out of our bunks to stop a German raid. We always slept with everything on but our shoes and puttees. Some did not even take these off. Following the word, shoes were laced with feverish haste and puttees wrapped any way so they would not come down. The rifles, which we had kept loaded and locked since coming to the front, were grabbed and bayonets fixed. We followed a trench down toward the bottom of the hill and on the double. It was just before daybreak and there was considerable artillery fire. We waited, but no Germans came our way. On a subsequent occasion as well, we came speedily out of our dugouts a little before dawn and "stood by" for a time, to return in a few minutes to our bunks.

I spoke of our sleeping with our clothes on. Our masks we kept on us, too, day and night, at the alert position. Wearing the mask reminded me of the stocks used by New Englanders in the early days to punish offenders. The big, clumsy mask rested on the chest, a few inches under the chin. A strap ever pulling down from the back of the neck held up the mask, and a string attached to both sides of the mask ran around the body to keep the mask from flopping about.

The result was whenever and wherever a fellow went he was thoroughly weighted down from tip to toe. The heavy steel helmet on his head, the ever-present Springfield rifle, the aforementioned gas mask, one hundred rounds of ammunition in his belt bearing down heavily upon his hips, and the ponderous hobnail shoes, with an incalculable trench gumbo enveloping them—the carrying of this load in the cold and wet, frequently staying up most of the night, digging trenches and what not, well, a fellow didn't want another war after that one.

As the only water supply was at the foot of the far side of the hill, near the company kitchen, water was indeed a scarce article with us. Naturally, bathing seemed out of the question with our bunch. However, I got into my head that I wanted to take a bath, and so I set out. The spring where I performed my ablutions was on the side exposed to German view, and while I prepared my toilet I could not but reflect what a nice situation I would be in should the Germans decide to throw over some shells in my direction, or, worse, should an attack be made. No shell struck closer than a few hundred yards away. If the Germans had the pleasure and the honor of seeing me just then, they doubtless saved their ammunition because of the realization that I very much needed the bath. A few days later a shell made a direct hit on a company kitchen a short distance from where I had done my washing.

One night a patrol of about thirty men went down to look over No Man's Land. A box barrage was thrown over, and when a check was made after the return of the patrol, Corporal Toth was missing.

Toth was an Austrian [Hungarian] who had served in the German army, later in the German navy, and while his boat was docked in New York he deserted, and later enlisted in the Marines. At this time he had been in the service a number of years. Toth was a peculiar fellow, in appearance and manner, and he had not been a favorite. Following the return of the patrol, as he was the only one missing, the battalion commander [Hughes], among others, suspected that Toth was a spy and had gone to the enemy trenches.

However, a lieutenant of the company, Joe Gargan, able and courageous, had a conviction otherwise. He asked for volunteers for a trip to No Man's Land to try to find Toth. Three of us, I think it was, prepared to go on the mission just at daybreak.

At this point the line passed through the outskirts of the shattered village of Trésauvaux. Although there was an overhanging fog, by the time we were ready to issue out into that sea of barbed wire entanglements, it was almost daylight and the lieutenant questioned the wisdom of leaving at that time.

But we went, the lieutenant leading the way. We proceeded in the direction of an isolated blockhouse. About 150 yards out we came to a fence, and beyond it, among some straggling brush, was the body of Toth. He lay on his back, his knees drawn toward his body, and on his ashen face and ears were dried splotches of blood. His mask was out, held by stiffened hands, as though he had been in the act of putting on the mask when he died.

There in No Man's Land that morning I viewed the first corpse I ever saw out of a casket. But we lost little time then in thinking the situation over. It was no small task for two or even three of us at a time to carry back the stiff and lifeless body through the tangles of wire.

When we returned to the company it was nearly chow time. No water, and when the bunch was ready to eat there was still blood on my hands. The spring was too long and muddy a walk, and in eating that bread and slum my stomach had a hard fight to keep in its normal position.

The day after we arrived at the dugout was Easter, and the remark was made what an inglorious Easter. Nine days later we relieved those on the front line, down near the base of the hill, at Trésauvaux. Only one or two platoons occupied the front line proper, however, as the remainder of us were in a wide, comparatively shallow trench a third of the way up the hill. Our bombproof dugout on the hill now gave way to a home that was only part of a trench, widened and covered with metal roofing and possibly a foot of dirt. If a shell made a direct hit now—good night! The dugout contained narrow, double-decked bunks, but as more of us occupied a sector than there had been of the French, there weren't enough bunks to go around.[3]

I've mentioned some mud we encountered. It is not possible to give a fair conception of that bottomless mud, which covered the face of the earth and adhered tenaciously to everything with which it came in contact. Everything was grimy mud—hands, faces, uniforms, and rifles.

A short distance from our own shelter was the officers' bombproof dugout, and the exit opened into the trench and faced the enemy lines. It was at this dugout that three of us took turns at watch, two hours on and four hours off. The other two were Chick Johnson and Finck. We later changed the watch to four on and eight off, which proved more convenient. Things would have gone along well enough had Johnson not gotten sick and been evacuated to a hospital. And it was decided that no one else could be spared to take his place. Consequently, Finck and I alternated guarding the officers' dugout, six hours on and six off. To one who had not tried it, or could not visualize the conditions, a guard of six hours, followed by six hours of sleep and leisure, might not sound unpromising. But the five or six days that Finck and I had the dugout guard were, in some respects, the worst I ever spent.

During the night the near-freezing temperature would not have been so near unbearable but for the humidity of the atmosphere. The night air fairly reeked with moisture and cut to the bone. And the mud!

Our chief duty consisted of noting any shells that fell in that vicinity and reporting them to Captain "Goophy" Cauldwell. He could nearly always be depended upon to be far back in his dugout, and it was said that he and Lieutenant Mills, whose duties also kept him inside, were half drunk much of the time. Just what was the captain's object in having reported to him the fall of the shells, I did not know. We were to be particularly on the lookout for gas shells, and it was explained to us the difference in the sound made by the unseen gasser hurtling through the air and any other shell. To this day I don't know whether the difference was real or imaginary. However, with a little experience there was no mistaking the dull thud of an explosion of a gas shell. A number of times the captain urged me to remain just within the entrance of the dugout, but for some reason I didn't spend much time there.

When the end of the watch came, sleep was the next thing in order. In the morning I came off guard about ten or eleven o'clock, and as the men had been up most of the night, all were sleeping. But there were not enough bunks for all, and I recall a number of times when I had gotten off duty there was not a bunk for me. One or more times I found an empty bunk, and when I had gotten into heavenly sleep the owner came along and demanded possession. Under such circumstances, if any sleeping was to be done, there was no alternative but to flop on the floor, which was scarcely less of a miry mass than the trench outside the dugout. When I came off guard at night most of the bunks were empty, but too often there was a "standby" alarm, a no-sleeping order, or I was welcomed with some other sleep chaser.

The result was that when I went on post again it was almost impossible to stay awake. We had been told the dire consequences for a man found asleep while on guard at the front. Notwithstanding the prospect of the death penalty that would follow, again and again during those endless hours I would try to drive off sleep by walking rapidly to and fro in the trench before the dugout entrance. Even these quickened movements sometimes did not rouse me from my semistupor. I even tried pinching myself severely, but my very nerves seemed dead. Notwithstanding the sleep preventatives, I feared that before I was done with the guard I would commit the unpardonable crime of going to sleep on post. I was fortunate enough at least to stay wide enough awake to remain on my feet.

I cannot leave the subject of the dugout watch on the Verdun Front without a few parting words concerning my co-worker and sufferer in the mutual sorrow—Private Finck. Finck was absolutely and unqualifiedly the most pessimistic being I ever heard of. And it was he whom I had to cheer me when going on and off this six-on, six-off watch. I veritably believe that had Finck been handed a check for a million dollars he would have complained that the amount was not ten million or that the donor had not cashed the check for him in the first place. Before entering the Marine Corps he had been connected, in some capacity, with the newspaper business, and he showed traces of a man of rare ability. But booze had burned him out, body and mind.

One of the things that made this guard so trying was the scarcity of food. While it is common knowledge that a good meal makes one feel better, it was not till then that I realized what a difference comes in a man's spirits when a stomach long empty has been filled. A number of times while I was on guard my friend Finck relieved me long enough for me to get some stew, French bread, miserable coffee, and possibly a slice or two of greasy bacon. And precious little was the whole; but I could not but help noticing the amazing difference in my spirits before and after I had partaken of Slum Jim's repast, that small quantity of ill-prepared food.

By this time our kitchen had moved to one of the few unshattered houses in the village, though there was fear that the white smoke from the smokestack would draw shellfire. However, the proximity of the kitchen had far from settled the all-important and ever-interesting, unforgettable topic of something to eat. Three days had passed and the men in back of the lines had failed to bring up anything for the mess force to cook. In spite of the injunction that a court-martial would follow, most of the fellows had, without order to that effect, disposed of the emergency rations. The four boxes of hard bread and the can of corned beef were eaten and forgotten and still no rations.

Edward Osterhout, one of the live wires of the organization, was granted permission by the captain to take a detail of men to the rear to try to get rations. About dark several of us, with rifles slung over our shoulders, wended our way through the trench that led to the rear and over the hill. Possibly two miles back we arrived at the ration dump at Mesnil, where we found other soldiers waiting for their rations to be brought up the narrow-gauge railway.

About midnight an ample quantity of bread and other food arrived for the 95th. Now to get it back to the company. For the few of us to take the rations up the trench and over the hill would have been an impossibility. Instead, the supplies were placed on a second narrow-gauge road, in a cart to be drawn by a mule and a French driver, I think. The miniature railway went to the right, along the base of the hill, and under cover of the night we would be able to get the rations within a few hundred yards of the company kitchen at Trésauvaux. That is, we could do this if there was no bad luck.

It was another dark night, and had the driver not had a track to guide him he could never have found his way. The mule, driver, and rations were off, but it very soon developed that the car wheels did not fit the rails. Every few steps the cart jumped the track, and it was with no little exertion that we set it right again. Frequently it was no sooner replaced and the mule started then off the tracks it went. Under ideal circumstances we would not have enjoyed this sort of thing, and, to repeat, the night was dark. We neared the front line, and with the news the German lines were not far away, the incessant rattling, banging car of rations seemed to emit ungodly sounds.

The cart now left the rails more than before. And then shells began to fall some distance away. Every shell that dropped increased our anxiety, and each time we set the cart back in position with nervous hands and feverish haste. Our journey was not more than half done when we had drawn quite near the line, which was occupied by the French. Every German across No Man's Land was deaf if he did not hear the thundering sound of that cart. One or two groups were ahead of us, and these men were experiencing the same trouble we were having.

Hitherto the shells had left a wide margin between us. But as we proceeded, each shell seemed to fall nearer. Then a whole host of howling, hellish messengers of death roared through the black night and exploded a dozen steps ahead of us. We dodged into a shallow ditch at the right, but the shells fell before we had time to think. Had the men ahead of us been blown to atoms? Investigation revealed that they were unharmed, and the track ahead was clear.

It was a great relief to get to the end of the rail line, where we dumped the rations on the ground. But we had not reached our goal yet. Each man picked up as much of the rations as he could carry, and it was with much effort that I kept in contact with the one just ahead of me. A sharp bend in the trenches at this point made it unavoidable for us to walk for some minutes in No Man's Land.

If I ever had hopes that I was following a man who knew where he was going, it was then. But try my best, several times the fellow ahead got out of sight and hearing. It was then that visions arose of

German trenches, bayonets, and deadly machine guns. To my joy they did not become a reality, and we arrived at the company safe.

If we did have an occasional shell to remind us that the war was still on, and though a fellow wondered if that mud could ever dry up, there was at least the great satisfaction of having plenty to fill those empty stomachs.

Another day came. If there had been rejoicing twenty-four hours before, many a Marine perhaps bemoaned the fact that he had ever in his life seen anything to eat. It was a sick bunch and not without cause. Somewhere in back of the lines, and without our suspecting it until too late, the rations—particularly the bread—had undergone a shelling of mustard gas. I suppose every man in that company thought he was going to die and was disappointed because he could not.

A few days later, when the effects of the gas bread were over and there were no fake alarms to occupy us as there had been on the hill, the higher-ups seemed to hate to see us without anything in particular to worry the life out of us.

A special night feature was put on. This consisted of a group of men taking a walk in No Man's Land (N-M-L), under cover of the darkness. I think only volunteers went on these patrols, though they had only vague ideas of what they were going for. Just what prompted the boys to go I don't know, either, unless it was the spell of going to No Man's Land. Possibly the fellows wanted a closer look at that phantom place, so far as the night would enable them to see. On the other hand, fear of being called a coward might have been a motivating force. Be that as it may, I shall not soon forget my trips to the Land of the Barbed Wire.

The remains of one shattered street in Trésauvaux projected some distance out into N-M-L, the best-preserved part of the village. By a freak of chance most of the exterior walls were left standing, while the walls between those closely built houses had been razed to the ground. This would afford a passageway for us to get some rods from the front line proper with a minimum of danger of being detected by the enemy.

It was another dark night that we started on that patrol. A Frenchman led. Instructions had been carefully given to us of the dos and don'ts in N-M-L, and we felt that death was our fate if we failed to carry out these instructions to the letter. "Noiselessness" was the watchword. One idle word, or a single false step, could instantly be the end of all of us. Should one of the illuminating flares go into the air, the thing to do was "hit the dirt"—and not spend a week getting down. But a fellow must keep his wits about him, and if for any reason a flare should go up and burst into glow while the man was yet on his feet, he was to remain standing, as stock still as a pyramid. By so doing he could easily be mistaken for an inanimate object.

It must have been nine or ten o'clock that we left that night on what was my first patrol. Quiet—quiet—but how were we to make our way noiselessly when our path lay along the ground where the shattered tiling from the roofs had fallen? Although we were still between the walls of the rows of houses, we were actually in N-M-L. As a foot came upon one of the tiles the resounding crack sent forth a most forbidden sound. And the darkness; I swung to the man ahead of me as the one behind held to me.

At last we emerged from the edge of the village, and silently—except for the beating of my heart—we entered through an opening made for that purpose into the endless sea of barbed wire.

We had advanced but a few steps when the silence was broken by the explosion of a flare pistol back in our own lines. Didn't the men behind know that we were in the N-M-L? The silent blessings the man must have received who shot that flare! But we were ready for it and had fallen. When the flare burst into a glow it seemed to have in it all the potentialities of a fiery devil. However, like most American flares, it soon descended, and we resumed our advance, cautiously and *quietly*. There would be an advance for some distance and then a halt for one awful moment, while I waited for half the Prussian Guards to swoop down upon us. Clothes were constantly hanging in the barbs, and a fellow did not want to become enmeshed and be left behind in that place!

Of the several French on the patrol, one was the next man in front of me, and when we had gone some distance he passed some word back to me *in French*. If I ever felt that my life hung on a thread, it was then. Whether I attempted to pass on the meaningless jumble I am not sure, but I have an indistinct recollection that in some fashion I whispered the meaningless jumble to the man behind.

When I volunteered for that patrol I was under the impression that after going out some distance from our lines, we would return again. But to my sorrow, I was evidently in error. We walked and walked—were we *never* going to stop? Every moment I expected us to come upon the German front line and then for the inevitable machine-gun fire. Since I was not one of those heroic souls that crave a large share of hazardous adventure, I had no great longing to get mixed up in the German lines at midnight.

We passed a small isolated house, and still there was no indication of the group turning back. Some yards farther on we found a spot where there was no wire, and here two or three of us were told to get in the prone position, with direction to keep an eye out. If ever an order was superfluous and unnecessary, it was this admonition to be watchful. Sometime later the remainder of the patrol returned and we went back to our lines.

The next morning I took a peep at N-M-L, in the direction of the blockhouse we had passed the night before, to ascertain just how near the German lines, and the jaws of death, we had gone. To my great surprise, I found this blockhouse was not more than two or three hundred yards away and not a fourth of that distance to the German trenches!

I made perhaps two other trips into the N-M-L while on the Verdun Front. On one of these about thirty of us went out to where it was thought that the Germans had been making nightly patrols. When we arrived at a wide space that was unoccupied by wire, the patrol was deployed and lay prone, rifles ready for action should the enemy encounter us. Strict orders had been given not to shoot unless we were attacked or considered our lives in jeopardy. The crack of a rifle would very likely bring a German barrage upon us. We lay for what I judge to be two hours on the wet ground, a cold, damp wind blowing upon us, which chilled us to the bone.

It happened that I was on the extreme right, with a tall, black-haired corporal on my immediate left. There came excited whispers from the corporal. Didn't I detect *movements* a few steps to our right?

I replied in the negative. Then my imagination began working, and when the corporal asked me a second time whether or not there was someone advancing toward us, I replied that I was not sure.

The words were hardly spoken when the corporal's gun rang out a shot in my ear loud enough for an exploding shell. A terrific shelling might ensue, and we lost no time in getting back to our line.

The fact that a bombardment of that part of the N-M-L did not follow the shooting of the rifle was attributed to the belief that the Germans also had a patrol out, but when the Fritzies left an active front to come to this comparatively quiet sector, they doubtless underwent no unnecessary risks and spent little time wandering around the N-M-L nights. But the man who shot his gun never heard the last of it.

Several times during these days I got into the observation post to overlook N-M-L and beyond. Our trenches, as has been said, were at the base of a hill. A wide valley was before us, covered with an interminable network of barbed wire, and in the middle of this space was a thread of small trees where it was reported a German sniper was located. At the base of the range across the valley, possibly a mile away, was the enemy front line, which could be seen from our side indistinctly. And that line and what lay beyond held for us untold mysteries and dangers. So far away were the enemy trenches that I never once saw anyone there.

And it was quite hard to realize that the shell of a village about us had less than four years before been homes. The now ragged walls had enclosed an unpretentious, simplehearted, and liberty-loving people, far removed from the turmoil and strife of the world. Goldsmith's *Deserted Village* came to mind again and again.

A few days after our arrival at Trésauvaux a rumor came to us that another company of our battalion, the 74th, which was in reserve some distance to our rear-right, had been gassed. In fact, the news bearer said that so many gas shells had fallen, many men fell dead in their tracks. He stated that of the original 250 only 25 were left able to do duty. We learned later that this account of the attack had been exaggerated, although most of the men in the company had to go to hospitals. It was true, too, that a number of deaths resulted. Among those gassed and evacuated to a hospital was Jesse Palmer.[4]

It appeared that our stays in new places had come to run in nines—nine days back at Sommedieue, nine on the hill, and now at the end of the ninth day at Trésauvaux we were being relieved to go to the rear. Just before leaving I was detailed with Lieutenant Mills on some sort of special duty, and while I was with him there was considerable rifle firing along the line. I do not recall any bullets hitting uncomfortably close.

And if some of the good folks back in the U.S. who imagined that every boy across the water remained unceasingly in a paroxysm of patriotic fervor and almost prayed for the opportunity to sacrifice his life for his country—if these deluded fathers and mothers could have seen conditions as they were, there would have been surprises, painful surprises. One of the men whom I regarded as one of the ablest, if not one of the finest, soldiers ever in the company, since coming to the front had made remarks that could easily have gotten him into serious trouble, with the severest penalty. Another talked in the same vein, and we will hear more of the matter later.

Many times when the boys did not get all they had a right to expect, and were not getting a square deal, there was grumbling.

After being relieved, no time was lost going back over the hill and through the trench we had come up some weeks before. Such an occasion was an example of a time when no orders were necessary to get quick action. Men who thought they were too hungry, sleepy, and tired to go anywhere had new life when the opportunity came to get them away from the front and the shellfire. The difficulty was to keep us from going too fast and crowding. As such main arteries of travel back and forth were sometimes shelled heavily, precautions were taken to avoid the danger of a large number of men being killed by the same shell. While still in the danger zone we were constantly reminded to go single file, about five paces apart. But to follow these orders was not easy when there was a great hurry to get to the rear.

NOTE: Before we left this position the boys were entirely out of tobacco, and under those circumstances having no smokes was a trying ordeal. A fine chap of the 95th, who was temporarily attached to the Intelligence Squad, visited us one af-

ternoon and with his arrival was rejoicing. He brought with him
a goodly quantity of Bull Durham.

While at Quantico I received a letter one day meant for another
Jackson in the 6th Regiment. His initials were N. R. [Norman R.] and
mine W. R. A few days after receiving the letter I made the ac-
quaintance of this man and handed him the letter. And at the Verdun Front he was one of the first, if not the very first man, of the regiment to be killed, though there were perhaps not more than a half
dozen killed in the regiment at Verdun. The 95th had lost one man
[Toth], with several gassed and wounded.

The front had been known as a quiet one, with a kind of mutual
understanding between the sides that there would be a minimum of
shellfire and other activities to correspond. And when the Allies and
Germans had recently come from a front where there was hard fighting, they were willing enough to let things remain as quiet as they
could. However, due to the inexperience of the Americans, with perhaps a difference in temperament, this kind of thing changed somewhat upon our arrival at the sector. Our loyal friends, the 12th, 15th,
and 17th Field Artilleries, could see no earthly use of those shells and
guns but to shoot them, and shoot they did. The usual result was that
the enemy retaliated by firing at the men on the front line, though
the boys on the big guns felt that they got their share of German artillery fire.

NOTE: Before going to the front we even heard tales of Allied
and German soldiers swapping jokes and tobacco, and probably such things happened.

The nearest approach to a battle at the sector came when our 9th
Infantry sustained an attack. One night a company of men in French
uniforms dropped into the trenches of the infantrymen. The Doughboys soon discovered that the visitors were Germans, and a lively battle ensued and the unexpected guests were quickly dispersed.[5]

But to return to our hike in the rear. After a hard night's march
we halted alongside the road where there were some wooden barracks, and here we were quartered. What a grand relief to get away

from that endless mass of mud and all the accompanying discomforts of life at the front!

A few hours later, when we were fallen out for breakfast, Sergeant Lynch dressed us down in no uncertain terms in his nasal, haranguing voice. The bawling out was for our appearing for chow as we did. And, in truth, it would have been hard to find such an unkempt-looking bunch: hair long and falling in strands down our necks, grizzly faces and uniforms begrimed with that Verdun mud, buttons missing, leggings tattered and muddy alike, and some of the company had dispensed with the use of leggings entirely. If anyone had heard Sergeant Lynch telling us what a careless, ungrateful set we were, and the hearer had not had a view of the objects of the sergeant's derision and sarcasm, the natural conclusion would have been that we had spent our whole lives in meticulous care to avoid barbers, clothing stores, laundries, and bathtubs.

Soon after our return from the front our dead were buried. The graves were dug a short distance from Sommedieue (which was not far from where we were then billeted). With the usual ceremonies several of us on the firing squad fired a salute over the graves.

A few days passed and one night we headed toward the front again. This time we left all surplus baggage behind, and this was a great relief. What was essential to carry was heavy enough. We expected to go again to the trenches seething with mud. However, our company, instead of going to the front line, was placed in support about a quarter of a mile behind the most advanced trenches. Our new abode lay in an abandoned rock quarry, fifty or a hundred yards across and terminated by perpendicular walls of rock ten to fifteen feet high. One of the platoons was quartered in a dugout made by digging into the solid rock. The fourth platoon occupied a rock-and-frame structure built against a wall of the quarry. And no mud was to be seen anywhere! Our new home was crowded but clean and even boasted of some small windows. No one needed to tell us that we were in luck. A fair-sized shell could wreck the whole structure, but there was little indication of recent shellfire thereabouts.

Just out of the quarry, and in a trench overlooking the valley beyond, I was placed on post. Down to my left, along which ran the front line, was the shattered town of Haudiomont. From my position

I had a distant view of the German side, though a projection of the hill to my left prevented my seeing the much nearer portion of the enemy lines. A part of my duties consisted of simply keeping an eye on the valley of N-M-L ahead of me; and I think, too, that I was to report to the major the falling of any shells nearby. At any rate, I doubtless felt my services could easily have been dispensed with.

One day while I was on post, the division commander, Major General Bundy, came to the front on an inspection tour. It is impossible for a civilian to conceive of the commotion resulting from a visit of the divisional commander. I don't remember whether or not we had been warned of his coming, but when he did put in his appearance it was a high time for buck privates like myself to be on the job. The general and his staff were being shown around and probably were informed of the utter futility of the enemy attacking that prepared and fearless organization.

Just about this time in the discourse on our virtues (I am supposing), the rounds of the general and his staff brought them to the valorous private on the observation post. And this was the first of the two times while in the Marines that I was addressed by the division commander. General Bundy stopped short and asked me several questions pertaining to my welfare and, among other things, did I have access to plenty of *water*. At the time I did not think the general meant to insinuate, but probably he intended to give me a loud hint.

It must have been shortly after the visit of the general that one fellow in the company apparently received an unusual stimulus, and he brought to the quarry a molasses bucket full of water. None of the men had washed for days, so hands and faces were far from snowy white. The man who brought the water, and nineteen more (I counted them), washed in the one gallon of water. My turn was next. While it was no time for a fellow to be very particular over his toilet, the sight of that water shooed me away. Instead of being the twenty-first to partake of the club bath, I walked a mile or more to a spring. The place had some camouflage near it to cut off the view from the German lines, and there were a number of fresh shell holes in the vicinity of the spring, but there was at least plenty of clean water.

While in the quarry, so few were our duties, and so remote seemed the enemy, that Lieutenant Mills conceived the idea of calling out the platoon late one afternoon for inspection and practice in the manual of arms. It seemed that the lieutenant felt the war could be won by snappy peacetime drills plus inspections. The inspection was just getting under way when an unlooked-for caller honored us. A screeching was heard in the air, and before we had time to bat an eye a shell exploded at the edge of the quarry. It is hardly necessary to say that the platoon "fell out" in less time than it had taken in assembling and with less ceremony too. No one knew how many shells might fall on the heels of the first. Nor did anyone stop to check the number of missiles Mr. Hun was sending over to liven the afternoon inspection. With an unprecedented unanimity we made for a dugout. In talking over the incident later, the part best remembered was the rapidity with which Lieutenant Mills found the dugout. In fact, it seemed that when the rest of us had scarcely had time to move, the lieutenant was hurrying into the dugout entrance as he shouted back breathlessly, and rather lacking in his usual dignity, that the platoon was dismissed. There were no more inspections in the rock quarry.

About a week in the quarry and we were to the rear again. The march, of course, was at night, and the guide lost his way, thus bringing down much wrath upon his head. Several hours of hiking later, the road led up a hill into a wood of tall trees, and we were quartered in one of the numerous barracks scattered through the wood. Like most of the bunkhouses in which we were to be quartered during months to come, the place had a dirt floor. The entrance was from either end of the structure, with rows of bunks, ends to the side walls, running down the left and right of the building, with an aisle down the middle. On the rude bunks was nailed some wire to keep a fellow from falling through to the "ground" floor. The place was dry and, with no shells to follow, we rather felt that we were "sitting pretty."

This was Camp Chiffoure and here about a hundred percent of us went looking for something to eat. The camp had a YMCA, but the invasions of that hollow horde of newcomers immediately reduced the stock of provisions to nought every time a new supply was brought in. This being the case, we had to seek other pastures. One drizzly day I visited another Y, some distance from the camp, where I was fortunate enough to obtain several chocolate bars. The relish with which I disposed of chocolate bars in those days was beyond measure.

Another day I made a trip with one or two fellows to a town several kilometers away, where we had the luck to get some canned fish, canned pears, with perhaps some other eats. Still another foraging expedition brought us to a French camp with a Y, where we bought a good stock of cakes, chocolates, and so forth.

The town of Verdun—that is, what was left of it—was reported to be about five kilometers away, and I decided that I would not let the opportunity slip of seeing the historic ruins. However, an MP thought otherwise. He stopped me in the road before I'd gone far.

At a Y in camp a chaplain one day made a talk to the boys gathered there. Although we had been in France about seven months, I think this was the second opportunity afforded to attend any sort of religious services.

Just one cloud appeared upon the horizon while we were at Camp Chiffoure. Someone concluded that we should make nightly trips to the line to dig reserve trenches. One evening just before dusk I left with a pick-and-shovel gang, each carrying our rifle and belt of ammunition, to go up for digging. On either this or a subsequent trip to dig, we passed a fortress. It must have been two hundred yards across, covered with dirt, and rising like a great mound some feet above the surrounding country. Like portholes of a ship, though doubtless much larger, gun holes formed a ring about the fortress. About the fort was a tangled mass of barbed wire, with other devices for arresting the progress of an enemy. And these formed a barrier that would be quite impassable until the endless confusion of wire was removed. We passed through a heavy forest and there were traces of recent shellfire, with holes here and yonder, and occasional broken limbs half ready to fall to the ground. After a long and arduous journey we came to the trenches that we were to deepen.

An hour's work and we started on our return. We seemed surrounded by a veritable wall of blackness. Who the leader was and how he found his way, I did not know; but through brush we went, across ditches, and over embankments that kept us in constant fear of breaking our necks by a fall. One man did go over the bluff and so hard was his fall that he crushed the canteen at his hip. My recollections are that the accident kept the fellow for several months in a hospital. To those who made the journey it seemed nothing short of an absurdity that a detail of a hundred men would spend most of the night, encumbered as we were, blundering our way through the darkness for one hour's work, when a dozen men, stationed a short distance from the trenches, could have done the work that so many had been sent to do. And we suspected that these trips were ordered to give us something to occupy ourselves, as much as for any other purpose.

On the next night men of the 95th were called upon to repeat the ordeal. However, the men, forewarned, had vanished. Only one man was in our bunkhouse, namely Private Jackson, and he would likely have been among the missing had he not thought a splitting headache would entitle him to remain in his bunk. Call succeeded call, but no man volunteered for a working detail. Buck Ashwood came in and, finding the illustrious soldier reposing, or trying to, forthwith commanded him to arise and prepare for the pleasant sortie. The private replied that he was incapacitated and received clemency at the hands of his superior. Yet soon after, the piping voice of Happy Summerlin was directed toward the self-pitying soldier, and nothing would excuse him but a written order from a doctor. A few minutes later this private of Marines, still suffering from the depression on the unfurnished floor, returned armed with the cherished writ to find that the working party had been given up.

After about two weeks at Camp Chiffoure we broke camp to hike farther to the rear. I cannot recall a single other long hike during the time I was in the service but with which I connect dismal feelings of heavy packs, cutting shoulder straps, and frequently other joy-killers added. It was a fine, clear April day, and as we left the main road to pass over broad expanses of rolling country, carpeted with short, tender grass, we could not but enjoy the contrast to the scenes we had gazed upon only a few weeks before. Probably our joy was accentuated by the realization that each step carried us farther away from the German guns, nights of sleeplessness, and endless days with empty stomachs.

About midafternoon we ascended a hill that overlooked Somme-dieue and descended the hill on what I suppose was the western side of the village. I say I "suppose," but in truth it is nearer a guess. With the exceptions of the very long trips in France, I usually had but a vague idea of the direction we were going, and even on the long journeys I probably didn't know anything definite as to the part of the horizon we had chased unless a map was produced. From this, it must appear that I am numbered with those who have eyes but see not.

A few hundred yards from Sommedieue we boarded French camions. Our destination, as usual, was probably unknown to us. Before dark, we passed through Châlons, which was General Pershing's headquarters. We also passed through most attractive farming country where spring grain covered the gently rolling hills.

Sometime during the night the truck in which I was riding stopped under some trees alongside a rock wall. This windowless wall was one boundary to the imposing edifice in which several of us were to repose during coming weeks. I do not know the exact nature of the quadrupeds who had preceded us, but I have not forgotten that my boudoir was on the first floor, and the only article of furniture of which the establishment could boast was a bed, if a spacious one, that was a by-product of last year's grain harvest.

It was the village of Outrepont, on the Marne. I had read so many times of "the bloody Marne," and heard the British speak so much of "the blaww-dy Marne," that I expected to find something other than water there when I first viewed it.

We drilled some and for a time I was on guard. My beat was along a road bordered with high cottonwood trees. Near one end of the section I patrolled lived an old lady who told me that the Germans had been there in the first battle of the Marne.

One day I met Jesse Palmer, who had been gassed back at the Verdun Front and had just returned from the hospital. His emaciated face and almost skeletal body were in painful contrast to the rare physique and buoyant appearance that had always made him conspicuous. Why he and others were evacuated from the hospital I could not imagine, as he was obviously far from fit to enter again upon duties of a wartime soldier. And the mistake was discovered, for he returned to the hospital.

In the village was a never-failing source of interest—a French camp. I can see now the cooks cutting up the esteemed carrots to flavor the abiding *soupe*. In fact, it seems that of many things during the war that want to play tricks with my memory, those pertaining to food and eating have remained the longest. True to form, soon after our arrival at Outrepont, we swept down upon the little French store. However, after the first Marines to have found the store had spent their money, there was little or nothing left to buy except sardines. One day the aroma of fresh bread attracted several of us, and we followed it through two or three villages. We, it seems, could not catch a bread wagon.

One of the boys—I think it was my good friend Bill Piggott—must have conceived the idea of cutting in twain the army of Kaiser Wilhelm. One day I found him across the street sharpening his bayonet on a grindstone. Several others of us did likewise, though I, for one, felt anything but bloodthirsty. Before this time an addition had been made to our equipment. Each fellow was issued a small entrenching shovel, or a pick about the same length, to be attached to the pack for future use. We were confident that neither could be used to advantage. Imagine trying to dig a hole with those toys! Why were those responsible for our getting these things so senseless, anyway?

As light as these tools were, they became very cumbersome to carry along and were always in the way. As the days passed, army-issue shovels disappeared. Also picks. Officers asked for explanations: why the shovel had been stolen, or dropped off the pack, or in some mysterious manner had deserted its owner. Instead of a pick or a shovel some of us were awarded a machete, which was hooked to the back or side of the ammunition belt. That heavy axlike implement was certainly a nuisance swinging on a fellow's belt or even from the back of the pack. It was on the day we left Outrepont that one machete that had been issued to Private Jackson was disengaged from the equipment and allowed to repose under the straw in the barn. Nor were machetes and entrenching tools all that were left behind. A number of recently emptied bottles stood in a military row behind the barn.

Notes

1 I can't quite figure out what was meant by the 5th having been in "third-line trenches" in the fall of 1917. I believe that this was a faulty memory at work. But his feeling of inferiority, probably common among the other newcomers of the 6th Marines, is a common attitude by "boots" toward "veterans." The 5th had been in France for more than six months before the majority of the 6th Marines arrived, and many of the officers and men were long-serving Marines.

2 Jackson's first words, crossed out, were "was possibly eight feet wide," which makes more sense than the corrected number. At four feet it would seem nearly impossible to navigate.

3 What Jackson probably meant was that not only were the French units greatly downsized by casualties but essentially the American units had at least twice the personnel and probably another half as well, more than what all foreign units had.

4 This disaster was brought about by inexperience and an unusual concentration of shells upon a reserve area. On 12 April when the 74th was in Camp Fontaine-St.-Robert, at least 220 men and all officers of the company were evacuated, all in serious condition. Forty of them died as the result of the shelling. See Clark, *Devil Dogs*, for complete details.

5 This happened to the 3d Battalion, 9th Infantry, commanded by Lt. Col. "Hiking Hiram" Bearss, USMC. For a complete breakdown on this event, read George B. Clark, *His Road to Glory: The Life and Times of "Hiking Hiram" Bearss, Hoosier Marine,* Pike, NH: The Brass Hat, 2000.

4: Northwest of Paris

SYNOPSIS

Meanwhile, after reassembling, the division began their move west to the region of Chaumont-en-Vixen in the Department of the Oise. They would now be in some of the most beautiful farmland of France. But it wouldn't last more than two weeks. The Marines were now to undergo more training, after which it was expected that the 2d Division would relieve the 1st Division up at Montdidier.

Training began at once and continued until 30 May 1918, when the troops were given time off for "Decoration Day" ceremonies. The following day they were to start a move northward to begin relieving the 1st Division.

About a seven-kilometer hike brought us to boxcars, which we boarded. It was about noon of the next day that we detrained in a most attractive town northwest of Paris, and the boys doubtless said "bon sector." But it was not for us to spend the rest of the war there. An afternoon's hiking brought us to another town that appealed to the eye—or should I say *stomach*. We were halted on a concrete walk, where we were to stop for the night. But some of us found it softer to pitch our blankets on a grassy spot some distance away.

The next morning we were on our way again, with many a strong expletive for the man responsible for always sending Marines, the 95th Company in particular, straight through the good towns of any size to quarter us in some "godforsaken place." Many of the men used to bemoan this sort of thing until I got sick of it. Perhaps about ninety-nine percent of the AEF thought other outfits were receiving better treatment than they were. As I think of it now, I wonder if we were not purposely billeted in small villages to avoid the recurrence of the fate that some months previous had befallen Marines in Paris and other French cities.[1]

The day's march was hard, and such was the pace set by the leader that even before it was well begun, our officers were commanding and threatening in vain to hurry along the straggling column. On and on, with short, infrequent rests. Our throats became parched. Several of us took several canteens each, where, with delay, we filled them from a weak flow some distance from the road. Many men dropped out of line, to join us hours after we had reached the destination and tell of the fine feeds they enjoyed while the rest of the bunch marched on.

Mile after mile we marched through a prosperous-looking country, with fields of grain as far as the eye could see. Late in the afternoon we passed through a town of about a thousand, more or less, where we left a road to follow a path along a fence, a field on one side, a meadow on the other. We came to a knoll, with several big spreading trees upon it, and beyond it were the walls of a French château—if that is not too dignified a term for it. Following a lane to the right of it, and what *might* have been the west side, we passed a stagnant pool, guarded by gabbling ducks, and found ourselves at the main entrance.

The "Farm," as we called it, like many we were to be quartered in later, was a quadrangular enclosure of stone. On one side, forming a part of one wall and facing outward, was the house of the owner. Behind at least two of the other walls were stables and haylofts. The four sides enclosed a large open space.

A good many of the bunch climbed an uncertain ladder to pitch their packs in a hayloft, though some of the rest of us decided to bunk down in what perhaps had served as a stable. Our equipment was hardly thrown off when, with the usual dispatch in such matters, we began looking about to ascertain what eats the place afforded. I got a quart of milk at very reasonable terms and think some of the fellows bought some eggs, but with the whole company of 250 quartered there, we were to be less fortunate in the future.

Outside the château was a grassy plot of several acres—a drill monger's paradise. Yes, wherever we went many things were denied us but never a drill field. Wherever we went the proximity of the never-missing drill field was ever lamented. There followed days of drill both here and along a road leading from the Farm. However, tents were later pitched on the drill field. This was our first experience at putting up tents, and as we placed them someone directing insisted that proper alignment be maintained in Tent Street. Among their other instructions the machine gunners were put again and again through the process of "breaking down" and assembling the French Chauchat, as well as the British machine gun, the Lewis.[2]

One day I went a kilometer or two to the last town we had passed, where I had some dental work done. I was to need strong teeth in the months to come! While I was in the village German planes came overhead, though I recall no bombs being dropped.

While at the Farm we had plenty of bread, the first time for more than two meals together since we had left the U.S. eight months before. That bread was filling and in those days that was the first requisite. But French war bread had much the flavor of sawdust, without the pleasing aroma of fresh sawdust. I fail to find something to compare with the texture of French war bread. Gun wadding might do, but gun wadding comes apart very easily.

In the evenings after drill we often went to a village below to a Y where on a few occasions I was fortunate enough to get some chocolates. I found Sandusky there, whom I had not seen since we left Paris Island. He was the most interesting *simpleminded* fellow I ever met. I never saw him again.

It was after supper one evening that I sat on my bunk in the hay, reading the letter I had just received telling of my brother Fred's death. While I read, an order came. "Roll up and stand by to move, thirty minutes to get out!" The "dope" had been floating rather freely that the division was going to southern France for a rest. But it seemed that thirty minutes was short notice to get ready to go to a rest area.

A few minutes later the familiar "Outside" was given and, with equipment on, the men left the dingy hayloft, descending the rickety ladder one at a time. The company was assembled outside the courtyard on a country road. Where were we going, when, and how? The time passed and no further orders came. "Stack arms" was given and we were ordered to fall out beside the road. Hours passed and no orders. What did they mean by breaking us out in such a hurry and then not starting somewhere? Night set in and the time dragged slowly. Some tried to sleep, but the cool, damp air did not encourage them and orders had been given not to unroll packs. Others were grouped about smoky fires talking about possible plans for the future and the bygone days "back in the good old U.S." When day finally broke, an almost endless stream of sky-blue French camions appeared on the crest of the hill. We were not going to hike at least. In a short time the men were crowded into the camions, each carrying twenty-odd men, and the endless stream began moving.

We soon found ourselves headed almost due east. Could it be that we were going to Paris? It was only about fifty miles distant. This sounded almost too good to be true. One of the fellows on the same camion as I tried to get information from our French driver as to our destination. But with his lack of French, or the Frenchman's lack of information, we were still at sea as to our destination. The procession was soon turning slightly to the northeast. That did not add a bit to the fast-withering hopes of a stay in Paris.

Notes

1 I'm not sure exactly what he is referring to. It was not very often that Marines got anywhere near large cities and if they were in Paris, it must have been on special duty of some kind. Perhaps something unpleasant happened during the parade in Paris on 4 July 1917.

2 Technically, Jackson was correct. The Lewis was invented by an American soldier, but when the less-than-"aggressive" U.S. Army refused to accept it, he sold rights to it to a British firm—which, in turn, later contracted with the Savage Arms Company to produce it for the U.S. Marines and, I believe, the U.S. Army. But eventually all Lewis guns were "rounded up" and transferred for use on aircraft. Instead, the U.S. Marines got to use French guns.

5: To Belleau Wood

SYNOPSIS

The Germans had broken through once again, for the third time in 1918, and instead of working over the British in the north, Ludendorff changed his tactic and decided to separate the French and British armies where they joined. To do so he would have to plunge in a general direction toward Paris. That would force Marshal Foch to pull his reserves back to place them before the "City of Lights."

The 2d Division of U.S. Regulars, a relatively untested force of about twenty-eight thousand young American men, was allotted to Marshal Foch to help put out the fire and, hopefully, stop the oncoming "Boche." No one expected that they would or, for that matter, could. Only they themselves were confident.

They were shipped eastward and in a day or so managed to form something of a line across the Paris-Metz highway, just west of the town of Château-Thierry. Another body of young Americans, the 3d Division, also called regulars, sent a machine-gun battalion to help delay the crossing of the Marne River at that town. Like their comrades of the 2d Division, they, too, would make history in the next few weeks.

Upon arrival, the 3d Brigade of Infantry took up positions on the south side of the Paris-Metz Road, while the 4th Brigade of Marines occupied the north side. Within hours they were both reasonably well organized and ready to entertain expected guests.

French soldiers were still falling back under pressure from the German armies, and within a day or two the Boche met some of the Americans lying in wait. At first they weren't sure of what was opposite them. Sustained and aimed rifle fire soon made them aware that this wasn't a French formation that had managed to hold their ground before the steamroller. For twenty days they would get a taste of what the "youngsters" had been preparing for them. The Marines and Doughboys would also find out that opposite them was a first-class military formation that could and did make them pay a high price for the ground saved and attained.

The 1st Battalion, 6th Marines, was first to arrive on the ground and for a few days would occupy positions facing along the northernmost part of Belleau Wood. They would go into reserve and then launch a major attack on the southern portions of Belleau Wood beginning on 10 June. After about a week they were relieved by portions of the 7th Infantry but within a few days would return for the balance of the Belleau Wood campaign.

When the noon came everyone was glad to get out and stretch a bit and partake of the delicacies of hardtack, corned beef, and cold coffee; while the bearded French drivers chewed away on their tough bread, first cutting it into small bits with their big clumsy pocket knives and sipped at their *vin rouge.*

We were soon off again, and those ahead of us whipped a cloud of dust into our faces. By this time all hopes of a "rest" were blighted. We would probably relieve the 1st Division at Montdidier. Almost before we were aware, we had come upon a place where some French soldiers were mounting a battery of large-caliber guns, pointing them to the northeast. That seemed strange, placing guns fifty or more miles behind the front. The story was soon plain; hundreds of refugees started passing us. The Germans were making a drive. By the time we got to Meaux, a town of fifteen or twenty thousand, refugees in countless numbers were passing us. Old men, old women, children, mothers with children in their arms, all trying to get out of the way of the oncoming Germans.

It was far in the night before the camions stopped, and we unrolled our packs by the side of the road to sleep. But it was not our good fortune. Hardly had we closed our eyes when an "Everybody up!" greeted our ears. We were soon headed toward the front, this time walking. After marching for a while, we could hear the French seventy-fives belching forth ahead of us. About daylight we met some worn-out retreating French soldiers. They told us that they had not had anything to eat in three days and that the Germans had advanced sixty miles in four days.

We came to a large farmhouse and stopped. We were marched into the courtyard and told that we could unroll and go to sleep. The place was just being deserted by its owner. The exhausted men were not too tired to eat. The place was alive with everything one could expect to find at the home of a wealthy farmer. French wine that had probably been in the cellar for a quarter of a century. The farm was alive with chickens, pigs, rabbits, and even young calves were soon slaughtered. What a feast we could have! The animals were cleaned and hung up; we would sleep some before cooking them. But the opportunity for sleep was snatched from us, and we had to leave the uncooked rabbits, chickens, and calves hanging there.

The middle of the morning found us continuing the march. The day before, we had witnessed the painful sight of fleeing refugees. Today we were to get a shock from which it would not be easy to recover. With their years of experience in warfare, we had admired, almost reverenced, the French soldiers. For my own part, I had come to feel that there was a certain invincibility about them. Inexperienced and untried, we were on our way to the front to help try to stop the onrushing Germans.

Then there met us on the road that day French soldiers, worn-out, haggard, and dejected, retreating in disorder from the oncoming Germans. They reminded one more of hunted beasts than human beings. We had regarded an experienced French soldier as worth several Americans, and now they were retreating. It would not have been unnatural for the Americans to despair at this turn of affairs, but I do not recall one word of fear or other evidence of a desire to turn back. As we continued along that tree-lined Paris-Metz Road, more and more of the French passed us. Their emaciated faces and eyes that reflected despair told unmistakably of the thousand perils they had witnessed.

We left the road to our right to turn into some fields. Toward evening we were deployed and resumed the march through the field of ripening grain. Coming upon rising ground, we saw a village ahead. As we advanced, two of the men, who had brought along bottles from the cellar, had to be separated in their drunken fight.

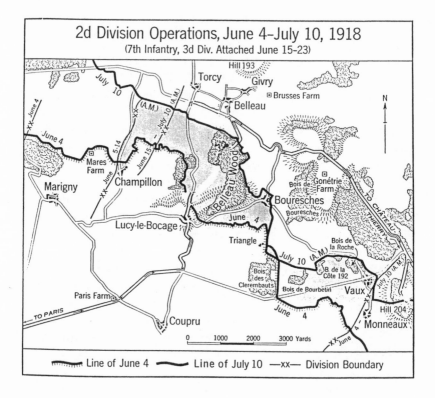

2d Division Operations, June 4–July 10, 1918
(7th Infantry, 3d Div. Attached June 15-23)

Line of June 4   Line of July 10   —xx— Division Boundary

When we went into the village on that bright June day, an air of calm serenity seemed to pervade its sunlit walls and green gardens. It was the village of Lucy-le-Bocage. Its population had recently fled and the sole occupants were a few French hospital corpsmen. These men cheered us by reiterating the predictions we had heard along the road, that *Paris would be taken in eight days.* *"Paris, huit jours"* seemed to be so firmly rooted in their minds that it would almost lead one to think that they had received an official statement that Paris would be surrendered to the hated "Boche" in exactly eight days. The French did not appear to consider at all the idea of their being stopped in the meantime. And how long before Lucy-le-Bocage would be taken? *"Trois jours"*—three days. They said this with the certainty of night following day.

More ammunition was issued to us, and just before night we began to move to the left, to the northwest I suppose it was. We walked along a path down a slight decline and passed the 75th Company, who were making an effort to dig in. Among them was Albert Ball, and I shall never forget the picture of him as he sat upon the ground with the despairing has-it-come-to-this expression upon his face.

The valley below was heavily timbered, and just in the edge of this wood we were halted for the night. We had not been there long when Peter Timmer began digging a hole between two saplings a few feet from me. I felt that Timmer must have a yellow streak. I was to learn.

We took a turn at watch during the night, and I was on for an hour. The night was quiet, and not until the next morning did any shells fall along the line. A few shells fell a few hundred yards to our left, and word came that four men of the 78th Company had been killed. The news was a shock.

About eight or nine in the morning Allied artillery fire attracted our attention. We were located on a gentle slope, and from an opening nearby we could see across the valley a mile or more away. In an open field were a house, set about with large spreading trees, and a small, thick wood a stone's throw distant. The house seemed to be the object of our artillery fire. Every few seconds a shell was dropped in the vicinity of the house, throwing clods and dust into the air, leaving where the shell had struck an irregular mass of black smoke. Such was the distance between us and the falling shells that we did not hear the explosion until some seconds after the black puff appeared over the place where the shell had dropped. However, the movements could not be seen with the naked eye, and for a few moments I watched with the aid of Lieutenant Wheeler's field glasses.

The shells had been dropping but a short time when, following the fall of a shell close to the house, half-crouching, hatless figures began to scamper in abandoned haste across the open space to the plot of wood—running for their lives. The sight was novel; strange to say, even amusing! Why I was affected by this tragic scene in the way I was (and the same on a similar occasion later) I do not understand, as I always took even a dogfight more seriously than those around me. Yet it was sport now to see these fellows, much like we were and with similar hopes and ambitions, running a race with death.

Before the day was far advanced we moved to the right a few hundred yards and formed a line, averaging a half-dozen steps apart. Within hours a few of the men began digging holes in a desultory sort of fashion. Gradually, all the men took this up, often two or three men digging a hole together. However, we must have taken turn about, as there could not have been many shovels among us. Two of us dug a crude sort of hole, and over our hole we placed a light roof of leaves supported by twigs. What good we thought this roof would do, I don't know. It was not to keep out the sun, as the treetops above did that.

Not having had anything to eat since noon the day before, we resorted to our emergency rations. A good many of us withdrew into the heavier portion of the wood to build fires, which served to cook bacon in our mess kits. It tasted good. In the midst of our cooking and eating a shell fell on the extreme left of 95th Company lines, followed by more shells in quick succession. And then it occurred to us that the white smoke from those fires passing through the treetops would in no way improve the chances of the Germans turning their guns in another direction. A cry became general to put out all fires.

Later in the evening a spray of machine-gun bullets came through our line. I was standing a step or two from our dugout when the bullets sang by and one zipped through the twigged roof of our dugout. Just after sundown heavy machine-gun fire began several hundred yards below us. Shortly, orders came for us to advance. A brief distance and we paused to fix bayonets. We had not had a taste of a real fight, and the men were exuberant over the prospect of getting into battle.

We crossed a road and soon came to the edge of the wood. Here we paused, apparently awaiting further orders. A raging machine-gun battle was going in the valley below us; however, a cloud of white smoke overhung it, so we could only hear. We were surprised that no bullets came our way. In the meanwhile several of the men had loosened their pack straps, allowing their blanket rolls to drop to the ground. These fellows did not know what lay ahead and they disliked the idea of being encumbered with a heavy blanket roll. Then a part of us were sent along a fence to our right. We met excited groups of

French soldiers. One of the men had told us that the Boche had captured the company kitchen and that they had not had anything to eat for three days. These men were evidently bent on getting out of the fray. Farther down the fence was a dead French soldier and then another. Both of them wore their sky-blue overcoats and their packs. One lay on his face. I couldn't tell where either had been hit, but here on the ground were two of the French whom in past months we had regarded as invulnerable—dead. Of course we had read where sometimes regiments and even divisions were wiped out. The sight of those two dead soldiers was a thousand times more impressive. Appalling! Without taking any part in the battle, or even knowing definitely the result, we withdrew.

And here I must go back some weeks or months. I have stated that while we were back at Trésauvaux, subsisting on emergency rations, the morale of the men was far from the best. The depression and discontent that pervaded the enlisted personnel had been fomented by events in the preceding months that I have not mentioned. And some of these things could hardly be calculated to engender a great fighting spirit among the best of troops. The mud-begrimed exterior and the emptiness within, along with the continued sleepless nights, coupled with the belief that we were not getting a square deal, resulted in grumbling.

I believe I have spoken of Corporal Ferris. He was one of the best soldiers in the company, though one of the youngest. Affable, inoffensive, he, like a lot of the bunch, grumbled some too. What others said was overlooked. But Happy Summerlin, who had recently been made sergeant, picked up a remark made by Ferris about something that "we ought not to do," and Summerlin branded the idle statement as *mutiny.*

When we went to the rear again, Ferris was "run up" for a general court-martial, which was indeed a serious matter. Ferris was thereafter under guard, pending trial. While we were at the Farm there came the unexpected order to leave for the front. When we got off the camions, I recall Ferris in the ranks with the marching column without a gun or other means of defending himself. It was with him that I dug my first hole. In the morning when the 78th Company men had been reported killed, Ferris went to the company with the hope of getting a rifle from a man who had been killed. For some reason he was unsuccessful. In the evening when the battle was on below, and we moved up with the expectation of reinforcing the French, Ferris went along still unarmed. In the excitement that followed I lost sight of him, and when the company withdrew he was not along. A few days afterward we learned that Ferris had been killed.

We were still following the road when dark came, and I remember seeing the glow of cigarettes of men resting at the roadside. Hour after hour we went on, we knew not where. There were now only two platoons of us, the others having been sent elsewhere. We came to an open space, and the order came to deploy.

Then Lieutenant Wheeler told us the Germans were ahead of us, adding, "*Thirty minutes to dig for your lives,* and the chances are *four to one against you.*" Anyone who doesn't think that such an order, under such bewildering circumstances, didn't get us moving is mistaken. It was time for action. But alas, alas, for the departed SHOVELS! And even my machete was gone. If I ever tried to use tact and diplomacy it was then, and with results. Without delay I sought a partnership with a man with a shovel. Mine was the transcending fortune to receive Piggott's permission to dig in with him.

If a set of men ever worked with a frenzied haste, it was then. Where the beloved shovels were not available, mess kits, mess-kit lids, bayonets, spoons, forks, knives, and helmets all were drafted into the trip to China. But the shovel that we had despised in the days before was now the master tool.

Down not more than six inches the shovel was prized against a rock and *broke.* In fact, we had struck almost solid rock. But this was no time to stop and weep. We were bent on *going down.* Not having much success at this, we picked up clods of dirt and rocks we could find about and placed them on the front edge of the shallow hole, figuring they would at least stop machine-gun bullets. To add to my distress I was placed some steps ahead of the company on outpost.

The half hour passed and, to our surprise, there were still no signs of our being dead. A little after daylight a blue line appeared along the edge of the wood ahead—the French were coming from where the Germans were supposed to be!

During the morning we shifted our position several times. In the edge of a grainfield where we halted a few moments I picked a few berries. I was not sure what kind they were, but they tasted good. Then we were descending a gentle, wooded slope. We met a party of French whose dejection disconcerted us. We came to a newly dug trench a couple of feet deep, which we followed. A small puddle of fresh blood in this deserted trench was most suggestive. The trench ended, and beyond was a row of scattered holes. Some of the men were left in the trench and dugouts. When we went a little farther, there was no trench and no holes. Here the last of us stopped. I was the last man, on the extreme right of the company. What or who was to my right I could not even guess. I looked with envy to my left at the men who had been lucky enough to have a dugout to get into. However, no shells had fallen in our vicinity since we had taken up our new position, so I don't think we were particularly concerned as to getting below the surface. Nevertheless, I felt lonesome with the next man to my left some distance away and no one on my right.

Along our line the trees were somewhat scattered. To the rear the trees were much closer together, and ahead there was a forest of trees, with a heavy undergrowth. I can see myself as I strained my neck and eyes to make out some stealthy Germans, gun in hand, crouching in the undergrowth ahead. A large tree was to the right and some steps ahead. I thought what a good bullet-turner this would be and adjusted my position accordingly.

It was about this time that we were told that we were opposed by Germany's best soldiers, the famous Prussian Guards, and that they outnumbered us *five to one.* Then the quiet was broken by the unexpected fall of shells to the left. And following this unwelcome surprise two of the men, who had decided the position they were occupying was *undesirable,* came with transcending speed down the rear of the line in my direction. It was as though one of the shells had released a spring in the fellows. They shot by. One of those on the flight was a dried-up, redhaired, boasting fellow; but on this occasion his characteristic chesty, flaunting stride was rather impaired, if vastly accelerated.

But for one thing, the first nonstop flight across the Atlantic would have been made right then. The interceding factor was the big bear-like voice of Buck Ashwood. I am disposed to doubt the figures of the learned gentlemen who first said that sound travels only a mile in five seconds, as the voice of Buck Ashwood overtook the flying warriors. What is even stranger, if possible, is that the departing squadron took heed. Crestfallen, they returned to the place that had witnessed their spectacular sortie.

If I have often been amused in thinking over this incident, what immediately followed seemed at the time anything but laughable. Several of those howling shells fell a short distance to my rear, one quite close. The shells continued to fall in quick succession. At that hour had a million dollars been placed on my right hand and one of those once-despised army shovels put on the left, and I given my choice, I would have rejected the million in the twinkling of an eye. Never in my days had I been possessed of such an overwhelming desire to get down into the earth. Our feverish digging of the night before was almost unsurpassable, but the human voice could not in a thousand years give the inspiration to dig that those shells afforded. With frenzied movements we used mess kits, along with the remaining accoutrement of chow warfare, and bayonets and helmets were drafted into the all-important approach to the heart of mother earth.

Then the shelling ceased. Two of the company had been wounded. One of these had a piece of his skull carried away. The other man wounded was Lieutenant Wheeler. However, he would not leave us until he was forced by a second wound to go to the rear. For his conduct he later received the prized Distinguished Service Cross.[1]

I had envied the men on the left for their trench and holes, but it was they who bore the brunt of the shellfire. With the lull, activities of the digging brigade ceased accordingly. Then hungry exhausted men swore they would never dig again. They would just as soon be killed then as later anyway. Furthermore, if a fellow was bumped off right there and then, he would not have to undergo the hell of shellings ahead. No, they would not dig another lick. In the midst of this kind of talk a shell would fall somewhere. With it declarations were immediately forgotten, and the onslaughts of the digging brigade were renewed with unsurpassed vigor. Many times, in months to come, was I to see this kind of thing repeated.

That night several of us moved forward and to the right to dig in. That very black night I attempted to dig my hole on the side of a sandy bank—I don't know why there—and all during the night the sand would give way, causing me to slip down the embankment.

That night a stillness reigned, in marked contrast to the fearful fire of the afternoon before. The very quiet made me apprehensive of a coming storm, as though the very jaws of hell were ready to swallow us up.

Many cautions had been given not to let a shrewd German in some manner deceive us and perhaps cause the whole bunch to be trapped. Suddenly, from a short distance out in the inky darkness of No Man's Land, came a strange, imploring voice!

"Camarade, je suis blessé."

Such an appeal from N-M-L that time in the night sounded suspicious, to say the least. But the one who had uttered the words was entering the line, just at the point of a mounted machine gun. The man who had cried out claimed he had been wounded in the back or shoulder. Buck was not taking chances. He felt and put his hand into a gaping wound. The Frenchman stated that he had been wounded several days before when he was left by his retreating comrades. Only by the greatest effort had he been able to make his way back to our positions. The poor Frenchman—or was he lucky to get out of it?—was taken back to a hospital.

And there were more changes of position. As we walked down a slope, we came upon the bodies of Frenchmen scattered about. In a moment Summerlin was ransacking their packs, and I don't know what else, to get whatever suited his fancy. I was amazed at his coolness and unconcern in doing what it took me weeks to learn to do, and then with a great sense of relief when I had finished the job.

I must have been at the end of the column, or for some reason was late arriving at the new position where the company had halted, just in the edge of the wood. I was told to go up to the left of the company to fill in as much of the gap as possible between our company and the outfit on the left.

I was making my way toward the edge of the wood through the undergrowth when I came upon a sight that horrified me. Before I knew it I was at the edge of an opening in the bushes and trees, and at my feet was a large hole six or eight feet across. In the hole were the mangled bodies of three Frenchmen. Against the back of the hole on the side nearest me leaned one of the bodies, nearly bolt upright, with the head and neck almost gone. The body of one of the other men presented a sight scarcely less ghastly. A time shell had evidently burst above them, and they had been in the act of crouching to avoid being hit.

The combined odor of the high-explosive gas, which still lingered there, and the decaying bodies, sent me hurriedly away. I think I reported the presence of the bodies. A few minutes later, when Buck was summoning a working detail, I lay low—it was to bury the dead men, I knew.

It is almost needless to say that I dug a hole in a different place from where I had intended digging it. About dark Rosenow and I began digging a hole together. I think some large shovels had been passed around, but whatever form of entrenching tools we may have had, they were used with vigor. A number of things entered in to stimulate our efforts. The ground was soft and, if my calculator was functioning at the time, in not more than an hour we were five feet or more below the surface with a hole about two feet by six. We figured the deeper the better, I suppose, but had a large shell hit near our hole we would have been buried like rats. That night brought but short and troubled snatches of sleep.

Another move, where we found holes already dug. There were more men than necessary to fill the front line proper, and my hole, along with some other fellows', was some steps back. All I had to do while there was just sit and pick out the joys of life afforded.

The days continued to be sunshiny without, though far different within. As I stayed in my dugout those days, it seemed that I was in a dream, a most unpleasant and unreal dream. I was in a daze, so sleepless were the nights. Yet a bit of troubled sleep was ours during the day; the morning seemed like the evening and the evening like the morning, and all a troubled unreality that made me rub my eyes to see if I was not in a ghastly trance.

The Germans had gotten their artillery in position so as to shell us in earnest. Our own guns were silent. They had either not pulled up or lacked ammunition. This was disheartening. Then our artillery began shooting over shells, but not to the enemy lines. Few of the shells went more than a hundred yards beyond our lines, and some hit in our positions. Knowing the experienced Germans greatly outnumbered us, continually harassed by their artillery fire, and then to have our own guns threatening us with annihilation every moment—the anguish we suffered could not be described. What in the world could be the cause of this bombardment by our own guns? Why was the range not raised? We asked one another the questions in vain. I later heard that there had been a spy in our artillery. I don't know.[2]

The sole artillery support we had was from a one-pounder not far to the rear. I can hear it now as at intervals this little gun fired into the enemy lines. And the Germans replied with their big guns, so we wished our one-pounder would stop. And it did, probably silenced by a shell.

The bombardment we underwent was almost enough to drive one mad, but added to this, a part of the time there was no food or water. The rations that did come consisted of French hard bread and French corned beef, known as monkey meat. The hard bread was the size of a biscuit, well browned and with a smooth, glossy top. When dipped in coffee for a moment the biscuit attained a mushy softness almost instantly. Without this immersion it had the physical characteristics of a brick. "Rain barred, a fort made of this hardtack would be impregnable, joking aside." The cans of beef held about as much as a teacup. Had water not been so scarce, this meat would have done very well as a substitute for something to eat, but it was salty as brine. When a fellow ate this monkey meat he was ravenously thirsty.

While in this position little else did we have to do but count our miseries. A part of the time we wandered along the lines, that is, until we learned better than to expose ourselves. Ahead of us was a field of tall, thick ripening grain. Some hundred yards out was a small ravine where the Germans were understood to be. Beyond was a gently rising swell, and near the crest of the hill some of the houses of the village could be seen. Over this hill we saw a man leisurely walking one day. Undoubtedly he was a German soldier, though he was too far away to know definitely. How strange it seemed—a German.

Yes, there was actually one of them. One or two of the expert rifle-men in the company had rifles equipped with telescopic sights, though no one fired.

Notwithstanding the trying circumstances, an occurrence here furnished no little amusement as men spoke of it afterward. When we got to holes where we then were, the front must have been un-usually quiet. At least conditions were such that Sergeant Hickey de-layed the all-important duty of getting himself a hole. When the first small shell did come somewhere in our direction, it seems to have penetrated Hickey's understanding that he needed shelter. In all haste he ran to the nearest dugout (which was covered with twigs and leaves, except for a hole at one end to go in and out). All was dark within. Upon coming to the edge of the dugout Hickey cried out in his own particular Irish accent:

"How many's in that dugout?"

"Three," came a voice from within. Hickey was bent on getting for himself a protected spot, whatever the method.

"Well, half youse come out!"

Whether the mathematical problem was solved by the three I don't know, but Hickey had to look for another hole.

Early one morning as a company of the 5th Regiment was drop-ping into positions to relieve us, a heavy machine-gun fire began along the line. I could see only drooping branches of trees just ahead and the grain beyond, but men about me began firing. I strained my eyes but could see no one. For a moment I thought the air around me was filled with passing German bullets, but on looking about saw traces of very few. I asked the men next to me if they could see any-thing to fire at. They said they did not. They just thought they should shoot since those on the right and left were popping away. I always had a dread of running out of ammunition, and it was no use firing till I could see someone to shoot at. The men a few steps to our left—as I later learned—saw the enemy approach in the old mass forma-tion, with several abreast, but none got to our line.

It was broad daylight and the incessant clatter of the machine guns had diminished somewhat when we were making our way back to the rear. I know of only one man who was killed at the time, Ferris, though he was a fine boy.

We made our way to the rear with feverish haste. Through wood and field we went. In one place there was all kinds of equipment left under a tree. To our left was a deserted farmhouse. We were in a dream. The sun was just rising, yet I could not rid myself of the feeling that it was late in the evening, so much had transpired before the sun had shone.[3]

We hastened on. It was impossible to get away too soon from that awful shellfire. However, our hurry was not such as to keep us from stopping at the edge of the village. On the side of the road was a ration dump, with French bread, salt pork, with maybe salmon and I don't know what else. We did not know or care who had left those rations there. We surely helped ourselves. It was June but Thanksgiving Day.

Protected by a clump of trees, a French seventy-five belched forth. It was the first time that I saw a piece of artillery in action. In the field was the stiff and swollen form of a dead animal, which had probably been killed by a shell.

Several miles hiking and we turned from the road toward a wood. A sudden and terrific explosion scared me stiff. I suppose for a moment I thought I was shot, and the vibration almost dislodged my helmet. A six-inch gun had fired a short distance away.

In the wood we were halted. A haven at last! But the choice of a resting place was unfortunate in the extreme. The surrounding forest was veritably alive with artillery, which fired unceasingly. While the firing of the gun would not ordinarily be taken for the explosion of a shell, the continual deafening roar that these guns emitted kept our nerves unstrung. During the days before, an explosion had meant danger—and beware. Though we now had no cause to fear anything, the constant explosions still brought home to us with overwhelming force the pictures we had seen and dangers we had escaped.

But these unpleasant sensations were not sufficient to curb our ravenous appetites. For four days—and it seemed that many weeks—we had hardly a half-dozen bites. The mess kits were drafted into service and we soon had a soul-filling meal. At first water was scarce, and I made an unsuccessful attempt to get a drink at a miserable seep not far from camp. Later we got water and chow at the company kitchen.

I spoke of digging in one evening with Rosenow. It was he that brought the boys the smokes when we were back in the mud at Verdun. A fine and intelligent fellow he was, from Wisconsin, I think. Months before he had been a most happy, optimistic fellow, but now he had become morose and his face haggard. While in the wood I bunked with Rosenow. Succeeding events caused me to remember quite vividly his confiding in me. He told me with feeling of the girl he had left back in the U.S.

There was a minimum of danger from enemy bombardment, but the continuous roar of our own guns about us disturbed me during the day and caused wakefulness at night. Three days of this, and on the night of 8 June we left our blanket rolls behind to leave for the front again.

And the battalion got lost. Shortly after, our amiable and unaffected major [sic] was relieved of his command and he did not return until some months later.[4] We spent the next day in a wood, where preparations were made for an attack the following day. Runners were selected to carry messages during the day from one organization to another. Jack McWilliams and I and one other were inducted into this service. The idea of chasing around, going here and yonder into places I had never seen before, with the ever-present possibility of passing through a gap in our lines and thus running into German machine-gun bullets—these and other dire possibilities were far from reassuring. And, too, if a fellow was running around by himself and got wounded there was little chance of medical attention.[5]

Most of that night we spent marching and halting, marching and halting. There was always something unnerving about that stopping along on a dark night. Standing on a road or an open field without any sort of protection was hard when the shells were falling around. A fellow wanted to get somewhere and dig in. A couple of hours before daylight we drew up in the usual position at the edge of the wood.

Several times when it was still dark a storm of machine-gun bullets rained over our heads. Nor were they very high over our heads either! My unselfish instincts prompting me, I used dispatch to get

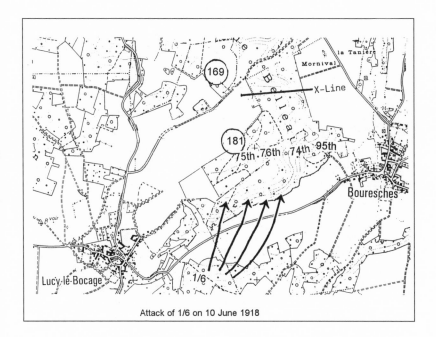

Attack of 1/6 on 10 June 1918

someone else between me and the bullets. While there was quite a
bunch of us huddled there, my attempt was in vain, for others were
trying to perform the same feat.

A little after the break of day we prepared to advance. A grainfield
lay ahead of us for a hundred yards, terminated by a gorge, and beyond that rose a low, heavily timbered hill. It was from this direction
that the firing had come earlier in the morning. *(See map.)*

Major Hughes—more familiarly known as "Johnnie the Hard,"
tall, imposing figure that he was—led the way, quietly, serenely. The
line followed to the right and left, walking with bayonets fixed. The
point of woods toward which we advanced was believed to be infested
with machine-gun nests. They would have free sway over the troops
advancing through the open field. It was the tenth day of June. Almost to the hour one year before I had been sworn into the service,
on Paris Island. As we began advancing that morning, somehow I
could not help thinking that time would be peculiarly appropriate

for the dropping from the 95th Company roster of the name of one redheaded Marine. In the middle of the field I passed a dead Marine, his bayoneted rifle sticking perpendicularly in the ground beside him. At a preconcerted signal from Lieutenant Smith, Jack McWilliams and I turned to our left to leave the company. The object of our going was to learn the exact position of the company that was to be on our left, when the objective was reached, and see that the liaison was established between that company and our own. This would avoid a gap in the line where the enemy might get through. Jack and I followed the ravine just referred to, in the direction of Lucy.

Arriving there we saw the effects of recent shelling. Sixth Regiment headquarters had been in the town and had just been abandoned, so heavy was the bombardment of the village. The village that but a few days before had been so quiet and peaceful had now assumed a fearful aspect. The only sign of life was an old cow, wounded by a shell in several places. The shell had struck beyond a wall, throwing a shower of dirt and rocks that now lay about us. Why we lingered in what seemed so much like a death trap I don't know, unless it was to ascertain definitely, if possible, the position of the company we wanted to see.

I knew I was turned around and had directions and positions hopelessly confused, but Jack said he knew the way. We were then crossing a grainfield. When we got some distance out, Jack had growing doubts as to his ability as a guide. Hearing the occasional spit of a machine gun in a forest a half mile or more to the left, we decided to go over to the outfit and try to learn the location of the company for which we were looking. We passed scattered trees in the field and the swollen body of a cow that had been killed by a shell.[6]

We had not gone a great distance from Lucy when we came to some holes or trenches, and they had evidently been left in a hurry. Blankets and equipment of various kinds had been strewn about the dugouts and in them as well. We did not think our mission demanded any great rush, so we paused long enough to pick up whatever appealed to us. This was indeed a rare opportunity. Even the hardtack had been a luxury, and we helped ourselves. However, even this acquisition dwindled in comparison with something else. I was now the possessor of an entrenching shovel, the kind that a few weeks before we *knew* were no good. We passed other deserted holes going in the direction where we had heard the machine gun.

While we were exulting over our new treasures, the machine gun opened up again—and bullets whizzed all about us! Into a dugout we dropped. What could this mean; could the Germans be over in that wood and nobody facing them? Possibly the line was back of us, beyond Lucy. The hole, of course, provided entire protection from the machine-gun bullets, but it occurred to us that the Germans would likely decide that the next thing in order would be *to send out after the Americans*. The idea of getting out of that hole did not appeal to us in the least, but we crawled out. Fortunately a small clump of bushes was between the hole and the place from which the bullets had come.

Half crawling, half walking, with all possible speed we made our way back in the direction from which we had come. For perhaps five hundred yards we retreated in this manner and were mighty careful to stay as low as possible. Not until we passed over the crest of a knoll did we stop for a breath. In our haste we had left behind the boxes of hardtack and the shovels. Considering our fright and haste, we had done well not to have left our rifles behind.

Later in the day I went alone to look for this 43d Company, and while waiting there I heard some dire stories of the effects of the enemy fire.[7] A fellow whose dugout I visited told me that one company that had gone over the top [he means 3/5 on 6 June] came out with only *eight* men whole. Most of those casualties had been from machine-gun fire. The same man who gave this depressing news showed me a dud that had fallen in the end of his dugout the night before. Lucky, and I suppose he realized it. When I returned to the company a second time, most of the bunch had dug in. Bergeman and I deepened a hole that we found.

Four years before, Germany had struck at the heart of Paris. Again she had marshaled all her strength for a fatal thrust at the capital and victory. A wedge-shaped line pointed toward Paris, and at the point of the wedge were the Marines. This battle Germany must win. Sixty billion dollars she had put into that war, undergone untold suffering and miseries, and had lost more than a million and a half of the flower of her manhood. She would lose the war in addition to paying the war debt. She would lose her position as a first-rate power, probably to be trodden under the heel of her enemies for decades to come. She could not lose this war. She had assembled her guns and best men for one more mighty blow. But she had been checked on the Marne by the 3d Division and to the west by the 2d Division. As stated, we were on the point of the wedge where she had concentrated her forces. She must go through and to Paris! To attain this goal those who stood in the way must be wiped off the face of the earth. A good start had already been made. I feel entirely at a loss to describe the events of the succeeding days. Bombardment followed bombardment. There was no way to know when the wood might be swept with murderous machine-gun fire or the deadly gas shells would leave destruction in their wake. They were soul-trying days. When a man left his hole he did not know whether he would return or if a dozen bullets would cut him down. Yet while a bullet might pierce a limb or even kill, a thousand machine guns could not give one that helpless feeling brought on by the approach of the overawing, merciless shells. They would carry him instantly to oblivion by covering him in his hole or with their terrible force blow him to atoms. These monsters of powder and steel put fear in a man's soul.

And the woods resounded with practically every sound known to modern warfare. Had that group been an older, less vigorous set of men, who did not seem to have such a dear lease on life, I think they would never have stood it—they could not. They would have turned their back to the enemy, or in desperation rushed madly into the face of fire, to bring an end to it all. Shell after shell dropped about us. Now one in front, another behind or on the side, ever with that hellish scream that accompanied them. At times during those hours they fell so fast that it was impossible to detect the sound and fall of the various shells. But all with an unearthly howl, a sudden rush of air, and for one terrible moment the shell seemed to be suspended in the air as though undecided where next to blast a life.

And as I have said, with the falling of the shells came the intermittent raking machine-gun fire. The enemy seemed to be in the point of the wood a few hundred yards away, but so heavy was the undergrowth there that I was unable to see the ones who were firing these death-carrying missiles. Guns from our lines fired repeatedly, but only, I think, at the spot where it was supposed the enemy ought to be. The crack of our rifles, the hollow rattle of the enemy bullets striking the leaves, or the *twang* after being turned from its course by a twig, the dreadful crash of exploding shells—this din kept my ears ringing. So loud and terrible was the crash of a shell that hit near that one was deafened. For a few moments the sound of enemy machine guns, as well as our own, sounded like a weak popping. Most of that day the air hung heavily with stifling gray smoke.

One of the most fearful weapons used by the Germans was the trench mortar. A shell a man could hear coming—if it wasn't coming too fast. There was at least a faint consolation in the fact that it might be heard and a fellow could dodge. Not so with the trench mortar. Instead of being sent over by the explosion of a gun, some other device projected them, and only when all was quiet about could the whirr be detected. There was no warning, just a terrifying crash.

Several of these projectiles from trench mortars fell near the dugout occupied by Bergeman and myself. They were not the cause of our greatest distress, just a painful addition.[8]

Bergeman and I sat facing each other at opposite ends of the grave-like hole. His hands shook as he rolled cigarette after cigarette. No sooner did he get one lighted than he was rolling another, his hands trembling so that half of the tobacco might be shaken from the paper before he got it rolled. Even now I can see his big eyes roll at the falling of each shell. If I looked as scared as he did, I presented a picture.

Then, without warning, another terrific crash, and the loose walls of our hole were caving in and coming down on us. We were out in an instant and took refuge in a vacant dugout nearby.

Many a time during those months did I hear the fall of a shell and wait for the loud cry or muffled wail of a wounded man. On such occasions, regardless of the hazard, a hospital corpsman we called "Buck" [Leonard Barker] could be depended upon to give aid. And now, while the shells rent the air and changed the form of the earth, Buck called for men to take a lieutenant to the first-aid station.

Because of the extreme ruggedness of the ground over which the wounded lieutenant was to be carried, it was necessary that several men should go along. The only exit that we found practicable was a ravine that was almost impassable because of the number of boulders. The whole back area was being shelled with high explosives and mustard-gas shells. A part of the ravine extended along the front line, and the men who had occupied it had sought cover from the harassing fire by digging back into the banks of the ravine.

The shelling indeed was terrific and left a fearful picture along our route. When we had gotten beyond the rocky part of the ravine, so many of the trees that bordered it had been struck by shells and fallen along our way that it was only with the greatest difficulty we could make any progress. The heinous sound of the pursuing shells still fell upon our ears as the death-seeking missiles crashed near us. The nauseating odor of the exploded gas shells, with the suggestiveness that always accompanied it, made us hasten with all possible speed toward the first-aid station.

The position of it was about a half mile from the line, in a culvert, under the road. Since this excavation was covered by several feet of well-packed soil and rocks, it afforded protection against all but the largest shells. Inside, the wounded received temporary dressings before being carried in an ambulance to the rear to a field hospital. However, outside the station, lying side by side, were the bodies of several Americans whose wounds were too severe. The lieutenant we brought in had a severe wound in his side, and blood trickled from his forehead. We learned later that he, too, did not survive.[9]

After our task was done, two of us, Shepherd and I, went to the town of Lucy for some purpose, possibly to get water. I have a somewhat indistinct recollection of being greeted there with a rain of shells. On our way back to the line we found the other two who had helped carry the wounded lieutenant, seeking protection from the shellfire between two large boulders.

Upon our return we found that the company had moved to the left and up the hill. Dark was coming. While the front was now quieter, the ordeal through which we had passed had demonstrated the wisdom of digging a hole as some sort of protection. It behooved me to get in a dugout with someone else, if such was possible. I managed to form a partnership with Weinberger and another fellow. Since they already had a hole dug some distance, I probably derived considerably more satisfaction out of the arrangement than they did.

Before noon of the following day the Germans began peppering us with shells. Most, if not all, of us again moved to the left, dropping a hundred yards or more down the hill. Here we would be in a position equally advantageous to repel an attack and yet miss the larger number of shells that were falling farther up the hill.

Whether the change was a good one I do not know, but the bombardment that followed can never be erased from my memory. So hard was the ground where we were that it was impossible to dig in. The only thing to do was hover under the edge of one of the numerous large rocks that lay about.

By about noon the shells were coming over with a frequency that was appalling. Never had I undergone anything that would compare with the horrifying shellfire that fell unrelentingly on the twelfth day of June 1918. It is true that the enemy thought us a little farther back than we were, and it was due to this circumstance alone, I suppose, that we were not annihilated. I crouched under a rock six or eight feet high and on the German side. Shell after shell screeched by with awful sounds, many of the shells seeming to go only inches above the rock. But one of these shells had to come a bit lower to strike the edge of the rock above me to explode and blow me to pieces. So fast did they come that many times the sounds of different shells were not discernible. One deadly explosive after another passed over, or fell nearby, with a rapidity that stifled the senses, and brought upon us almost frenzying madness.[10]

Anything in the world in preference to cringing there by that rock, helpless in the unremitting shellfire. I did not expect to come out of it alive and would gladly have given an arm or leg to know I would survive it. The helplessness that one felt is inconceivable. It would have seemed a thousand times better to face an army of machine guns with my bayoneted rifle in hand and a chance—though but the shadow of a chance—to act, to *do* something, to be opposed by an enemy where there was the opportunity to fight back. What was our chance against artillery fired from miles behind their lines? There was no alternative for us but to stay where we were and wonder if the next moment might bring the end. Two terrible hours passed before there was any indication of a cessation.

I do not now recall the casualties of any except those in that immediate vicinity. During the bombardment men were shifting frequently from one unprotected spot to another, with a bit of hope of finding a place more secure. On the other side of the rock, and little over an arm's length from me, Bacon had received a wound in the hand. He was to receive wounds on two other fronts before the war was over. To my left half a dozen steps Weinberger, who had sought protection by piling some loose stones about him, was wounded by the third shell before he could get out. To my rear, less than six feet, Caskey's life had probably been saved by a steel trench mirror he carried in his shirt pocket. A piece of shell had torn a hole several inches long in the thick steel plate, with no worse than a shock to Caskey. The mirror had been directly over his heart.

Following the shelling we went some distance through the woods to our left again, where we dug in. Water was very scarce and I became intensely thirsty. The gift of a drink of water from Parker, a princely fellow from St. Louis, I will never forget. While the shelling was not as heavy as it had been, constant firing continued about twenty-four hours.

On 13 June, led by Captain Kearns, who had recently joined us, we moved yet again to our left. Still in the woods, our destination was on the upper edge of a steep incline, a timbered valley ahead, and a grainfield some hundreds of yards to our left front. And there we were to experience more soul-trying days that I can never forget. The rain of shells at times was terrific. As I have said, a man can go into the worst kind of bloody conflict for a few hours, but day after day of merciless shellfire tears the nerves to pieces. Time after time we thought a lull that greeted us might be prolonged but as often were doomed to unbearable disappointment by the heinous shriek of a shell to be followed, very likely, by many others. Repeatedly, when a period of quiet seemed imminent, the comparative silence was broken by howling shells that made the blood run cold.

The shells that came over were of various sizes, but the gun that harassed us most was probably an Austrian eighty-eight that shot from our left front, seemingly less than a mile away. Day after day, this gun belched forth, shooting upon us direct fire. Because of its position, and possibly because it was the only eighty-eight used in that part of the sector, the report of the gun had a distinct sound. Nor were we long in learning to recognize its "voice." A heavy *a-rup-rup* that it emitted had enough evil in it to have been the earth itself bursting open. Then as quick as a flash a shell whistled over our heads—if we were fortunate enough for it to go over.

Of course, if a shell is to be a direct hit, there is no good in dodging; but if it falls anywhere in a radius of three to a hundred feet (depending upon the size of the shell and the nature of the ground on which it falls) the danger is minimized if one is lying flat upon the ground. But in the case of the eighty-eight, the shell followed so soon after the report of the gun had reached our ears that we had practically no time to get down. This was particularly disconcerting, and perhaps that one gun did more toward unnerving us than all the other guns farther back put together.[11] Most of the time we were in our holes, averaging perhaps three and a half to four feet in depth. If we were standing, there was not time enough to bring our heads down into the dugout.[12]

Muck and I dug in together. Muck was a good-natured, simple-hearted fellow, hung together with less care than Ichabod Crane. He hailed from a farm in Michigan. His unmistakable corn-row step and manner of expressing himself branded him as a farmer from a farm remote.

Behind the lines Muck was usually in the best of humor; and when there was any carousing, he was on hand to do his share, scorning even a pretense of abstinence. "You are likely to get kilt anyway, so you had just as well have a good time while y'ar livin'," he would say. But Aesop was right when he said circumstances alter cases.

During the days when Muck and I shared misery in the hole together, I could not but observe his new attitude toward the Here and the Hereafter. The day before we left Quantico we were given Testaments by the American Bible Society. For the rest of the period of our service the man who never deigned to be seen reading his Testament nevertheless carried it in the pocket of his OD shirt. At this time I had been quite closely associated with Muck for over a year, and Bibles always seemed the subject furthest removed from his mind. But to come to the point, at the present time and under the circumstances given, Muck assumed an entirely different attitude toward the Book. Much of the time we sat in opposites ends of the hole, facing each other. During hours of greater danger each lay stretched lengthwise along the holes we had burrowed into the sides of the dugout. This position was far from comfortable, though physical comfort was of only secondary consideration. In this position we usually faced one another, only Muck would not be looking at me—he was extremely busy in a nervous perusal of his Testament. But his power of concentration was not such that he was oblivious of his surroundings; when a shell came howling over, I could see the look of utter despair on his lean face. I was probably engaged in the same manner as he, and the terror may even have been more pronounced on my features; but I could not, even in those grim moments, but get a faint amusement from Muck's terror-stricken countenance.

Had there been any way in the world for us to occupy ourselves, we would have been blest. Perhaps only one thing made it possible to endure the days. Ever there were rumors—a thousand rumors: that we would be relieved and go to southern France for a rest, that the war would end at an early date and we would go home, et cetera, et cetera. Long before, we had learned (we thought) to beware of all good news, but still we would clasp at the last straw.

On one particularly trying day the rumor was strong that we were to get relieved that night. Late in the afternoon the harsh, grating sounds of German planes came to our ears. By that time sufficient shells had fallen in the wood to render the treetops so thin that they no longer served to intercept the view of enemy planes that flew over. The harsh, irregular grind of the planes came directly over us, and for some minutes there were eleven German planes overhead. All these over our lines and not an Allied plane in sight. This kind of thing was most disheartening. Now that the planes had visited us, we were feverishly anxious to get out of the line. They would probably send a corrected range to the artillery and we would pay. But no relief that night.

Just about the break of day a battle usually raged along the line to our right or left. A sharp crack of a machine gun or rifle would break the morning stillness. Then came an increasing clatter-clatter of machine guns, while we wondered what might be the fate of the boys who were being attacked or were doing the attacking. Sometimes artillery would come into play during the rifle and machine-gun battle, the artillery firing at one another or, more often, at the men in the lines. There were momentary lulls in the firing of a machine gun, and then the rapid fire again. Or the gun might suddenly cease, to fire no more, which often meant that the enemy gun had done its work. The gray smoke of battle often enveloped us, though we might be some distance away.

Just at nightfall was a favorite time for attacks from one side or the other. With the coming of night it was usually much quieter than during the day—but never so quiet that I could get anything like good, sound sleep. In fact, the sleep I got during the several times I was in Belleau Wood was almost negligible.

During the night, when most of the men were making at least the attempt to sleep, it was necessary that each take his turn being on the alert every few steps along the front—this to prevent a surprise from the enemy. The night guard was not an enviable occupation, and it was my fortune to miss it while at the front this time. In fact, the machine gunners did most of this, from a point forty or fifty steps beyond the line proper. In this exposed position it behooved the man on guard, for his own welfare not to mention the safety of his fellows in the rear, to keep *awake*. I recall that Owrey, Wasser, and maybe Piggott had this night watch most of the time. Nor were they particularly in love with this phase of soldier life. Back at Outrepont both Owrey and Wasser had boasted of the number of Germans they would kill when we got to the front. They didn't seem to feel quite that way now.

During those endless nights, as stated, there was comparative quiet. However, the occasional crack of a rifle caused a fellow in his hole to wonder if the Germans, in the blackness of the night, might be slipping upon us. And then a fellow thought of home.

In case of an attack, of course everybody wanted to be ready. I used every precaution to have my equipment in shape to make a move at any time. The rifle was kept loaded at all times and on the bank in easy reach. The combat pack, too, must be handy to slip on at any moment's notice. The belt of ammunition was supposed to be kept on at all times, I believe; but with its hundred rounds of .30-caliber army cartridges, and a bayonet and canteen attached, it got more than heavy during a week or ten-day turn at the front.

Most of the time more or less gas hung about us, the larger percent of which was mustard gas. One day a shell exploded not more than three or four steps in front of my dugout, leaving in its wake a heavy mass of black smoke, which set us all to coughing violently. Tears flowed freely. Owrey and Piggott's dugout was a little to the right of the falling shell, and they were affected much the same as Muck and I. Perhaps the shell came down nearest me, and I figured that I was pretty badly gassed. Yet the idea of being gassed and leaving my loyal comrades to go to the hospital added none to my flow of tears. For perhaps fifteen or twenty minutes I coughed and sniffed and cried. I was just about to leave to go to the first-aid station when I, like the rest, began to cough less. Soon, to our sorrow, we found our heads clearer than when the shell fell. The shell had been only high explosive and not gas at all. We really should have known this at first, but so severe was the coughing and choking for a few minutes that we perhaps thought that the Germans were throwing over a new kind of gas.

I failed to state that while on our way to the present position we passed the bodies of a number of Marines strewn here and there.[13] And now in front and to the left of our dugouts, a dozen steps away, were a number of dead Germans, with a dead Frenchman or two, their pockets turned inside out. While the bodies were doubtless suggestive of what might happen to any or all of us, I think that their nearness gave us little thought.

It might be wondered why the bodies had not been buried. Some days before our arrival a burying detail had been sent into the wood, we were told, but so hostile was the enemy fire that it was deemed inexpedient to try to bury others at the time. On several occasions, when it was unusually quiet, two or three of us ventured to take a look at things a hundred yards or so behind the line. The first time I went on one of these trips I was alone. I came upon bodies that I thought were of Negro soldiers, though it seemed strange that I had heard of none on that front. On closer observation, I saw that they wore Marine uniforms, and I knew that no Negro ever wore one. The faces were turning black with age.

But a short distance away was a dense thicket, the tall, slender trees in many places but a few inches apart. A fierce battle had raged here on 10 June in which the Americans had driven the Germans out. And praise be to the man who led the charge! Later his superb gallantry cost him his life. It took a man of supreme courage to face that formidable position. I've never seen anything like it. The thicket was veritably alive with machine guns. Nor had the Germans who fired them been the *"Kamerad"* kind, which many Americans had been undeservedly heaped with praise for *capturing*. The German gunners had shot from shallow dugouts, and most of them had died at their guns, bolt upright, and I think I recall one who still had the trigger in his lifeless hand. Few, if any, shells had fallen there, yet the saplings and brush were almost mowed down by the literally thousands of bullets that had gone through there. How the Americans had captured a position so near impregnable, I do not know.[14]

Not far from the edge of the thicket were the bodies of several Americans, the price paid to take the machine-gun nests. I went into the packs of a number of them to look for hardtack. Just now, I would not greatly relish food that had been in close proximity with a corpse several days, but when a fellow is really hungry, such a consideration is of no consequence. However, as I looked for food sometimes personal articles dropped out of the pack, such as letters, a Testament, and so on. And these made a fellow think of the probable loved ones back home, who had likely not gotten the news of the boy's death. But such thoughts were quickly forgotten when I got back to the company.

Others in the outfit made trips back of the line to search the dead, salvaging razors or other such articles as met their fancy. While I had no scruples about taking what could do the dead no good, I always drew the line after looking for something to eat. It was safer in my dugout anyway.

The wandering we did was usually some distance back of the lines and in such other places as we were not within the range of enemy observation. However, when we had been in the present position for about a week, the 7th Infantry, which had not been on the front before, came up and dug holes immediately to our left. And instead of lying low during the day, as we cautioned them to do, they wandered along the most exposed places with the unconcern of a squirrel shooter. The result was that night they got their baptism of fire. Shell after shell dropped on them, with murderous accuracy. Although we were to their immediate right, the only shelling we caught was where our part of the line joined theirs. The cries of agony from wounded and dying came increasingly to our ears, until we were relieved and were out of earshot.[15]

During our stays in Belleau, many details of men made trips to Lucy for water or rations or both. Although such journeys carried one farther from the enemy, they did not necessarily mean getting farther from danger.

The first trip I made to Lucy-le-Bocage, after our first time there on that serene afternoon of 2 June, was about two days later, when we were in positions from which we were relieved the first time. When we were staying at the deep dugouts back at Verdun, the day seemed unreal, the morning often like the evening, and evening like the morning. During the early days at Belleau this muddled sensation was accentuated. And on this first trip back to Lucy, with the mingled sensation of fear and the feeling that I was in another world, I can never forget. As I walked through the green woods for some distance, I recall how wholly out of place those scars of shattered shell holes seemed, where the trees, the bushes, the grass—everything—had just burst forth with all the verdant freshness of spring. I probably made haste to get out of that troubled chaos of grim incongruities.

The peaceful Lucy set amid yellow grainfields of but a few days before now had been the scene of many falling shells. The quiet serenity of past days had been supplanted by a danger that made the life of a hunted beast to be envied. A wild desolation now marked the village. Shattered walls and village streets with scattered debris now met the eye on every side. And between those walls was no place to be when shells were falling near. The risk of being struck by shell fragments was enough; the thought of a heavy mass of brick and mortar falling heavily upon one seemed the most terrible destruction.

While in the village, I was told by one of the company mess cooks, I think, of a lone civilian who had refused to leave. A shell had come through the wall of the old woman's house and passed through her body, of course killing her instantly.

This was the last time I went to Lucy during the day. The enemy artillery was too wide awake for men to go along the unhidden paths in broad daylight without throwing over shells. And the thought of passing along one of those paths alone was anything but comforting. Shell holes, in or near the path, still smoking from the explosion of but a few moments before, the rank, hellish odor of the high-explosive gas they emitted—these did not tempt a man to loiter. And along the way, here and there, were always to be found the bodies of those who had gone for rations or water along the same path and a shell had gotten them. "Poor fellows." But the sympathy for the unlucky boy was for the time displaced by reflections whether the passerby might not be overtaken by a like fate. A fellow felt relief leaving such scenes behind. And should he be making the trip alone, the sound of an approaching shell struck terror in him that he did not experience when in his dugout. If a man was to be killed, of course one place was no worse than another. However, there was a greater likelihood of being wounded, and the thought of getting a leg or an arm blown away and no one near to aid gave the suggestion an added horror.

There are no words to describe the feeling when a big gun opened up across the lines and with lightning fury there came a gurgling, hissing, roaring shell. There seemed to be a moment when it was poised in the air, as though to pick its victim, then to burst a few feet away with a thundering crash that seemed to tear the very earth apart. This kind of thing struck terror to the bravest. But if the shells missed, thoughts were soon running to what might be ahead.

As I have said, the ration and water details first went to Lucy during the day, later changing the time to after sunset. Still later the village was abandoned for all purposes, so great was the danger. For some days or weeks it was perhaps the sole watering place for several thousand troops. Men were detailed from each company to gather the empty canteens, one man carrying a dozen or more. The Germans, with their usual alacrity, were quick in observing the hour the water details arrived in the village. Since there were not more than two springs, and these did not have a generous flow, there was always a rush and jam to fill the canteens and get out and away from the shells, which often fell in quick succession. The Germans seemed to have the very springs located.

And those shells! The greatest fear I had was being in a village when it was heavily shelled. There would come the deep report of a gun, as though a gigantic volcano was erupting, a heinous, roaring shriek, with fearful moments of suspense terminating in an ear-splitting explosion that brought hollow, resounding echoes belonging to another world. This was followed, not infrequently, by a wall weighing many tons toppling heavily upon the ground, hurling a shower of bricks fifty or a hundred yards.

And woe to the man within the walls! The thunderous crash and the hollow, mocking echo sometimes came with such overwhelming force that the deafening sound set the ears to ringing. And there were times when those shells came in such quick succession that a man was left in frenzied bewilderment, not knowing which way to turn. Here, as on the front line, quite often a fellow got the idea that another place here or yonder was safe and had a kind of immunity to shells. Many a time I surmised thus to find the cherished spot a torn shell hole or soon to become a mass of wreckage.

The one place of protection that could be found in a bombarded village was below a French house in a wine cellar. These cellars were made of brick and rock, with an arched roof of the same material. Some of the cellars had an added protection, since several feet of dirt and rock had been placed over them, in the rooms above. Such shelters as these offered security against all but the largest shells.

After a company water detail of half a dozen or more men had filled their canteens, they often hastened to the nearest cellar to wait till the Germans decided to give them a rest. In fact, it was not unusual for such a group to remain in the cellar the greater part of the night. It might seem that even the remote possibility of a night attack at the front would have made it imperative to return as soon as possible, but as well as I remember, it was taken as a matter of course that if the town was being shelled, the next thing in order was an *abri* or some other place that afforded protection.

The security furnished by one of these underground vaults permitted a temporary relaxation of the nerves that could be conceived only by the person who had undergone that awful, nerve-breaking strain. Once in the cellar there was nothing for a man to do but just sit there in the dark, making the most of the time that he was out of great danger. Yes, and listen to the indistinct, shrieking howls and muffled explosions of shells falling in the distance.

When a shell struck very close, the feeling of uneasiness was very pronounced. A direct hit by a big shell would probably either blow those in the cellar to pieces or leave us wounded with a mass of brick and cement pinning us to the earth. The thought of the walls above tumbling down upon us was far from pleasant.

Indistinct recollections come to mind of stories of narrow escapes, told by men who had taken refuge in the dugout and by others who had undergone some harrowing experiences while above in the village.

One night the wall of the adjoining house was struck by a shell and crashed to the ground with a thundering roar. We then sought another dugout and felt we had made a lucky change. The place must have been some kind of headquarters. It was lighted, had bunks in it, and a telephone that was not infrequently used by one of the occupants. This hole in the ground was incomparably more inviting than any palace I ever gazed upon. My, but how I envied those fellows in there! And leaving time must have been particularly delightful.

Nor were high-explosive shells the only kind that greeted us while in Lucy. On one occasion in particular we got a quantity of mustard gas. We immediately hauled our masks out and having them on was anything but pleasant. The tight band that secured the mask to the face often gave a headache, and that noseclip of the early American mask was often so painful that I have seen men deliberately pull off the masks when there was an uncertain quantity of gas about. At this time we had a French mask that afforded comparative comfort. However, the construction of it was such that it did not give protection for more than a few minutes at a time, and so it was replaced by the American mask. On this particular occasion I think we could not have worn the mask less than *three* hours, the longest I ever wore one.

While the mask was on, the rubber mouthpiece could be removed and with his one "lung" of air a fellow could hastily say a few words. Following the remarks, which in all probability were not understood by anyone, the speaker had to hurriedly thrust the rubber tube into his mouth for a breath of fresh air. Should he inhale before taking the mouthpiece, he would not get a full breath and the sides of the mask would be drawn against his face. The conversations carried on in these dugouts of pitch darkness, by men with masks on accompanied by the noise of falling shells—these conversations must have been of a very happy and enlightening nature.

Before dawn approached, we had to get out of the deep dugouts and on our way. By this time the German artillery was likely quiet, but the thought of facing another day like the previous ones was painful to dwell on. However, daylight could not find us crossing the open fields.

With canteens of water, cumbersome cans of coffee, and loaves of bread with about the physical properties of pasteboard, we made our way back with all haste possible. Nor was it an easy task carrying these rations, especially the cans of coffee, along rocky ravines, through thick undergrowth or chaotic masses of fallen trees, with the added burden of a rifle slung on the shoulder constantly catching on twigs and whatnot. The falling of a shell or two somewhere nearby made the situation complete. Even though the coffee cans were provided with some sort of top, it is surprising that more of the cold liquid was not spilled. It was a temptation to drop coffee or bread when a big shell whirred by. However, I never knew any rations to be lost or left behind on such occasions.

A host of experiences I had going to and from the front line have faded from me. All seem to have melted into one weird recollection of shells, gas, and dead men.

In a letter home I wrote: "When we arrived and took the sector from the French, I thought, well, here is the end of the 2d Division. Throwing a bunch of inexperienced men like ourselves up against the flower of the German army seemed worse than murder. As soon as we had relieved the French and they were gone, I expected the Germans like a big snake to be ready to swallow us up. But ask any of the old Dutchmen who were up against us!" If the war was to be won by the Allies, we were sure that the Marines would do the winning!

The glory of at last being relieved must have been unbelievable. But as we went back we caught a raking fire. Buck Ashwood, who was but a short distance from me, got a shrapnel wound in the leg as we hurried along. Krieger had been wounded some nights before and died on his way to the hospital. It had seemed that there was something invincible about Krieger. It was to me always an unreality that he could be among the number who had drilled and fought with us the last time.[16]

A hike of some length—we never complained of the length or the speed when we were going away from the front—and we were halted. Our blanket rolls that we had left behind some weeks before were produced, but many of them had been ransacked so that the original owner found few of his belongings. Although it was about the middle of June, the weather was disagreeably cool, and a fire in a neighboring camp felt good. We again lined up for chow, and this doubtless seemed strange. Yes, and rumors, of course the camp was rife with rumors.

A few hours here and trucks carried us fifteen or twenty miles to the town of Nanteuil, a clean little city on the bank of the clear-blue Marne River. We figured we had a good thing of it here. A Y offered some recreation and sweets as well. I quote in part from a letter I wrote home from Nanteuil on 19 June:

> You should have heard the boys who relieved us talk about the Marines! They say the Marines were all they had heard for a week. And the French! "American soldat très bon, très bon." Many civilians who were deserting this part of France when we were on our way are now back again, so you can imagine their gratitude to us. The German prisoners taken could hardly believe that we were Americans. Even the officers taken thought we were Canadians. The German soldiers are told that there aren't more than ten or fifteen thousand American soldiers in France, and that the submarines are sinking the transports as fast as they leave the American harbors.

So, we were some shock to the morale of the German soldier.

At the front our company had lost probably about fifty percent in killed and wounded. After our arrival in Nanteuil we were to receive new men from what was known as the 4th Replacement Battalion. As indicated previously, our bath of shellfire and weeks at the front had given us an exalted opinion of ourselves. Strangely enough, in those days, the man who had seen action had thrust upon him certain superior traits. He was someone to be revered. The man who had not been to the front seemed effeminate and of a lower caste. Just how such an attitude came to exist I do not know, but such was the feeling toward all noncombatants.

The 4th Replacements had not fought and automatically fell into the nonfighting class. Most of the older men of the company had enough sense to avoid saying anything to them that would be offensive; but the new men humbled themselves before the least deserving who had been to the front. However, we were to later realize that the men who joined us at this time were, as a class, a superior type of men.

Among those whom I was later thrown in close contact with was Cpl. Alexander Mascia. He was a big, sturdy, heavy-visaged fellow with a good fund of common sense, a lot of bulldog determination, and he was honest from the ground up. In the months to come he did not fail to see many flaws in the general run of things, nor was he reluctant to express himself. But for courage when iron nerves were needed, few could equal him. Another of this group was Moose Taylor, who had left college to join the Marines. He proved an asset to the company. One of the men who joined us whom I came to know best was A. W. Robertson, who was later affectionately to be known as "Bobby." He was a rather short, thickset fellow from North Dakota, who, like Taylor, had left school to enter the service. He was of Scotch descent, and he had inherited all the hardihood, with other good qualities, of his race. Although hotheaded at times, his anger was usually a righteous one. He proved himself an admirable leader, being respected, feared, and at the same time almost idolized by those who knew him.

Since new men were in the ranks, regardless of our training or theirs, it was deemed necessary that we go out along the bank of the river each day to drill and practice in the various formations. It was generally felt that we were getting a bad deal in having to train this way after the siege we had undergone. There was a profusion of crabbing.

After about a week at Nanteuil we rolled our packs and hiked perhaps half the distance to the front, stopping in a wood along the Paris-Metz Road, over which we had been once or twice before. Shallow holes were dug, as it was felt that the Germans might get their long-range guns into action. However, during our several days there we were not molested. Although we had come nearer the front, rumors were still current that we would leave any time for southern France or some other *bon* sector; these notwithstanding, there were almost unmistakable indications that we were to leave for the front again. My gas mask, which I had been issued back at Champigneulle, was condemned, and now I got a new one of a somewhat better type. Then, late one evening, orders came to roll packs. It developed that my old friend Bergeman was not, however, ready to leave. He had gotten it into his head, or wanted to, that he was to remain in the rear in the capacity of cook, mule skinner, or something else of that order. I can easily imagine his feelings when he was told to roll up, to go along with us and face it again.

Some distance from the line the Germans shelled the road with gas shells. All masks went on almost as one. The night was so black we could see little at best; but with the masks on and the eyepieces becoming increasingly clouded by proximity to the face, making our way was difficult. To this was added the discomfort of carrying the packs at about twice the pace we should have taken. After perhaps half a mile, almost smothered, we got orders to remove the masks. So nearly exhausted were we before the order was received that we were almost ready to fall from exhaustion.

As we came into the shell-torn woods and neared our former positions, I heard one of the new boys behind ask another "what that awful *odor* was." The poor fellow had some things to learn. He did not seem to have suspected that dead men had lain in that wood for a month. Until he called attention to the odor, I had not noticed it. Get used to that awful shellfire I never could, but the strong odor of putrefying bodies, with the scent of high explosive and mustard gas that always hung in the wood—these had come to seem a part of the place. The result was we had practically forgotten that the decaying bodies had an odor.

We dropped into holes left by those before us, and my hole was but a few steps from the one I had when we'd left the line about ten days before. As I slipped into my shallow, half-covered dugout, I overheard one of the new men remark dismally to his companion in misery, "This is a dog's life, ain't it?" The one who made the remark, I later learned, was a green fellow from West Texas, with a drawl in his voice and general deportment that soon branded him as a Texas curio. Although this was not a time to make light of anything, I got a faint amusement from the disparagement in the fellow's remark. The fellow had scarcely gotten a taste of what he was yet to enjoy.

More of the heavy shelling like we'd experienced when in the sector before was expected, but compared with the baptism of fire we had gotten, the days were not bad for us. Most of the shells hit a hundred or more yards away, and the number of them was small compared with what it had been. I, for one, was duly thankful that the Austrian eighty-eight had been silenced or had found amusement elsewhere.

However, what we missed was more than made up for by the 9th and 23d Infantries, who one afternoon made an attack on the town of Vaux, a half mile or more ahead and to the right. The town was situated on a woody slope, and the fighting had not long been in progress before the country was veiled in smoke. The attacking men underwent a terrible shelling. Shell after shell burst about them, but they continued to advance and took the town. Coincident with this battle an airplane fight took place overhead.

Only one thing do I recall worth mentioning that happened while we were in this position, and for this poor Hickey, the brunt of a thousand jibes, was responsible. A gallon can of apple butter was brought up with the other rations one night, and there was some disagreement as to the best way to open the can. Hickey, as usual, was forthcoming with a solution for getting the fluidlike apple butter. Simply place the can on its side and cut all the way around it, he urged. It did not occur to Hickey that the disadvantage of losing the contents was worth consideration. Perhaps the contents of the can were to be divided and sent to different parts of the line, but the solution to this grave problem I do not remember.

After about three days here we moved to occupy a part of the line far down to the left, where we dropped into some holes at the edge of the wood overlooking a wide stretch of open country. Apparently the Germans had first held the position, as a number of Maxims were in use along the line. One was the heavy Maxim, mounted on a large base and weighing several hundred pounds. Of course, the guns might have been brought from elsewhere by Americans, but there were other indications of a former German occupation in that vicinity.

To our left front five hundred yards was a wooded slope that we supposed was occupied by Germans. Far to the front and right was an open valley, terminated by a mountain range a mile or more away. At the foot of this range, almost directly in front of us, was a small village. A day or two after our arrival in our new position, we derived no little pleasure in seeing the working of some of our own artillery. In the days past, so many hours had we been harassed by enemy fire, and part of the time by both the German artillery and our own, that we now derived a peculiar satisfaction out of hearing the deep bark of our big guns in the rear. This followed by a momentary silence, then a slow, drowsy whine, while high in the air a huge shell seemed to be taking its time on the journey of destruction. Then a kind of drowsy roar, as though the shell was lazily turning over, followed by a sharp, tearing, grating sound, as though the body had suddenly been transformed into a wild beast of irresistible speed and ferocity. A moment of silence, then a crash and there appeared simultaneously an irregular mass of smoke, with black clouds of dirt flying into the air. The shells fell so far away that we could see the effects of the explosions while, for some seconds afterward, we were still hearing the shells in the air, to be followed, of course, by the sound of the explosion. While these shells did not fall very often, their size—probably ten-inch or larger—made up for the infrequency of their fall.

Sometime after our arrival a rather small-calibered gun not far within the nearest part of the German lines opened up and threw shells so close over our heads as to send our hearts to our mouths. The shells seemed to barely clear our dugouts and, with lightning speed, to strike the higher ground several hundred yards to our rear. The enemy evidently thought us farther back, as the range of their guns was not corrected, and the shells continued to do little or no harm.

One morning we waked to find earthworks thrown up not far out in No Man's Land. This was somewhat disconcerting, to say the least. There was much speculation as to what the Germans had done and *would* do. A night or two afterward the ring of picks and shovels that came from that direction caused increased concern. There was little telling what the Germans might not be preparing to make life miserable for us, or to get rid of us entirely. Whatever their plans had been, they did not materialize. While they worked away one night, our artillery turned loose on them and they made a hurried departure. I was after rations at the time, but I later heard the boys speak of hearing a wagon quickly rattling away from the entrenchments when shells began dropping about.

The danger to water and ration details bound for Lucy became so great that company mule skinners now carted these supplies up in the night to a point as near the line as was safe and practicable. Two of us went together one morning with as many canteens as we could carry, but for some reason we were late starting. All about the cart others were crowded, trying to fill their canteens from the faucets, which were working very poorly. Day was beginning to break before the last two of us could get to the tank. We made haste to fill our canteens before daylight found us in this exposed area. But nearly all the water was gone, and what little there was oozed out of the faucets very slowly. I tried to get the much-desired liquid more quickly by taking off the top of the water tank and setting canteens below, but for some reason the attempt was unsuccessful. It was getting light and only a few of our canteens were full. Returning to the company with some of them unfilled was unthinkable as long as there was any water to be had.

The carts were in the edge of the clump of trees, surrounded by an open field that had recently been the scene of a hard-fought contest. That Fourth-of-July morning had been unusually quiet. Then a shell dropped far down about the front line. Another followed close on the heels of the first, though not so far away. Another, another, and another in rapid succession, each bursting shell falling closer to us and the water carts. We did not have time to think twice before the whole volley was directed toward the carts, and with murderous accuracy shells fell all about us. I jumped from the cart and ran through the clump of trees. I made a dive for a gigantic shell hole, which for some reason had been the burial spot of two men. A shell struck almost under me—I did not know exactly where. The smoke of the shell had not lifted when, half kneeling, half crouching upon the ground, I found myself coming out of a daze. My helmet, which had been securely fastened under my chin, had in some mysterious manner fallen off *behind* me. The shell had stunned me but I seemed to be whole.

The spasm of shelling was over, apparently. However, I and my companion on the cart—who had sought shelter with the same fervor and alacrity that had characterized my own haste—were unanimous in the conclusion that this was no place for us. We returned to the company with part of the canteens unfilled, but with the conviction strengthened that Sherman had had his subject well in hand when he gave his memorable, if short, discourse on war.

Though the Germans used illuminating flares on all the fronts we were on, there was something about them at Belleau that impressed me especially. I can picture myself now as I went feverishly to or from the line, while ahead or over my shoulder (the Germans were on three sides of us at this time), the enemy flares could be seen rising above No Man's Land. For me there was something appalling in the sight of them, a subtle indication of impending disaster. Although maybe there was a hushed silence along the line, one of these flares shot noiselessly into the air, dropped like a rock for some distance, and when the parachute had opened a light of dazzling brightness hung as though fixed in the air, often remaining in the air ten or fifteen minutes. In fact, so slow was the descent of these flares that when seen at a distance it was sometimes impossible to determine whether they were flares or actual stars.

I never learned to determine with any degree of accuracy the distance of these flares, or star shells as they were sometimes called. I have seen them go up when they appeared unbelievably close. Many times they seemed to be so near that I thought that the Germans *must* have broken through our lines and were but a short distance away. On a quiet night the sight of one of these flares seemed to give to the hushed stillness a terror, an omen of dire consequences. Likewise, when shells wailed over our heads or dropped mercilessly about, the going up of a flare from the German lines seemed to increase the horror of it all, to portend an awful fate that was soon to overtake all.

• • •

On the night of July Fourth, a month and two days after we arrived at the front, we were relieved [by the 26th Division]. It was generally felt that we had made our last trip to that front. However, this could have been no more than a surmise, as about all we could really know was that we were in the war and would probably stick around until the war ended or we shuffled off.

With inexpressible enthusiasm we made all haste to the rear. Legs that had been almost too tired to move now bore a swing that could hardly have shown more pep had the chances of coming out of the war whole increased geometrically with each step taken. When day came we still hiked on, and probably with no complaint at the rapid pace that had been set. Our stay on the line had been nothing as bad the first two trips up, yet the strain was such that as we got out of danger the nerves that had been tense for days gave way and demanded rest. As we hiked along we passed a detachment of 26th Division men camped at the roadside. They showed a fine spirit of friendliness long to be remembered in bringing coffee to as many of the fellows as our few minutes rest permitted.[17]

It was the famous Paris-Metz Road along which we hiked. At intervals along the road, to the right and left, we were surprised that the French had dug reserve trenches, with the added protection of wire entanglements in front of them. The precaution was doubtless a wise one, but at the time it seemed to us that the French had put a disproportionate amount of confidence in the trenches themselves, rather than in the hold-or-die spirit that had prompted the American leaders. But the American generals and soldiers were not wearied by four years of war.

About noon we turned into an inviting grove and pitched camp some hundreds of yards from the Marne. In the afternoon I started along a beautiful path toward the river for a swim. But for some reason I turned back, later to enjoy a visit in a fruit orchard. In my rambles I visited a house where French soldiers were enjoying their wine and who offered me a drink.

Far in the night we were waked by what seemed the almost frenzied voice of Major Hughes, shouting, "Everybody up!" I could imagine but one reason for being waked in this manner, that THE GER-

MANS HAD BROKEN THROUGH THE LINE AND WE MUST
FACE THEM AGAIN. The night was black, and the command had
been given to get on our clothes and roll packs with the greatest possible haste. All the horrors of the war and the dangers we had undergone flashed before me in a chaotic and hideous picture, and
now we were to face the awful conflict again.

We were soon retracing our steps of the day before. We met artillerymen on the way, which seemed strange. Finally, it dawned upon
us that our surmise regarding the attack was a mistake. The company
camped in the wood several days then moved to a pine grove that
had been planted. It seemed most strange to see row after row of
trees a foot or more in diameter at regular intervals, as though they
had been just set out there.

One afternoon orders were given for a company formation. When
we had assembled, a list of names was read of noncommissioned officers raised in rank, as well as the names of new ones that had been
made. A considerable percent of the survivors of Belleau were made
corporals. However, it was the greatest surprise of my life when my
name was read among those created corporals. Morrison and others had told me in the weeks before that I was to get the "stripes,"
but I had thought them only joking. To my enlightened mind it was
as though I had had a great responsibility thrust upon me. I compared myself with corporals that had been made in the past in the
company. Most of them were older and I was sure quite superior to
me. What had they meant by making *me* a corporal?

My mind in a troubled daze, I immediately went to see Captain
Kearns to have this grave mistake corrected. I found him outside the
grove, in a little nook surrounded by a native growth of trees and
shrubs. He was alone, and I proceeded to tell him (doubtless in a
blundering, stammering way) that I wasn't the fellow for the job and
did not want the place as corporal.

Captain Kearns had just come from the States, was hard boiled,
and unused to men in the ranks advising him. Just what reply I anticipated, I don't know, but I do know the trouble I got was a surprise. In very blunt language he told me something about this being his business, and that when he got ready to reduce me "it
wouldn't take an act of Congress to bust me." This ended the brief

interview, while I returned to the company, looking forward to an early day when my incompetency would bring me to the grade of private again. I don't know why I took the matter so seriously, but my feelings in the matter were not quick to wear away.

Not many days after my bawling out, we hiked back to the town of Montreuil and there pitched our rolls under some scattered trees. A rainstorm necessitated our seeking shelter, and a number of us took to the loft of a barn that boasted of plenty of soft, dry hay for bedding. And this flop, with walls and roof for protection from the driving mist, we appreciated in the extreme.

There were no long drill hours to harass us during our stay on the side of the slope at the northern edge of Montreuil. However, frequent visits to the Y, in the lower part of the village, with sometimes several hours in line to get a box or two of cakes and chocolates, suggest that our fare at the mess hall was not everything it might have been. I made a number of trips to this Y with Corporal Moss, another man who had come over with the 4th Replacement Battalion. He had not long been out of St. Paul. His fair complexion, rosy cheeks, and large animated eyes made him seem effeminate in a way, but something about the fellow had an attraction for me. I think it was to Moss that the West Texas cowpuncher back at the front had made the despairing utterance about the taste of life he had gotten being a "dog's life."

Since all the civilian population had left the village over a month before, we did not hesitate to confiscate anything that met our fancy. In a field nearby we helped ourselves to potatoes, though they were hardly larger than marbles. We secured grease somewhere and fried the potatoes in our mess kits with fuel from cans of "heat" indiscreetly stored in the barn below us by some army outfit. It was perhaps with Moss again that I explored various articles left by the former occupant.

Notwithstanding the luxurious leisure, there was a too-suggestive artillery fire and bursting of shells a mile or more to the north and west. Of course, we were not in danger of shells falling so far away. But they fell with startling regularity, and what was there to prevent the range from being raised at any time to include a town that had as many troops quartered in it as did Montreuil? It was not so much the possible danger as the suggestiveness, in the booming, of what we had experienced and what might be ahead.

Only the activity of the German artillery about sunset each day, it seems, could account for a strange gloom that pervaded my spirit as night drew near. While there was no sentiment connected with it, a song beginning "When evening shadows fall" I heard the first time then, and I cannot now disassociate the song from those days.

In the late afternoon of each day an air battle took place over us or between us and the line. Though sometimes these engagements took place so far away that we could not tell the Allied planes from the German, we watched the fights with keen interest. Sometimes in the dim distance the planes could be seen only with difficulty, as to escape enemy bullets or maneuver for a better position they glided back and forth and up and down like so many insects.

Lined up at intervals of several miles apart, parallel to the line and at about the same distance from the front as we, was a row of Allied observation balloons or sausages. Since they were to our right and left, not infrequently we could while away the hours watching their doings. Since both enemy and our planes were more active in the latter part of the day, it was then that we watched closer for a move on either side.

One evening a number of us had been watching an air battle and had seen it subside when a German plane—out of nowhere, it seemed—dropped upon a sausage balloon not far away. Shooting into it with the specially made ignition bullets, the flyer had the balloon in a mass of flames before we had time to take in the situation. While the plane flew away, the balloon began falling in a shapeless, rolling mass of rubber, boiling in its own flames. The balloon observer had lost no time in jumping out. Some distance downward like a bullet he shot before his parachute opened. But as he then slowly descended, his danger was by no means past. The burning body still hung above him. Then, falling into one compact mass, the flaming balloon dropped, missing the observer and his parachute by a narrow margin. From the time the plane dropped unexpectedly out of the sky it could have been but a few seconds. Then as unexpectedly as before, the plane came into sight again and dropped upon the next sausage down the line, for it, too, came down in flames. One of the boys looking on wondered just how many Iron Crosses the kaiser would hang about the neck of this flier for this job.

It seems the folks at home had not heard from me for a long while, and a letter of inquiry came to the company office. On 14 July, I answered and expressed the great joy that had been mine in getting several letters from home during a recent stay on the front line. Reading material must have been very scarce, as my letter expressed great desire for "seconds" of *The Literary Digest, Outlook,* and such other magazines.

The life of the service was rumors. Rumors, ever and always. Chief among them now, as had been the case before, was that we were to spend some time in southern France. One afternoon French camions came into town and we boarded them. (It was on 15 July.) Undoubtedly we were going somewhere! To the south we turned. This was the direction of both Bordeaux and the incomparable Paris. Our spirits were fast on the upgrade.

After passing through the town of Meaux the column of trucks swerved to the west. That turn began to unsettle things. On and on we went, the westerly course changing to the northwest. I think I speak for the rest of the bunch when I say that there was no business in that direction that I wanted to attend to. Then an ominous sign met our eyes—an observation balloon! And now our course turned to the north and the inevitable front.

Notes

1 Later he also received a Navy Cross as well as a group of other awards. It was his third wound.

2 Undoubtedly someone's vivid imagination. German "spies" were everywhere, according to those in the know—the privates in the front ranks. The gunners weren't as well experienced as they could have been; ammunition was not always foolproof, consequently "shorts" were not uncommon in the war, or, for that matter, in any war.

3 This happened on 5 June on the high ground opposite Belleau Wood on the Lucy-le-Bocage–to–Torcy Road. It was Maj. Benjamin Berry's 3/5 doing the relieving. See Clark, *Devil Dogs*, for full details. Major Maurice Shearer, temporarily in command of 1/6, went into XXI Corps's Reserve, back west along the Paris-Metz Road in the vicinity of the Paris Farm.

4 The "major" was really Capt. George A. Stowell. He was responsible because while he was leading his battalion back toward Lucy-le-Bocage, an element in the rear took the wrong turn, becoming lost from the main body. Because of this Stowell was relieved of command of his 76th Company by Maj. John Hughes. See Clark, pages 137–138. But he came back later and performed at his usual high standard.

5 Jackson implies that he was mainly very concerned with saving his skin, but it is evident that he wouldn't have been selected for the most dangerous task of company or battalion runner if he didn't have a certain level of courage, cunning, and common sense.

6 This is confusing. It appears that at this point, Jackson and McWilliams were slightly northeast of Lucy. The woods were to their right and the fields to their left front. They were looking for the remnants of the 47th Company, 3/5, which may also have included a few members of the 20th Company. This was following that battalion's bad beating on 6 June when they attempted to take Belleau Wood and most of the exposed battalion had retreated back to the high ground from which they began their attack. But not all. Some of the 47th/20th may have remained in their wooded section just above Lucy, trying to hold what little they had managed to gain.

7 Jackson has evidently confused the period and forgotten that it was instead the 47th Company. The 43d Company didn't show up in the woods until a few days later and then they were far to the north and nowhere near 1/6, his battalion. After ten years anyone could be expected to forget a detail like that. Read Clark for a complete account of the entire period.

8 Jackson was scared for good reason. Major Hughes had led his battalion into a portion of Belleau Wood but stopped long before his objective. That is something neither Jackson nor his buddies would ever have known. By staying there and not advancing, Hughes left the battalion exposed to concentrated artillery, and especially gas, shelling. Why Hughes stopped and failed to advance farther as ordered has never been satisfactorily explained. It was a serious situation and in a few days caused horrendous casualties to 2/5.

9 Checking my records I find only one officer casualty from the 95th Company that day and he, First Lieutenant Smith, was listed as killed in action on 13 June. Possibly this officer, whom he didn't name, was from another company of 1/6, but even there I cannot locate anyone who fits the pattern except Smith. The other possibility is that the officer was a U.S. Army officer, which records I do not own. They were numerous in the 4th Brigade at the time.

10 Many of these men, in all armies, would suffer what was then known as "shell shock." Some, the unfortunates, would spend much if not all of the balance of their lives in mental institutions. Apparently, none afflicted, however modestly, ever quite got over it.

11 These shells were known as whizbangs.

12 As we can tell, from the foregoing, after ten years Jackson was still in a state of shock over what he had experienced during this relatively short period of time. It helps prove that being the target of artillery was the most horrible part of static warfare, as far as the troops on the line were concerned. Jackson's exposure to, and fears of, shelling will dominate the balance of this book.

13 These were Marines from 3/6, which had launched an attack on 6 June and in which the living had suffered for about three or four days in the same general area that 1/6 was now occupying. In fact, 1/6 had not advanced as far as had 3/6.

14 Jackson is not correct. The attack in that immediate area on 10 June was by 1/6. The attack that fits with his description was that

launched by Maj. Berton Sibley with 3/6 against that place on 6 June. And Sibley did not lose his life during the war.

15 The 7th Infantry relieved the 4th Marine Brigade, which had been shot to pieces by mid-June. The untried infantry took a beating during their short stay.

16 The battalion was relieved on the night of 16–17 June by 2/7.

17 The American leadership ignored much of what the French and British had experienced and learned during the war. Consequently, at least in the 2d Division, or perhaps only in the 4th Brigade, men and officers spent an inordinate period of time in combat. The French calculated that any longer period than three days on line was too much to expect from anyone. The Marines at Belleau Wood spent as much as fifteen days without rest. And most of that time they were not fed, but survived on hardtack and so on.

Lieutenant Colonel Hiram I. Bearss, sometime CO, 5th Marines, later CO, 102d Infantry. Holder of Medal of Honor, DSC, and Legion of Honor for his acts at Marcheville, September 1918.

Brigadier General Wendell C. Neville, 4th Brigade CO. He received the Army and Navy DSM, the Legion of Honor, and two Croix de Guerre.

Colonel Logan Feland, CO, 5th Marines. Feland received the DSC, Army and Navy DSM, and five Silver Star citations.

Colonel Albertus Catlin, CO of the 6th Marines. He was made a member of the Legion of Honor and received two Croix de Guerre.

Lieutenant Colonel Julius S. Turrill, CO, 1st Bn., 5th Marines. Turrill was awarded the DSC and the Navy Cross.

Lieutenant Colonel Frederick M. Wise, CO, 2d Bn., 5th Marines. He became CO of the 59th Infantry, then the 8th Brigade, 4th Division. He was awarded both the Army and Navy DSM.

Lieutenant Colonel Charles T. Westcott, CO, 3d Bn., 5th Marines.

Captain LeRoy P. Hunt, CO, 17th Co., 1st Bn., 5th Marines. Later CO of 1st Bn. He was awarded the DSC, Navy Cross, and four Silver Stars.

Captain Charley Dunbeck, CO, 43d Co., 2d Bn. 5th Marines. Dunbeck received the DSC, Navy Cross, and four Silver Stars.

Major Henry L. Larsen, commanding the 3d Battalion, 5th Marines, from just before Blanc Mont through Bois to the Meuse River campaign. He earned a Navy Cross and three Silver Star citations plus a Croix de Guerre.

Major John A. Hughes, CO, 1st Bn., 6th Marines. Hughes was awarded the Navy Cross and three Silver Stars.

Major Thomas Holcomb, CO, 2d Bn., 6th Marines. Holcomb received the Navy Cross, Legion of Honor, and four Silver Stars.

Colonel Harry Lee, CO, 6th Marines. Lee was awarded the Army and Navy DSM and the Legion of Honor.

Lieutenant Colonel Berton W. Sibley, CO, 3d Bn., 6th Marines. Holder of the Navy Cross and three Silver Stars.

Major Frederick L. Barker, commanding the 1st Battalion, 6th Marines after Soissons. Remained through the Meuse River campaign. He earned a Navy Cross and at least four Silver Star citations plus the Croix de Guerre.

Ernest C. Williams, CO, 2d Bn., 6th Marines. Recipient of the Medal of Honor, the Navy Cross, and three Silver Stars.

Major George K. Shular, CO, 3d Bn., 6th Marines. Holder of the Army and Navy DSM and Legion of Honor.

Private Elton E. Mackin, author of remarkable memoir *Suddenly We Didn't Want to Die*. Photo taken in Germany, 1919. (courtesy Wallace Mackin)

Officers of the 2d Battalion, 6th Marines, leaving Belleau Wood after being relieved. From left, lieutenants Gordon Grimland, and George L. White, USN, Capt. Graves B. Erskine, 79th Co., Capt. Egbert T. Lloyd, 80th Co. Capt. Randolph T. Zane, 79th Co., unknown, 2d Lt. E. J. Stockwell, USA, 79th Co., Maj. Thomas Holcomb, 2d Bn.; 1st Lt. Cliffton B. Cates, 96th Co.; 2d Lt. John G. Schneider, 80th Co.; 1st Lt. Amos R. Shinkle, 78th Co. (courtesy Larry Strayer)

Three privates of the 16th Co., 5th Marines. Sitting from left, Paul Lubawski; J. E. Mason; standing, Henry P. Lenert, (recipient of Silver Star and Croix de Guerre for taking 78 German prisoners at Belleau Wood on 25 June 1918). (courtesy David Fisher)

From left, Pvt. Joseph A. Keller, 95th Co.; Pvt. Arthur G. Marsh (with BAR), 79th Co.; 6th Marines. Marsh, along with another man, carried a wounded officer back to safety through terrific machine-gun fire. (courtesy David Fisher)

Belleau Wood after the German, French, and American artillery had made it look this way. The view is what the Marines saw as they tried to take what was left of it. (courtesy USMC University archives)

Private Edwin T. Beach, 23d Machine Gun Co., 6th Machine Gun Bn. Photo taken before he went to France, when his uniform was still clean and new. (courtesy Jerry Beach)

Unidentified group of soldiers from the Headquarters Co., 2d Engineer Regiment. Possibly taken in Germany after the war because they appear to be reasonably well dressed. (courtesy David Fisher)

Battery F, 15th Field Artillery, 2d Artillery Brigade, 2d Division, in support of the 4th Marine Brigade at Belleau Wood on 5 June 1918. The 15th was usually the 4th Brigade's artillery support throughout the war. (courtesy USMC University archives)

Official portrait of 2d Division CO, Maj. Gen. John A. Lejeune, showing his various decorations, including the French Legion of Honor. Most likely this photo was taken shortly after his return to the United States. (courtesy USMC University archives)

General Pershing frequently awarded decorations for heroic acts among troops of the AEF. Photo taken shortly after Belleau Wood because officer on extreme left (wearing a French helmet) is Brig. Gen. James G. Harbord who commanded the 4th Brigade. The officer holding his right hand to his face appears to be Maj. Gen. Omar Bundy, CO of the 2d Division. The others are unidentified. (courtesy *Marine Corps Gazette*)

Group of senior Marine officers in the trenches, Verdun sector. From left, Maj. Holland McT. Smith, 4th Brigade Liaison officer; Brig. Gen. Charles A. Doyen, CO, 4th Brigade; Lt. Col. Frederick M. Wise, CO, 2d Bn., 5th Marines. (courtesy USMC University Archives)

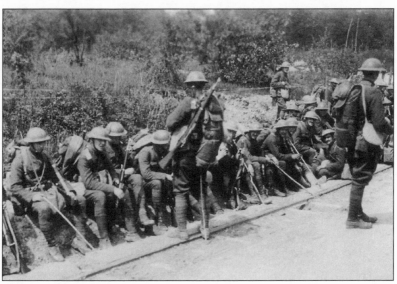

Marines resting on a roadside in France. They are probably just returning from the Verdun Sector, May 1918. (courtesy USMC University archives)

Marines digging graves for dead German soldiers at their command post in the Verdun sector. (courtesy USMC University archives)

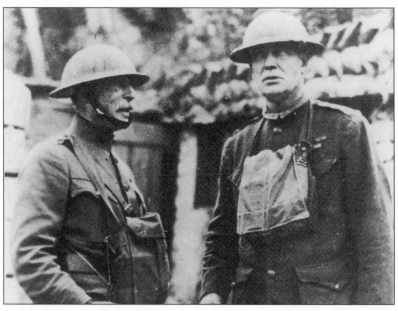

Major General Bundy, 2d Division CO, talking with Col. Albertus Catlin, 6th Marine's CO, in the Verdun sector.

Marines in the Belleau Wood area, preparing to resume their forward movement toward the front. Note the horse drawn, wheeled vehicles. (courtesy USMC University archives)

Group photo of the officers and men of the 23d Co., 5th Marines in Waldbreitbach, Germany, 4 April 1919. This was just after the 23d Co. of the 6th Machine Gun Battalion had been transferred as an infantry company to the 5th Marines which had suffered immense losses during the war and from the men who had been discharged early from the regiment. (courtesy Jerry Beach)

Marines mounting camions for a ride, to or from Belleau Wood. Probably before, because their uniforms appear to be in good shape—that wasn't the case after the June fighting. (courtesy USMC University archives)

The 6th Marines parading in Washington, D.C., 12 August 1919. (Signal Corps photo, courtesy Larry Strayer)

Fifth Marines headquarters group, taken just after the end of the Belleau Wood campaign. Seated from left, Col. Wendell C. Neville, CO, and Lt. Col. Logan Feland, assistant CO. Neville was awarded the Army and Navy Distinguished Service Medals and the Legion of Honor. Feland was awarded the DSC and both the Army and Navy DSMs, plus five Silver Star citations and six Croix de Guerre. (courtesy *Marine Corps Gazette*)

The last parade of the wartime 6th Marines, showing their colors as they marched in downtown Washington, D.C., on 12 August, 1919. (Signal Corps photo, courtesy Larry Strayer)

Major General John A. Lejeune, 2d Division CO, pinning Croix de Guerre on Pvt. E. E. McCormack, 83d Co., at Leutesdorf, Germany, on 4 January 1919. (USMC University archives)

Two German strong points on Blanc Mont. (USMC University Archives)

Brigadier General Wendell C. Neville, 4th Brigade CO, pinning Croix de Guerre on Maj. Gen. John A. Lejeune at Leutesdorf, Germany, on 4 January 1919. Neither man was tall, but Neville was obviously the taller one. (Signal Corps photo, courtesy Larry Strayer)

Group of Marine enlisted men of the 79th Co. 6th Marines, in heavy marching order. Probably on a regular route march while stationed in Germany. (courtesy David Fisher)

Headquarters of the 6th Marines while in the Verdun sector. The buildings were probably left over from the previous occupants who would have been from the French army. (courtesy *Marine Corps Gazette*)

Each of the Rhine River patrol boats mounted machine guns as "heavy" weapons for the watch. These guns are German Spandaus. Effective and accurate, they were more popular than were the French Hotchkiss the men were used to. (courtesy *Marine Corps Gazette*)

6: From the Frying Pan into the Fire: Soissons

SYNOPSIS

The officers and men of the 2d Division would not expect or get much of a rest following their exertions all during June at Belleau Wood. The wood was a disaster for the 5th Marines; now it was to be the turn of the 6th. Foch and his staff planned a major assault against German lines around Soissons, where lay the right hinge of the German thrust southeastward. In order to ensure complete surprise, assaulting units were brought to the scene rapidly and under cover of night. The 2d Division was especially discombobulated. The manner in which they were brought, and the method used to get them to the field of battle, nearly destroyed any effectiveness the three regiments assigned to the first day's attack might have had. The 9th Infantry and the 23d Infantry, each had a difficult and abusive approach on the morning of 18 July, but what happened to the 5th Marines was unconscionable.

The Marines barely made it to the battlefield in time. They had been, like the 6th Marines, forced to march along the same highway for hours and without any break, and then had to run several miles to try to follow the artillery barrage. They and their comrades of the infantry somehow managed to drive the Germans back a great distance before the day ended.

On 19 July it was the turn of the 6th Marines, all alone, to take up what the other three regiments had covered the previous day. They, too, were the subjects of terrible military management, primarily the staff of the French Tenth Army, and were not ready to attack for some time after the artillery barrage began. In fact, it was about over and the German infantry and artillery were just waiting for them. Needless to say the regiment was badly handled that day.

• • •

All night we rode. At daybreak we left the camions, hiked for a while, then turned to the side of the road and unrolled our packs. But we were not destined to stay there long. On we marched in the direction of the front, with no sleep and empty stomachs in the bargain. Then for a downpour of rain, which would not have been bad on a July day but for the mud that followed. Mile after mile we trudged on in that mud with scarcely a rest.

Our course had lain along an open country, with rolling grain-fields to the right and left. Then the road entered a forest, and the farther we went the muddier became the road and the heavier the traffic upon it. We met some wagons coming from the direction of the front, but the bulk of the travel was in the direction we were going and toward the front. The road stretched for miles without a bend. An interminable lane of mud, with the dark pine forests rising like two walls on both sides of that sea of mire, men, mules, and vehicles of various descriptions. An endless concourse worked its way along. Covered wagons, drawn by four to six mules, pieces of artillery of every description, following heavy draft horses that seemed even too light for the road, followed by a string of caissons, ration carts, water carts, men riding and men walking; the whole world seemed to be worming its way forward along that dreary, lanelike road of mire. Not in New York or anywhere else could such a seething mass of men and vehicles be seen on one highway. Trucks and wagons broke down in the middle of the road. It was necessary then for the endless stream to turn to the right and left, like a giant monster of a snake dividing itself, and, the obstruction past, uniting again. The mud was so deep and heavy that we could trudge along only with the greatest difficulty. Marching on the side of the road was even worse, as there we had to cope both with the mud and frequent heavy undergrowth.

Mile upon mile we labored on, almost to exhaustion, yet very little rest. Far in the afternoon we turned out to the right of the road to get an issue of four bandoleers of ammunition. Previously, we had carried two, but never had four been hung on us. Now 240 rounds hung from our necks and shoulders. This was in addition to the 100 rounds we always carried in our belts, not to mention the additional load of the rifle and mercilessly heavy pack, which seemed to all but pull the straps through our shoulders. The bandoleers were swung over the head and hung down on the chest and stomach. Two were on each side, pulling together so heavily as to necessitate a constant readjustment to prevent choking the carrier. In fact, so tight were they that the blood vessels in a man's neck could be seen to swell tight from the pressure. Since it was a court-martial offense to throw ammunition away, the safest thing to do was keep it, though not a few of the fellows finally in desperation threw one or more of the bandoleers away. When night drew near we still moved forward, though by now the officers had given up in their effort to keep the ranks in order.

Some rations were consigned to the company, with this load added to the overwhelming burden. It was a sack of French hard-tack, I think, that Morrison carried a long way.

Before nightfall we passed where a shell had recently fallen here and there among the trees along the side of the road. The sight of these shell holes, together with the nauseating odor of lingering high-explosive gas, brought back to us with sickening reality what we had experienced and would probably have to go through soon again. The ground had become more solid, but our equipment felt only heavier. In the middle of the road a shell had fallen not more than a few hours before and, so mangled was the mass there, we could not tell whether one horse had been killed or two.

The great stream that filled the road had dwindled until our column was all in sight. To the right of the road was a small house, which was the worse for the shelling. However, I concluded that we were farther from the front than I had first thought, as one of the higher officers—Col. Harry Lee, I think—was making the place his headquarters. A turn in the road and we halted at last. The men pronounced this the worst hike we had ever taken; that is, those who were *there* said it was the worst; a large part of the company had fallen along the roadside from exhaustion many miles to the rear. We flung ourselves into the ditch on the right of the road.

Water, water—it seemed that I would die of thirst. Across the road was a ditch of shallow dreggy water that had been drained from the road where countless teams had been drawn during the day. Although every kind of foreign matter was at the bottom, and even sus-pended in its inch or two of depth, I knelt down and drank. I had drunk all kinds of water, I thought, but nothing like that before. I felt the chances good for it to put an end to me, but such a prospect caused no alarm, as I might get bumped off unceremoniously very soon anyway.

Not long after our arrival some French "baby" tanks drew into the wood near us. Their presence meant something was going to hap-pen, though there was no knowing the result.

With dark came a drizzling rain, and slight protection did we have against it. Little sleep did we get that night. About four o'clock in the morning a tremendous artillery fire burst forth from all about us. The surrounding woods roared and thundered with guns that we had not suspected of being near. Such an earsplitting din as filled the air we had never heard. Had a man shouted, I doubt that he could have heard his own voice.

Of course, such a roar put an end to all thoughts of sleep. And as terrible as was the sound, there was a mingled sense of satisfaction. The Germans were at last getting some of their own medicine it seemed. We understood that at dawn the 5th Regiment was to go over, and at about daybreak the heavy bombardment ceased. There followed a rolling barrage behind which the advancing troops were to drive the Germans. By the middle of the morning the artillery fire had practically ceased.

Late in the morning we received a beautiful ration of snowy white bread and molasses. And did we enjoy it! Not many times since leaving Quantico do I recall our getting American bread. When it wasn't hardtack, most of the time we enjoyed the asbestos-textured French bread.

But we could not enjoy forever the luxurious fare of all the bread and syrup we could eat. The order came to move up. We met a small detachment of British troops, the first we had seen since we were in Le Havre. Farther along the road, and the surrounding country showed increasingly the effects of the month of shelling this part of the front had seen. At a place along the roadside we found wounded Marines, who told that the Americans had swept all before them. Far-ther along German prisoners, the first we had seen, were being lined up to be taken to the rear. Most of the captured men appeared to be privates and seemed to be very glad to be out of the war. However, at the end of the line was a haughty, stiff-necked German officer wearing a monocle, who made no demonstrations of joy. The war was going our way and we were all in high spirits. Artillery passed us going to the front at a gallop; the horses themselves seemed to feel the flush of victory.

Later in the afternoon a German plane swept down upon the marching column and shot into the ranks. What other casualties resulted I don't recall, but one of the men of the 95th received a bullet wound in the face, the bullet lodging in his neck. Never before had I seen an enemy plane come down so low. It appeared barely to clear the denuded trees beside the road, and the black crosses under the wings seemed to reflect all the atrocities that Germany had been credited with committing. So quickly had the plane come and gone that I think no shot was fired at it.

Soon after the plane had passed over, we moved into the wood to our left and dug in. Hardly had we gotten down when orders came to move. Not more than three or four hundred yards at most did we further penetrate into the wood, when we dug in again. This thing was repeated until we had dug the *fourth* hole before night, and all in that vicinity. "Some management," the fellows declared, but the "fellows" weren't running things just then. We had done enough digging for one day, at any rate.

It might seem that I would have been exhausted from what we had been through the past two days, but I went exploring in another part of the wood, finding a number of shell holes of tremendous size. Water was very scarce, and in an open space out from the wood was a well where hundreds of men sought water. The water was difficult to access, which accounted for such a large number of men congregating there. It seemed such an assemblage in the open would offer a fine target for the German artillery, but the guns must not yet have had time to move back into new positions and set up firing again.

During the afternoon a large number of tanks passed along the edge of the wood. There were possibly two dozen or more of them.

An observation balloon a short distance above the ground, and an-chored to an automobile made for the purpose, shifted back and forth near the wood in a manner I did not understand.

An hour or two before sunset we began to advance through the stretch of open country that we had faced for some hours. While we saw no opposing enemy, it was then that I first saw anything that matched the mental picture I had had as to what a battle looked like. The sight was thrilling. From the rear and ahead of us could be seen columns of men marching over that undulating plain. To the right and left were batteries of seventy-fives, belching forth one shell af-ter another, and after each shot the guns were moved forward a few feet. The picture was made complete by the appearance of a column of several German prisoners. Their only guards were one man at the head and another at the rear. These Germans were of course glad to be out of the fray, as the two guards could have been easily over-powered.

Before dark we deployed along a slope and dug in. A battery of the seventy-fives was in operation ahead of and to the left of us, and it was with no little interest that we watched them.

Early the next morning we were on the march again. Our path led us through woods and isolated swamps and later along a railroad. That a railroad had been captured seemed wonderful, in fact, almost impossible from the supposed invulnerable Germans. On a timbered hill to our right was a well-camouflaged battery of German guns that they had left in their flight the day before. An increasing exhilara-tion came as we advanced. At the end of a valley we found the vil-lage of Vierzy, the streets of which had been renamed by the Ger-mans. First was Ludendorff Strasse. Farther along was Kaiser Wilhelm Strasse or some other *"strasse."* Had His Majesty Kaiser Wilhelm II been present to witness the defense his namesake had received, he would probably have been little gratified.

All of us were in high spirits on that morning of 19 July 1918. The day was not done. Emerging from the basinlike valley, we found our-selves in a grainfield that stretched far ahead. Although it was broad daylight—about eight o'clock—and not a cloud flecked the sky, preparation was being made to go over. Ordinarily, making an attack at such time was unthinkable, but the Germans had started on the

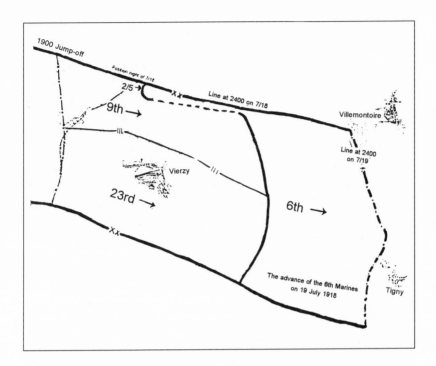

run the day before, and it was doubtless felt that their morale was broken and we would encounter little further resistance.

We were to be in the second or third wave and would not likely be called upon unless casualties were very heavy in the first wave. We fixed bayonets, formed combat groups, advanced some distance through the high, thick grain, and halted.

The field ahead of us rose gently to a distance of perhaps six or eight hundred yards, and the view was broken only by a long shed of some kind to the right front. Until we had gone into the field we had little idea where the enemy was and what was his strength. A fearful slaughter was to ensue. A few angry shells began to fall, and we got low. A number of shells hit uncomfortably close, leaving behind them, in place of the ripe grain, black, irregular holes that reeked with the nauseating odor of high-explosive gas and, above, shapeless masses of black smoke.[1]

The troops ahead began the advance and we followed. Under such shellfire anything in the world is better than remaining still and doing nothing. Frequent sprays of machine-gun bullets nipped the wheat about us. One shell after another fell in quick succession. Many of the shells came from artillery on the hillside not more than a mile away and were fired *point blank* into our ranks. So many shells were in the air at once that the ear was unable to detect the course of each separate shell: a terrific explosion a few steps to the right or left, in front or behind, was the first knowledge of the coming of these fiendish missiles. We had been deployed, though there were still scattered troops ahead. The line was now at the crest of the rise, and, unless my eyes deceived me, I saw the Germans in their retreat about five hundred yards ahead. But with their retreating they continued to pour upon us a deathly volley of steel.

The 95th Company was on the extreme right of the advancing Americans, and three of us were on the right end of the company line. French Algerians were supposed to be on our right, but they had failed to appear. As a consequence much of the fire they would have drawn fell upon us. Several times in weeks before, I had been particularly fortunate that the brunt of heavy shelling missed me by some yards, but an inconceivable number of shells now fell under the three of us who had somehow gotten separated from the main body of the company. Two or three shells, like insuperable demons from hell, would fall appallingly close, bursting almost simultaneously. As we tried to dodge from one or more shells here, our ears would still be ringing when we almost ran into the path of more, to have the earth shaken under us by terrific explosions that every moment threatened to hurl us into eternity.

The senses ceased to function normally. Only in a vague sort of way did I comprehend that the ranks to the left were being shot to pieces. However, as my eyes chanced to be in that direction, something caught my gaze with an almost paralyzing reality. A shell made a direct hit on the line, and a pack and helmet went spinning high into the air. Yet there were minutes such that had all the world, more than a dozen steps away, ceased to exist, we would not have realized it.

As the three of us dodged here and there, it so happened that I got in the lead, with Rosenow a step or two to my left rear and Wright just behind him. In the midst of the volley of shells of every size, from one-pounders to ten-inch, a small shell fell just to my left. Partly due to the hardness of the ground, it did not penetrate more than two or three inches, but spit forward like a rock thrown on the surface of the water. Looking over my shoulder, I saw Rosenow—who had been scarcely an arm's length away—sink to the ground with an almost inarticulate "Oh, God!" The little shell had made almost a sieve of the lower part of his body. From his waist downward at least fifty shell fragments must have penetrated. I started to take out an emergency kit, but I saw that he was dead. A fine fellow, who had but a few weeks before confided to me of the girl he had left back at home, now dead by my side.

Anywhere else I would have been appalled by the so sudden passing of a friend, but in the anguish and stir of battle one was not affected so. Perhaps a fellow had become somewhat inured to death. With all respect I say that his passing was to me, at the moment, as under other circumstances, as at another time, seeing a dumb animal die.

When I saw that Rosenow was gone, I turned to Wright, who had been dazed by the shell's explosion. He was on the point of turning back. Dazed as he was, he thought he was shell shocked or had met a worse fate; but I persuaded him to come ahead with me. We hurried to come abreast of what was left of the company, but I don't know whether we caught up with them or not. I may not have known at the time. But as I went ahead a sergeant, of the 75th Company I think, stopped in front of me and asked me to tie up his arm, which had been badly torn by a shell between the shoulder and the elbow. The bone, I believe, had been shattered, and to keep his arm from giving him unnecessary pain while he walked back to the first-aid station, he had me take the bandage from his first-aid kit and secure the lower part of his arm to his body. Before the sergeant went to the rear he gave me his Marine razor and a pair of field glasses. The razor I stuck away somewhere, but the field glasses were too bulky to bother with, so I dropped them.

The first-aid job done, I started forward to catch the outfit, which by this time must have been nearly out of sight. However, one of the three "Shepherds" of the company came crawling toward me, his left leg dragging stiffly behind him. He begged me to bandage the wound. He seemed to think that he would bleed to death soon if he did not get attention. A machine-gun bullet had gone through the upper part of his leg. By the time I had put a bandage on the wound, the outfit was not to be seen at all. With the line broken as it was, there was little telling into whom I might run should I try to find them.[2]

Shepherd and I dropped into an open dugout at our side until the worst of the shelling was over, and I went back to the village with Shepherd and another wounded man. On the way we saw two or three disabled tanks. Of one of these I carry a vivid mental picture. A foot or more of the top of the tank had been blown off, and the Frenchman who had been driving it sat bolt upright, with that part of his head just above his eyes cut off as though with a knife.

In Vierzy were countless wounded men. Among others I recognized was Schuler. At the time I supposed his wound was not severe, but I learned later that he did not survive. With Schuler, as had previously been with Eddie Small, Krieger, and others, it was hard to realize he was dead. A virility, a dauntless spirit—I don't know just what it was that characterized some men that made it hard to imagine them anything but strong and active human beings.

When I got back to the town, it seemed I was almost famished of thirst. Getting water out of a well with an improvised bucket and rope was no easy task. After getting the water I looked about for some 95th man to return to the company with, someone who had been with the company and knew its whereabouts. I started with a man named [Clayton E.] Hunt or Hunter, but when we were at the edge of the village he went back for some purpose and I saw no more of him. In a little while numbers of 95th Company men were in the town. They had brought wounded back, I suppose. I approached one after another of them regarding a return to the company, and all told me that except for the few 95th men in the town, 95th Company was a thing of the past.[3]

I ran across R. H. C. Shepherd, and he and I made several trips to the grainfield to get wounded. As we had no stretchers, more improvising was done in preparing a makeshift stretcher of two rifles and a blanket, the edges of the blanket rolled lengthwise on the rifles. Carrying the limp form of a wounded man three-quarters of a mile is an undertaking, to say the least.

The grainfield was strewn with men who had fallen, men wounded in almost every conceivable way. How we picked the few we took back I do not recall, perhaps those who seemed to be suffering most or whose wounds were bleeding fastest. Along the length of that battlefield there must have been thousands of dead and wounded. My recollection is that not until later in the day were any others carrying wounded. Men begged us to carry them back. It must have been hard to be refused.

Carrying the men was most exhausting, especially because every step we took further opened the wound, thus necessitating the greatest care to handle them carefully. The use of rifles as stretcher supports must have proved unsatisfactory, as I left my rifle in the field. This gun had been issued to me at Paris Island more than a year before. At this time I was one of the few who had kept their Springfield all the way through. Some of the fellows had gotten their guns mixed and other guns had been lost. It was not without a good deal of sentiment and pride that I hung on to the old rifle. I had left mine behind, knowing that I could pick up another at any time. However, I did pick up the old "fusil" later in the day.

On one of our trips to the wheat field we saw a German plane sweep down within a hundred yards or so of us, upon a disconnected trench in which was located a French first-aid station. While committing this dastardly act, the flier fell victim to an unexpected enemy. As the German swept down within twenty or thirty feet of the helpless wounded and those administering aid, concealed French machine gunners turned upon the plane. Hardly a second seemed to transpire from the time that the dark plane dropped down for its work of destruction, the black crosses (the very sight of which almost made the blood run cold) startlingly distinct and ominous, until plane and flier had met their end.

Only the exploding of a shell could have happened quicker. The aviator dropped suddenly out of the sky as from another world, fired upon the aid station, in turn was fired upon, when he crashed with bullet speed to the ground. Flames from the gas tank jumped high into the air, and in a moment the exploding of the plane's supply of ammunition sounded like a half a dozen machine guns firing at once. I think it was not more than a minute from the time the plane appeared until the plane and pilot lay a charred mess upon the ground. It seems that curiosity would have led us to a closer view of the ruined plane, but something must have caused us to shrink from the spectacle.

In the afternoon I saw take place what I never saw repeated. Shells had not ceased to fall at random both in the town and on the field. We were carrying a wounded man and were just emerging from the grainfield along a sunken road. A shell of small caliber struck forty yards to our right, sent up some dirt and dust, and ricocheted across the road in front of us to fall on the left of the road.

Before the day was far advanced, the town had perhaps several thousand wounded in it. Most of these wounded were in a large cavern that had been dug into the face of the bluffs fronting the village, far back into the solid rock. Deep in the caves the rows of closely laid bodies rested. Many of the men were strangely still. Of course, the doctors and hospital corpsmen were kept on a great strain caring for the countless wounded. The number of ambulances to take back to hospitals those who had received temporary dressings was but a drop in the bucket, and even the trucks that had been drafted into the service of removing wounded had, after many hours, made little or no impression. German prisoners under guard were now being used to bring wounded into the town, while others worked as Shepherd and I did.

The excitement and strain of this day of days did not take away our appetites. On the rather exposed bluff overlooking the town, and getting more than its quota of shells, there was a ration dump. For whom the punk [bread] and other supplies had been left was a small matter. Later several of us from the 95th ate chow in a shattered house. Those who last came from the lines told more and more of the slaughter wrought by shells and machine guns.

Like others I spent most of the night in a second underground vault near the one spoken of. Toward morning, word came that the remnant of the 95th had been relieved and had already passed through the village on their way to the rear. By about the middle of the morning the company had gotten together in the edge of the wood, which had suffered from shellfire during the month of fighting that sector had seen. At eight o'clock the morning before, the 95th had gone over with a company strength of nearly 260. This number included the cooks and mule skinners who did not go over, as well as several who remained behind to guard packs. This last group were known as the "twenty percent," and in case the rest were killed they were to form the nucleus of a new company. Of about two hundred in the company the day before, less than forty remained. Unreal of unrealities! One could scarcely believe his senses—that so many of the group whom we had hiked with and lived with were now wounded or killed!

Upon referring to the Honor Roll I find first among those killed at Soissons the name of Captain Kearns. It was he who had given me the rating down a few weeks before when I had insisted that I did not want to be a corporal. He died while men were carrying him off the field. Next on the list is Sergeant Farrant. He was small and not vigorous looking; but as one of the old-timers in the service, he was worth much to the organization. Next among those killed at Soissons I find the name of Sergeant Hindman. He was a tall, slender, dark-complexioned fellow, with small nervous eyes, black and penetrating. Hindman, too, had served several hitches in the army and Marine Corps. As a man of sound judgment, ability to lead, and experience in the service, he could have risen high but for his drinking habits.

Farther down the list of killed are John Kochis and Bill Piggott, both of whom I was told had their heads blown from their shoulders by a small shell. Kochis was a simplehearted fellow I have spoken of before. Piggott and I had been closely associated since the company was formed back at Quantico. Piggott was far from handsome, but he possessed a fine spirit and an indomitable will. He had worked in Ohio rubber factories—for Goodyear and Firestone, I believe— and his account of his duties in these places had been of no little interest to me. In months past Piggott and I had engaged in no little rough-and-tumble wrestling. He was somewhat stronger than I and the only time I remember throwing him was in the orchard back at Champigneulle. At Belleau he was prevailed upon to carry a French Chauchat; this with the understanding that he would be relieved of it when we left that front. But he was still carrying the machine gun when we went over at Soissons. The fact that he was a machine gunner naturally drew enemy fire, while artillery fire came point blank from the opposite hill.

Numbers of others killed, and whom I did not know so well as those already mentioned, I shall pass over, as well as the numerous wounded. Now it was but the shell of the 95th Company—strange and sad it was! Charlie Slaughter had not been with the company for some time, having gone to the hospital for an operation. Albert Ball had received a serious wound at Belleau and was out of the war. But I knew that Jesse Palmer had gone over, and I went to the 74th Company to see how he had fared. Poor Jesse was among those who had paid the price.

As I have said, after he and others were gassed at the Verdun Front, they were sent to a hospital, soon after to be returned to their companies. It was soon obvious, however, that these men had not sufficiently recovered to resume the exacting duties of active soldiers. They were returned to a hospital. About this time we went to Belleau Wood. With glaring headlines French papers extolled the heroism of the Americans, who were credited with saving Paris. Nor did the Marines fail to get their share of credit. The accounts of what was transpiring were too much for a fellow of Jesse's type. He went AWOL from the hospital to his company at the *front*. But he joined the outfit on the eve of its departure to Soissons.

Unreal of unrealities, that one so strong, so full of the joy of living, possessed of so keen a mind, with optimism that refused to be daunted—Jesse was no more! I am tempted to recount memories of him as I knew him as a student, football player, school yell leader, and teacher, but I shall not pause for this now.

When I returned to the company that morning, I found Summerlin, with the assistance of others, making a list of the dead. The names were to be cabled back to the States. As I came up, Summerlin hailed me as one risen from the dead—my name was to have gone in among the killed in action. Someone had thought he saw me as I "got" it. I defended the fallacy of this statement as well as I could. The mistake was not an unnatural one, as so many had been killed and so few remained.

Though we were out of the fight for a while, it was not our privilege to enjoy unbroken peace and tranquility. Soon after our arrival in the edge of the wood, a battery of French 155s opened up not more than a hundred yards to our rear. Under other circumstances we would have enjoyed a sort of revenge in hearing the fire. But with our nerves torn by the recent disastrous struggle, we wanted to get away from the frequent roar, which was a too-near resemblance to the soul-rending crash of a bursting shell. Sleep was so broken that it was almost like no sleep.

The wood in which we were had seen a raking shellfire. The trees were practically stripped of their foliage. Many branches lay on the ground, while other limbs dangled uncertainly in the wind. It was a day or two after we came to the wood that a small group of boys, quite without warning, had fall among them a heavy limb. It fell upon William Stavely, crushing his skull. The boy whose optimism and genial humor had so often cheered us was killed before our eyes. There was something appalling about the tragedy, and a gloom was thrown over us all. Another limb fell and fatally wounded a second man, Paul Quattlander. We then moved out in the open. It seemed that mocking fate had overtaken us that any of our number should meet such a violent death at that time.[4]

It was several miles to the front line. We were waked one night by ominous sounds: back at the front a battle was raging. A battery, certainly not more than a mile away, was firing in our direction. The nearness of the guns could mean but one thing—the Germans had broken through! We would now have to face them again, the fighting had been worse than in vain, more dangers must be undergone, more lives sacrificed. These thoughts ground at the very soul.

Shortly we were deployed and advanced in the open to check the oncoming Germans. Flares went up, seemingly not more than a half or quarter mile ahead. We then stopped. In not more than an hour the battle had ceased; what we had feared had been averted.

This, like many other episodes in the war, I never got a satisfactory explanation for. It was said that German artillerymen, who had hidden in caves by their guns when the Americans passed, under cover of darkness came out of their holes to vent their wrath further upon the Americans. I do not know whether anyone was killed. There was at least one who was scared. In the course of the next few days citations were read to us, in which the higher officials had commended the actions of the men at Soissons. Of course, this was not unexpected; but the fact remained that we were still at war.

Several days passed and no orders came to move. Rumors drifted in that we might return to the front, but the shattered condition of the 6th Regiment, we felt, would prevent our going to the line again right then. It was said that Colonel Lee, who slept but a short distance from us, had received orders to carry the regiment to the rear but had refused at first to make the men hike after undergoing what we had. This may have been only a rumor. When we did finally roll up to leave, we could only hope as to the direction we would take. The winding road through the wood kept us in constant fear as to where it might lead. The road had such turns that part of the time we seemed headed straight to the front again. But we were going away from the front and that night camped by the side of the road.

Less than a week before, I was adamantine in my conviction that if I was ever removed from that hellish shellfire, with a dry place to sleep and enough time to sleep, I would *never* complain again of my lot. How little did I know myself! Only a part of a day at the roadside and all were quite restless. We wanted again to come in contact with civilization.

Notes

1 Jackson's memory is failing here. His battalion, 1/6, was placed on the right flank, 2/6 on the left, and 3/6 in support. In a very few hours, 1/6 and 2/6 were shattered and 3/6 was in bad shape. The Germans were well dug in and just waiting for them. More than half the regiment were casualties. The whole story is in *Devil Dogs,* and it is a revealing chapter in military mismanagement.

2 There was one Pvt. Andrew L. S. Shepard and a Pvt. Royal H. C. Shepherd in the company. I cannot locate a third. This wounded man must have been Andrew Shepard.

3 Not quite, but almost. The entire battalion was badly hurt and the right flank had been exposed to three sides of abuse. The 6th Marines went into that battle with 2,450 officers and men and 1,150 came out a few hours later.

4 The 6th Marines had been pulled out and were billeted at and near Translon Farm, where they suffered from intense enemy artillery fire, causing broken tree limbs and a number of casualties from it.

7: Time for Rest

SYNOPSIS

The 2d Division had been badly used in two major battles and one exhausting session in trenches that lasted the better part of two months. All told, the months of March through July had been busy ones for the division, which had now served on three fronts. They were in need of replacements, reequipment, and especially rest. Someone at Chaumont, AEF Headquarters, apparently agreed, so they were assigned to a relatively quiet zone south of the St. Mihiel salient and north of Nancy along the Moselle River. There they remained until early September, when they were once again called upon to force their will upon the Boche.

The company was on the march again. Our way led through yellow grainfields and past small villages, isolated and lifeless. Our destination was the uninteresting village of Mantagny [Martigny?], where we quartered in barns.

During the week here the company was reorganized and I was transferred from the 4th to the 1st Platoon. We did not drill a great deal, and I took advantage of the hours off to explore the country. One day I took a pistol out some distance in the open for practice. If it was to be supposed that I might need to use a pistol in the near future, I should have had a lot of practice that I did not get.

One morning we hiked to a town some miles distant where we went through a decootyizer our first time. I had been lucky in avoiding cooties, as I had gone through the Verdun trenches without getting them. Cooties glory in dirt, and I had taken every opportunity to bathe. But when we went to Belleau Wood, I became inhabited.

At the decootyizer all the bunch took a hot shower, while our clothes went through a washing and steaming.

Then for a trip in boxcars. I think that this was one of the several times we passed through the suburbs—and slums—of Paris, and Alexander, hopeless Alexander, took French leave. On the trip we doubtless enjoyed the usual fare of hardtack, corned beef, and tomatoes. This combination may be dietetically perfect, but a less palatable concoction could hardly be imagined. And how ungrateful of me, even for a moment, to forget the coffee, that milkless, sugarless, coffeeless coffee. During one night on this trip we stopped, to be served with French coffee. This liquid was probably flavored with coffee, instead of dried chips or something else equally tasty, but rum had been added. This drink was despaired of even by the company rum hounds.

About forty-eight hours and we sighted sausage balloons some miles to our left. They looked too much like war. But for once we went toward the front without going all the way. Midafternoon we arrived in the town of Nancy, in northeastern France, and we detrained to line up on a platform. The one thing I remember definitely about our march out of the city was *passing* a large and tempting fruit stand.

Several of us, however, followed the company, remaining in Nancy for a while, to guard some supplies, I think. When we had hiked some miles from the city, we reached a fine vantage spot and looked back on the town in its basinlike enclosure below us. I thought the view one of the finest I had ever seen. Farther along we stopped at a café by the road where we drank something to cool us off. Later, a truck carried us some distance. On this trip we saw our first Italian soldiers. All seemed to have the uniforms of American generals. The fact that all Italians were "star" men was the source of no little jesting in the future.[1]

After some miles over a region of low hills, we arrived at our destination. The town was larger and more attractive than we were used to. The sight of the women workers, clad in men's garb, was new to me. We were quartered in houses built for the munition workers. Four of us occupied the room I was in: the two Bucks, and I think the fourth was Moose Taylor. We felt we were swimming to have quarters in those two-story houses, which were clean and dry. There was no drill to take the joy out of life.

The getting and spending of our money occupied no small part of our thoughts during the war. While the sum each man was to receive was most definite, the time he would receive it was most uncertain. At least this was true of us. In September 1917 we received our pay on the first day of the month (for the previous month, of course). In subsequent months we were paid anywhere from a week to nearly two months afterward. And the man who left his regular organization because of wounds or any other cause sometimes went an indefinite period with no pay. Times were hard. If Uncle Sam did furnish food (sometimes) and clothes, a fellow needed money for toilet articles, tobacco, and the like, not to mention little luxuries that sometimes met his eye. If I remember right, a man returned to our company at a later date who had gone thirteen months without one cent pay.

And when there was any money among the bunch, a lot of borrowing and lending occurred. Sometime before going to Soissons we received pay, for two months, I think. While I had taken from this money for payment of ten thousand dollars government insurance, together with a monthly allotment I still had more after being paid than I felt I should spend. And we must have been so situated just then that money orders could not be sent home. Since a number of fellows, for one cause or another, were broke soon after payday, I loaned a little money to three of the boys. Later, I was unexpectedly in need of money and borrowed small sums (as much, perhaps, as I could get) from three others. Soon after, we went to Soissons. The three I had borrowed money from were killed; the three who borrowed from me came out of the fight without a scratch.

And when a fellow had the money, usually he was in a dried-up French village—if in a village at all—where the most palatable delicacies obtainable were dried fruits, canned fish, and very inferior candy. And not infrequently, when something in the small French shops caught the eye, the French government prevented their being sold to us. An American might offer two or three prices for the edible, but the French shopkeepers would shake their heads and wave their arms and say a lot of things that did not tell anything.

In the town where we were at this time I tried to buy one of these forbiddens, but my effort was in vain. However, a purchase made by one of the other three in the room I occupied, I shall not soon forget. The prize was a piece of cheese, dear to the heart of a Frenchman. Could the novice entirely lose the use of his olfactory organ, it is possible that in the course of a decade or two he could eat this kind of cheese without any disastrous effects, but not before, unless that person be a Frenchman. The odor of French cheese! I know of but one thing in the world that has an odor comparable to it. And that is not, or *shouldn't* be, where water is abundant. But to return to this particular cheese. Though without the training back at Belleau, I suppose the eating would have been impossible. However, the whole cheese was not eaten at one time; nor had we been so hardened but that it was necessary between lunches to suspend the remainder out the window.

While in this town we received more replacements, bringing the company again up to full war strength. When we were ready to hike out of town, my helmet was missing—the helmet I had received before going to the Verdun Front—and for sentiment's sake alone I was sorry to lose it. But I was no little embarrassed, too, at losing so necessary a part of my equipment.

On this hike I first noticed one of the new men of the company. He was a rather large, big-jawed fellow, with a copperish-yellow complexion, by the name of Penn Howard. What he had in his pack I do not know, but it was of enormous proportions. With that, he seemed to carry the pack with less difficulty than many of the older men of the company carried their smaller ones. The man seemed to have been a preacher, with pronounced religious views. This, with certain peculiarities, caused him to be the butt of an increasing number of jokes. Howard had not been with us many weeks when there was a marked change. He was losing much of his spirituality, such as it was before.

That night we spent in some wooden barracks by the road. The next morning the journey was not continued, and I explored some strange country in that vicinity. In the afternoon we were on our way again. Unmistakable signs appeared that we were moving toward the front. Along one side of the road, suspended somewhat like clothes on a line, was an endless stretch of camouflage. It was composed of heavy, burlaplike, varicolored material. Night came on, and from the darkness torrents of rain swept into our faces. There came to our ears the occasional boom of a gun in the distance ahead. Our spirits were not high that night.

On the march we had passed through many villages. We now passed down the long street of still another. We looked forward to spending most of the night in trenches. It was a pleasant surprise to turn from the street into a large abandoned factory, where the company was quartered on the second floor.

We were in the town of Dieulouard, on what we later spoke of as the Toul Front but which was officially designated the Marbache Sector. Although it was about two miles to the front line, the sector was a quiet one; so we would not likely be troubled a great deal by the activity of the Germans. However, enough shells and bombs had been dropped to rid the town of nearly all its civilian population, and many houses had been injured or wrecked. While we were at Dieulouard, the screech of a shell now and then sent my blood down about sixty degrees. Who paid for their fall I do not know, if anyone in particular, but there were times when one after another screeched over, to hit in the far edge of town.

A church in the village had attached to each of two columns near the center a bomb of gigantic size. The two had fallen and torn up the rock or concrete floor for a radius of ten feet or more, but they had failed to explode. Their failure to explode was likely regarded by the church people as an act of Providence, which accounted for their removing the explosive materials and attaching the shells of the bombs to the columns. These bombs could hardly have been less than seven feet long and from one and a half to two feet in diameter. They were the largest missiles I ever saw. Not far from the church, between shattered walls, was a hole of enormous size. Until about two months before, we were told, the railroad had been used to that point. But the station was bombed and now all supplies were hauled from the next town back, by wagon or truck.

We had not been in the town long when one night we were greeted by the sawing, grating hum of German bombing planes overhead. Those who had not already done so got emphatic orders to "dowst the glim." The cry rang out to "put out that light!" The fellow who was slow blowing out his candle to prevent being spotted by the bombers received a shower of epithets far from endearing. It was anything but amusing to know that an enemy was above with explosives that could blow one into mincemeat. At such times I was always tempted to get out in the open, where there was less chance of a heap of bricks coming down on a fellow. But the others remained inside and so did I.

A canal paralleled the road in front of the factory, running on into enemy territory. One night we followed the canal some distance and spent several hours digging reserve trenches. While we were there, Allied planes crossed over to bomb Metz and German planes endeavored to bomb the city of Toul. It was a thrilling sight when enemy planes were no great distance away, while numerous and powerful searchlights nervously raked the heavens, trying to locate the planes.

About Metz there must have been forty of these lights, of almost unbelievable brilliance. It was a spectacle when all these shafts of light played across the heavens, and there could be heard the constant roar of antiaircraft guns, shells screaming through the air, and explosions in the air. It must have been an experience to be in the air during such times.

While at Dieulouard I did not get out of my habit of exploring the country around. One of my tours was in the direction of the front. It might seem that by now my curiosity as to what was going on at the front would have been satisfied, but I imagined that when I had proceeded some distance I would get to a vantage point where rare spectacles would meet my gaze. As I walked along, a shell falling no great distance away dampened my ardor considerably and I was soon on my way to quarters again.

I found other things of interest. Back of the old factory was a bluff, where observers with glasses spent the day. Here I put in some hours with them. Not far away was a fourteen-inch naval gun. I was anxious to take a peep at this; but a fence, camouflage, and guards prevented a near approach.

Some shoes that for some reason were unsuitable, I made an effort to return. The supply sergeant would not accept them. I did not want to be further burdened with a big, heavy pair of hobnails that I could not use. I did feel that I was equal to the burden of some extra francs, and a Frenchman gave me ten francs for the shoes. Had this little transaction been called to the attention of somebody or other, I suppose that I would still be making little ones out of big ones.

We hiked from Dieulouard in the night, as we had entered the place. We passed through Toul and stopped at the village of Harmonville, where a part of us were billeted in wooden barracks. The need of some dental work caused me to go with others about three or four miles away for a three-day stay. During this prolonged absence I hiked over once to see the company. Nor has a visit to a peach orchard been forgotten. However, the dentist left town before my work was done and I returned to Harmonville.

The company had left for a rifle range, and several of us put out to catch them. A truck that picked us up carried us somewhat out of the way and as far as Toul. We must have had recollections of stories of hard-boiled MPs there, as I lost no time in getting out of town. We found the company camped in the edge of a beautiful green wood, beside a canal. Up a long wooded hill and some distance farther we reached our destination. We were quartered in barracks during the days of practice on the range. When we left the range, our destination, as usual, was unknown to us.

I was surprised to return to the town of Favière, where I had gone for the dental work. My recollection is that during the days, we whiled the hours away pretty much as we chose. I remember particularly going to the railroad station to get a paper for the latest war news. We always waited with bated breath for good news from the front. Where a Paris edition of the *Herald, Tribune,* or *Daily Mail* could be had one time, a French paper could be had ten. The result was that in time I learned to glean the gist of war news from French papers.

It was about 7 September that we left Favière, hiking toward the front. We came into a village a black, rainy night and were quartered in a barn. I made my bunk with Sgt. William Speake, one of the new men, quiet and unassuming. Packs were unrolled by candlelight, with thankfulness that we had a roof over our heads, though concerned over some shells falling possibly a mile away. Like a thunderbolt came orders to roll packs. My sensations were not unlike the time when we were roused one night back at Belleau.

Soon we were on the road again. As it was no great distance from the front—though we did not know just how far—smoking along the road was prohibited. A company marching along a road would make a fine target for a bombing plane high overhead. But when we stopped along the road for a rest, some of the fellows were "just *dying* for a smoke." And when someone had the audacity to strike a match, he received a volley of: "Put out that match!" "Dowst the glim!" "Do you want to kill us all!" These, with many more exclamations that would not do to print, caused the man to be more thoughtful afterward of the general welfare. However, while some enraged men threatened to all but tear the perpetrator limb from limb, such as this was usually followed by a sort of aftermath, with expressions from a disgruntled "crepe-hanging rum hound." Burned out on all the bottled wares and exhausted from the hike, he would reflect, with all the commiseration in his soul, that we would just as well die there as later and be hiked to death. And the man who voiced this kind of sentiment was the last to procrastinate when a shell hit in his vicinity.

There followed several days in a wood. The small pup tents did not keep a fellow dry during those dreary days of rain and mud. About this time I sent twenty dollars to my mother, through a YMCA. Somehow I had the feeling that if I did not send that money home, within a few days some stranger would take it from my corpse. It was understood that we were to go over the top at the St. Mihiel Front, and the long-established lines were considered impregnable. The Germans, it was said, had endless barbed-wire entanglements and an intricate system of trenches, which would prove a most formidable barrier for attacking troops. We expected this to be the hottest thing we had gotten into. Numerous jesting remarks were made about So-and-So not coming back, with an accompanying smile that was somewhat forced.

Notes

1 He probably means that all the officers had stars on their collars indicating rank.

8: St. Mihiel

SYNOPSIS

Moving north from Marbache in early September, the 2d Division was assigned an active role in the almost all-American attack upon the salient created so many years ago by the German army. The planned attack was for ten American divisions, mainly along the south side of the salient, and four French divisions, covering the tip and northerly side, to advance and close off the long-occupied salient. Pershing's further plan, to advance and take Metz, was canceled by Foch with pressure from Haig.

The 2d Division would take its place approximately in the middle of the attack. The newly arrived 5th Division (regulars) would be on its right flank while the also new 89th Division would be on its left flank. It was the job of the 3d Brigade of Infantry to lead off on 12 September with the 4th Brigade in support. The 6th Marines followed the 23d Infantry.

Major Barker and his 1/6 plus the 73d Machine Gun Company were on the division's far left flank as liaison with the 89th Division. The 95th Company would be part of that liaison until 1/6 rejoined Lee's command on 13 September. It would be part of the force that relieved the 23d Infantry that night. On the fourteenth there was a period of several hours when the first and second battalions lost contact with each other and with Lee. The first was in the Bois de la Montagne, where they encountered the enemy and drove them westward. A primary problem during this period was the lack of liaison with the 89th Division, which had failed to advance on the division's left flank. Because of this the Boche pressed the regiment hard and the losses suffered were higher than previously suffered at St. Mihiel. The 4th Brigade was relieved on the night of 15–16 September and by the twentieth were entirely out of the lines.

• • •

And we were on the move again. A cold mist was falling and I had a headache. Our destination was another wood. Later in the day some chocolate bars were passed out. This was significant. There was also an issue of hand grenades. If any doubt had existed as to which direction we should go, the chocolate/grenade donation removed the doubt. Some of the companies in the woods were getting hot chow, but before the tardy 95th Company cooks arrived and prepared anything, it looked like we were going over with an empty stomach, except for the chocolate.

It was perhaps somewhat after midnight that we moved forward. A miserable night we spent in the cold, drizzling rain. The raincoats we wore were of the cheapest grade, so that they were practically worthless. There followed endless hours of marching a short way, then standing in the cold, penetrating rain. The column would move forward an uncertain distance, then, for reasons we did not know, would stop again for an interminable period. There was but to stand and wait; one could not sit down in the mire that covered the earth.

While we stood in the darkness, artillery opened up about us. Behind, ahead, and to the right and left, a multitude of guns poured out their volley of death. I had not realized there was so much artillery on the Western Front. As far to the right and left as the eye could see, the guns belched forth; and as they fired in the distance it was like a thousand plays of restless lightning. If the spectacle was grand and fearful, one shuddered at the deafening explosions of the guns, the roar and shriek of the shells. And at what moment might not the German artillery turn upon us! As we gazed and listened, spellbound, toward the lines, a fiery substance could be seen dropped by someone or something. Day was breaking and men going over; could it be the enemy planes were dropping the terrible liquid fire upon advancing troops? We never learned.

We were now in the shell of the village of Limey. For four years the town had been just behind the Allied lines. Nor had the naked and forbidding walls seen their end of destruction. As we passed through the streets an occasional shell shrieked menacingly over. Above a cellar was the Red Cross sign. The place was already doubtless filled with wounded. Countless raincoats were strewn about the drenched streets. Men who had gone before us did not wish to be burdened with those things.

We were soon out of the village and, single file, the column entered a shallow communication trench. Hand grenades were scattered on the banks of the trench. In one place was seen a sack of a dozen. We had heard stories of what would happen should a machine-gun bullet hit those grenades, and the men felt, too, there would be little chance of an opportunity to use them. Two or three bombs I had carried all night now joined the rest.

In making an attack the men in the lead, who were to do the fighting, were usually followed by several times their number. These "supports" would not become involved in the fight unless the resistance proved too much for the first wave. This first wave stood the brunt of the enemy machine-gun and rifle fire, while frequently the men following caught the greater artillery fire. The organization that was to go ahead was determined by seniority. During most of the war the 95th Company had a junior officer as captain, which resulted in our being in support more times than we would have otherwise.

Going down the zigzag trench to follow up the advance, we soon found ourselves on a rise, to see destruction and desolation ahead of us. Some hundreds of yards ahead there stretched a sea of barbed wire with trenches beyond. The advancing waves were just reaching the crest of the rise, and ahead of them moved the terrific rolling barrage. We were passing over what had been No Man's Land for four years, and the earth was a chaotic mass of shell holes. Some shells fell about us; and one, hitting a short distance ahead, sent singing strands of barbed wire over us with lightning fury.

Before we were aware, a piece of artillery was drawn up beside us and put into action. Certainly the Germans were leaving the country when the artillery was brought this far forward. Half an hour later, perhaps, we came in sight of a forest, beyond a depression ahead. Just before we entered the forest, about fifty German prisoners issued from it. What was there finer on a fellow's spirits than to capture prisoners—or even to see those that had been captured!

We were now passing through such a maze of vines and underbrush that much of the time I could see no one to my right or left. Presumably, the first wave had cleaned out the wood, but so many hiding places were there that any moment we might come upon Germans who had concealed themselves. At an opening in the trees we came upon a deserted, half-submerged dugout. And the men who had left were evidently in a hurry, as steam was still rising from the kettle. Fellows who stopped long enough for a closer look found potatoes in the kettle.

Finally, we came to a road, where we paused for a rest, taking the packs off to rest tired shoulders. Those shoulder straps from the packs had been pulling down, without a moment's cessation, for nearly twenty-four hours. We had not been able to sit down once during that time. During the few minutes we rested along the road, several snarling shells hit in the woods about us. If during the sweeping victory of the hours before we had come to the conclusion that the war was about over, the terrible roar and splitting crash quickly dispelled such hopes.

One shell struck at the edge of the road, two hundred yards or more to the right. A moment later there was a singing in the air and a ragged piece of shell the size of a man's index finger, the force of it almost spent, that grazed my hand to half bury itself in the earth a few feet away. The cut went little deeper than the skin, though bled profusely for a slight wound. As one of the hospital corpsmen, Buck, I think, was near and unoccupied, I got him to put a bandage on it.

The same shell had hit almost under Captain Black, killing him instantly. He had joined us just before we left for St. Mihiel and the boys regarded him as a princely fellow. A first lieutenant, John Popham, who had recently joined us, then took charge of the company. He was an amiable, easygoing sort of a fellow, but not the man to command 250 men at the front.

Several hours more passed before we came to the edge of the forest. During the morning, numbers of 95th men had been killed by shellfire and more wounded. Among those killed was Sergeant Speake, whom I had bunked with several nights before. While in the woods the companies had become more or less disorganized and men lost. We now faced an open prairie, with the town of Thiacourt a mile away. Orders to move forward were given by someone and we ventured out in the open. We swerved somewhat to the left and into a bit of valley where the Germans had left a narrow-gauge railway.

At this time I was sent on some mission, the nature of which I do not now recall. Returning to the position where I had left the fragment of company, I found it gone.

Among other places that I looked for the company was in a deep ditch or ravine thirty feet wide. Here were men of other organizations. Built into the sides of the ravine were bunkhouses that had been deserted by the Germans. There was also a large German truck, which seemed quite intact. They had evidently been in a hurry when they left. In answer to my inquires I was several times directed to the position of the 95th Company, each time to be disappointed. I finally decided to give up the search until morning.

The quiet that had reigned for some time was broken by a gun—seemingly not more than a mile away—firing upon us. If the German gun was no farther than that, how far away must their front line be? Some of the fellows busied themselves digging into the embankment, preparing for the night. Others found pieces of corrugated roofing, which they felt would provide some protection. Being away from my own company caused me a certain uneasiness and I was undecided what I should do. I started to dig into the side of the ravine but later went out into the open, where a few scattered men were digging.

Sometime before the break of day I returned to the ravine and went into a deep dugout where there were others. I don't know if I slept any before daylight or not. However, I doubt that I could have remained still for very long without going to sleep, as it must have been forty-eight hours or more since I had even dozed, and this under a mental and physical strain, with little nourishment. About daylight an officer hollered down into the dugout for all to come out, as an attack was expected. One of the men, Sgt. George Bell, who had joined the 95th but a few days before, was in no hurry to come out. It was not until the officer threatened to go down with his pistol that the man, later to be christened "Dugout" Bell, came out of the hole. However, the expected attack did not materialize.

The next day I resumed my search for the 95th Company, though it was not until later in the morning that I found it on the Beney-Thiacourt Road, several hundred yards from the latter town. For a day or two to come men who had gotten separated from the company straggled in. The bunch were stretched in a ditch along the side of the road. I joined Sergeants Washburn and Dowel. A drizzling rain was falling, though one of us was fortunate enough to obtain somewhere a wagon sheet, which turned off the water.

We had read much in days before of how the folks "back in the good old U.S." were having meatless, wheatless, and other -less days; but the three days since we had gone over the top had been practically *eat*less days for us. Although at the time our company was a mile behind the front line proper, still the company cooks saw no reason why they should endanger their precious lives by bringing us anything to eat. In fact, 95th Company cooks had on previous occasions won for themselves the reputation of taking numerous (*too* numerous) precautions to keep Mary from becoming a widow.

In spite of the strict order, "Don't eat them until you get the word from an officer," our scanty emergency rations had disappeared several days before. Of the several dangers to which we had fallen heir, too heavy a diet was not one.

At this time it was the job of the men ahead of us to do the fighting (unless we should be needed to help sustain and attack); so our time had been spent merely in staying in the ditch along the roadside, wondering what the future might have in store for us and reflecting upon those glorious days back at home when a fellow could go to the table—yes, actually go to a table—and not have to take his mess kit with him; but find there a plate and knife and fork, with the remainder of the accoutrement of table warfare, waiting for him. These, not to mention all the bread a fellow could eat, and coffee with not only sugar in it, but honest-to-goodness cream and——but why torture the soul with the impossible!

At last came rumors that might result in shortening our fast days. It was reported that in the shell-torn town of Thiacourt, a half mile down the road, there was an apiary abounding with honey. Upon making inquiries, several of us found the location of the rumored treasure to be inside the garden, which was surrounded by a high stone wall. As we reached the entrance of the garden, a soldier came out with a big honeycomb in his hands, with the finest-looking honey imaginable dropping from its panes. The surprise of a lucky forty-niner was not to be compared to our thrill when we viewed a dozen bee gums inside the garden wall. The possibility of being stung by some of the vigilant inhabitants did not dampen our ardor in the least. Now to fill those empty stomachs at last.

But, alas, what a surprisingly short time does it sometimes take to change plans! No, it wasn't the bees. But from far over in the German lines came a deep a-rup-rup, like the peal of distant thunder. This thunderous rumbling was followed by a slow, familiar—though far from friendly—whine, a rush of air as in a storm, then a brief, hellish moment that could not have been more horrifying had a thousand mountains been crashing down upon us. There was a tremendous explosion, and the earth shook under us. If the German who had fired that shell was an ally of the bees, he was certainly a friend in time of need. However, he showed poor judgment, not to mention wanton waste of materials, in following the first shell with a second. It was not only superfluous, but *uncalled* for: the honey had lost its attraction—we were off!

Upon our return to the company one of the boys told me that at Xammes, a village in plain view a mile ahead of us, we would be able to get something to eat. This information might have been music to our ears, but the Germans had recently played a tune with their artillery that put hazard into the possibility of filling our stomachs by going to *that* town for the "filler": during our three days along the road the Germans had shelled the town constantly. The proposed foraging expedition had offered abundant opportunity for grave reflection. Timmer, who had been urging me to go, soon understood that despite my growing cavity amidship, I was a strong adherent to the idea that even a hungry soldier *above* ground had advantages over a full one *below* it. So Timmer came to realize that strategy must be resorted to if that soldier went with him. He told me that I was mistaken in thinking all the shells fell into the town, that most of them fell between us and the village.

"Watch the next one, Jack, and see if I'm not right," he said. The next shell did go between our position and the village. As it did, something—or, more accurately, the absence of something—inside me said go ahead.

So we went, going far out of our way to avoid the shelled area, thus entering the town on the far side. There we found every indication of recent civilian occupation, and their hasty departure was in evidence on every side. Lace curtains still hung at several windows, and a McCormick reaper stood under a nearby shed. A cow seemed undisturbed by the recent disappearance of her owner and evinced her share of cow composure as she ate turnip leaves in a garden.

But we had not come sightseeing. Upon opening the door of a large building near the edge of the village, we found high stacks of what appeared to be pound boxes of butter. A closer examination of the contents of the paper boxes revealed a delicious, sugary compound that tasted very much like honey. What a shame it was that we had to leave so much of it!

A short distance away there was a second storeroom where we found two hogsheads of apple butter. Upon tasting it we decided that the Germans had surely been in the rush of their lives when they left this. But how were we to carry any, even had our arms not been full of the packages of artificial honey? Upon further observation we found along the wall of the room a number of large gunnysacks, filled tight. Opening a sack revealed smaller sacks of German hardtack. The pieces were about the size of soup crackers, though heavier and somewhat sweet. Can you recall the most toothsome morsel you ever tasted? Multiply the deliciousness of it by ten. Then, provided that your imagination is of a superior sort, you can begin to have a faint idea of the deliciousness of that hardtack when dipped in the apple butter! In a shed, a few steps away, were stacks of German war bread. It was dark, heavy stuff, with an odor like spoiled potatoes, but it was bread and would *fill* a fellow.

We loaded ourselves with the various findings and returned to our company. They were a lot of hungry and curious men, so the supplies did not last long. We tried to convince them that there would be no great danger in going to the town themselves, but few could be convinced.

Upon a second trip to Xammes I decided to explore a bit. As I opened the door of a house only recently deserted, a half-grown rabbit scampered across the floor and hid himself under a bed. The surprise of the rabbit could hardly have been as great as that of his visitor. In the far corner of the room a safe had been left open, containing many kinds of peculiarly designed dishes. In a lower shelf was a dish of dried figs; a bowl of greens sent forth a musty odor; and some biscuits, to judge by their aroma, had some more of the sour potatoes in them, with a finisher of Limburger cheese. On the stove I found a teakettle, which could be used for taking back some of the prized apple butter. A wardrobe in an adjoining room—well, the "madam" and mademoiselles had left town in a hurry too. A bed in the room looked fine enough, so far as comfort went, for Louis XIV. Upon raising the snow-white counterpane, I found a *feather* bed.

The recollections of my own bed having been in muddy trenches, again in boxcars, and at present in a roadside ditch, with a single blanket separating me from the ground—all these not altogether pleasant recollections gave me an idea. If a German shell came over *that* night with my number on it, there would at least be the kicking out on a feather bed.

In a few moments I emerged from the house jubilant over my late prosperity; my pockets bulging with dried figs, the kettle on my arm, and the priceless feather bed over my shoulder. I soon had the kettle filled to running over with the apple butter. And some bags of hardtack must go along. Nor could all the packages of artificial honey go begging. But how was I to carry such a load half a mile when I could not even get it all in my arms? No sooner was I loaded and had taken a step or two than a package of honey or a half-dozen sacks of hardtack came tumbling to the ground. Without the feather bed I could have made the trip with comparative ease, but leaving it behind was about as far out of my mind as going over the top without my rifle. And the kettle of marmalade, too, was quite heavy; but I was determined to bring it along if it took till midnight to get back to the positions. Out came my pocketknife and I cut a hole in the tick of the bed. Into it I dropped boxes of honey and sacks of hardtack among the downy feathers. As I turned to leave, I saw that something had been overlooked. There were enough cigarettes in the building to last the 95th Company a year. So several cartons of German cigarettes were thrust through the hole in the bed, to fall into the feathery world with the hardtack and honey.

And since I had such a heavy load, why should I return by the roundabout path I had come and gone by before? I started on my return by a more direct route. I passed what had recently been the home of someone, but a German shell that had fallen a few hours before had left only a ragged wall, a heap of stones, now smoldering ruins. The hasty reflections on the fate of the house automatically quickened my steps. When I reached the edge of the village I found fresh shell holes, surprisingly numerous. There was scarcely a piece of ground the width of a man's body that was not deeply pitted with the scars of bursting shells. A number of these shell holes along my course were still smoking; and the nauseating odor, too, of the high explosive told me that not many minutes before, shells had burst on the ground where I was then walking.

The route I was taking led to some barbed-wire entanglements that the Germans had placed there before their retreat, to help check any advance of the Allies.[1] While I was picking my way with difficulty through an opening in the entanglements, pausing every few steps to loose the feather bed from barbs in the wire, the German artillerymen waked again and dropped a shell into the path I had passed over but a few minutes before. Mud and singing strands of barbed wire that followed gave me an exceedingly creepy feeling. I was tempted to drop bed and all, but kept them and got back to the company safe.

Just as I arrived I heard an unusual sound behind me. A fellow was coming from the village with something I had overlooked. He led a big roan horse that the Germans had left in their flight. The horse was drawing a sled, and on the sled was a big keg of beer.

Along with the French civilians the Germans had occupied the town of Thiaucourt for the four years the war had lasted. And until the attack of a few days before, I think the town had never been shelled. It was with boundless curiosity that the boys roamed the village, to pilfer this, to scrutinize that. It seemed almost unbelievably strange that we were now in a town on which the Germans had put their almost indelible stamp, which the invulnerable Germans had so recently occupied. At the edge of Thiaucourt was an electric plant, rendered unusable, of course, before they abandoned it. What a contrast to French modernness and ingenuity, that a town of this size in time of war should have electricity. We could not but draw like comparisons wherever we went. However, any satisfaction we got in wandering about Thiaucourt was purchased at the price of continued fear that a shell would fall upon us. Perhaps a third of the houses in these few days had been struck, if not totally wrecked.

I think it was but a few hours after we arrived on the road that troops passed through our lines to push the Germans farther back. They had gone but a short distance when a merciless shellfire fell among them. The black masses of smoke from bursting shells were thick among the advancing lines. Soon a large number of wounded were being carried back to the first-aid station.

One day a fierce battle raged on the hillside beyond Beney. If those shells were well aimed, certainly many a man lost his life on the hill. So heavy was the shelling and so thick the smoke that it seemed the very hill itself was being consumed by fire. How many lives might not be lost there, what suffering must there be, and how many deeds of heroism performed! A vague mystery shrouded the view of a battle in the distance. It was not unlike reading a vivid account of a heated battle of long ago.

One day Allied planes appeared from the rear, and a short distance ahead they met the Germans. One of the boys said he counted 140 of our planes go over, and it seemed the Germans had them outnumbered. I had seen some planes do some hairbreadth stunts back of the lines, but it seems that it takes a battle and flying bullets to bring about the real thing. And such a battle as it was. Planes, like enraged hornets high in the air, flew back and forth, up and down, while tracer bullets streaked the sky. So high were the planes most of the time that we were unable to ascertain who was getting the better of the fight. I saw four planes fall in almost that many seconds, though I was unable to tell whether they were Allied or German.

There was something about seeing a plane fall and a man going to his death in this manner that I had not experienced when witnessing the death of a man on the ground. There was an awfulness, a tragedy, in the sight unlike anything I had ever experienced. One of the falling planes came from a great height, about two miles we thought. As the plane sped downward, the flier disengaged himself and was hurled through space like a bullet. It seemed the battle lasted an hour or two. Perhaps it was over much sooner than this.

On a partially wooded slope, maybe a mile away, one day we saw a German plane sweep low over a wood. He was met with a volley of machine-gun bullets and fell nearby in an open field. Later we were told that the flier, riddled with bullets, was removed from the plane and taken to the rear. Only a short time after the fall of the plane, the Germans began throwing over shell after shell with the object of destroying it. When we last saw the plane, apparently it had not been struck.

At what seemed about two o'clock in the morning following our fourth day on the road, we were surprised by the order to move. It looked like we would get into it. I still had with me some of the German rations I had gotten at Xammes. The rations were in a white pillowcase, and this would make too good a mark for a German machine gunner, I reflected, if we did go over. To turn loose the eats after going to that trouble to get them was not easy. I must have left the sack behind but carried some hardtack in my pack. As we crossed the road into a field, the outlook was anything but promising. I thought for a moment how safe and snug it would be had I lain in my blankets when the others came ahead.

Later, we remained some time on a road—waiting for what, we did not know. Shells falling a short distance away increased our nervousness. Anyplace but a road in the night when it is being shelled.

As day was breaking we went ahead. Passing over a rise, we were trudging through a field. Every moment I expected the order for attack formation. Instead, we neared a wood and the company was halted in a segregated patch of bushes. Shells began to fall here and there. When there was any chance of trouble with Germans, in months past, we had heard again and again, "Don't crowd; keep your distance!" Now we were jammed up so that one large shell would have killed and wounded a large number. Some men from another company were a short distance up the slope and one or more were wounded.

Some of us moved several yards from the main body of the company. Shells continued to fall unpleasantly near, yet no orders were issued to advance or even scatter out. I crossed the fence into the main body of the wood. Here I could watch, and in case the company got orders to go I could join them in a few seconds.

Hours dragged by. Many of the company were scattered here and there, getting low when a shell approached. When the wood was more quiet, men wandered about, gazing at the barracks the Germans had left in their flight. Several times during the morning the hollow rattle of machine guns came from somewhere down in the valley and bullets flew past us. Troops were supposed to be ahead; but just where they were, as well as the location of the enemy machine guns, was a puzzle to me. A few hundred yards ahead the wood seemed to terminate in a ravine of thick bushes and trees. Beyond was a half-obscured precipice; and still farther, we were told, was the town of Jaulny, which the Americans were attempting to take.

Men from other companies, too, seemed to have nothing to occupy them but to look out for the next shell. It must have been in the middle of the afternoon that Burt Wright and I were sitting on the edge of a shallow dugout, our feet dangling in the hole, eating hardtack that I had brought from Xammes. Suddenly a shell whisked over and, Pow! hit about a yard from us. I don't recall just what Wright did, but I think that he was the kind of fellow that would not, under the circumstances, postpone unnecessarily shifting his position. Enough for Wright. In a marvelously short time I came to the conclusion that a deep dugout nearby was the place for me.

Whether it was due to a shell or my heroic effort to preserve for future use the soldier that Uncle Sam had spent his hard-earned money lo these fifteen months in nourishing with hardtack, that coffeeless coffee, and abiding stew—whether it was due to a shell, I'm not sure. But it was then that I parted company with the old rifle I had gotten down at Paris Island and the pack that had been issued me soon after. I had both near me when the shell fell. Whether they were blown to atoms, as I at first believed, or whether some fellow made himself a present of them, I never learned. But I did regret parting with them. Very few men had gone through even the Château-Thierry scrap without exchanging rifles one or more times, or losing one. So I took pride in having kept mine, till—!

In connection with losing my pack was an unusual coincidence. Back at St. Nazaire my sister had sent me a Bible. With few exceptions the boys carried Testaments; but I doubt there was another Bible in the regiment. I had wanted to return the Book, but was unable to do so. It was throw it away or carry it along, and into my pack it went, notwithstanding its bulkiness. I carried it to the front one time after another. Finally, I got Leslie Spindler, one of the mule skinners, to relieve me of it for a time. With the next trip to the front the pack in which the Bible had been carried was no more.

With men of my own and other companies I stayed in the dugout an hour or more. I then went above, to see what might be going on. Returning to the place I had last seen the company, I found it had left. Among men scattered about in the wood was the battalion major, Frederick Barker. I inquired of him the whereabouts of the company. He summoned a runner, who started through the trees and bushes, me following. The runner had gone a hundred yards when, without a word, he turned about and led the way to a dugout where there were perhaps seventy-five or a hundred of 95th men. The dugout was dark and I must have been under the impression that all the company was there. However, it developed later that the main body of the 95th had gone ahead.

Sometime in the night the men of the 95th returned. The company had been relieved and was on its way to the rear. The boys had gotten into a close place, in an isolated position, and had come near being surrounded by the Germans. A shelling had come and two men had been killed, Sergeants Mayer and Mastin.[2] This was the second time I had missed something the company got into; and while at the time had I been with them I probably would not have objected to being elsewhere, it has since been a source of regret to me. It was my own fault, in a way, that I had become separated from them; and in either case had I to do over I don't know just where I should do differently. But I am sorry that two of the times that the outfit came in closest contact with the enemy I was not with it.

Day was breaking when we got back to Thiaucourt, and we waited there for a time for some detachment of the company to join us before we went farther. Most of the day and part of the next we spent in a wood an hour or so from Thiaucourt. As we lined up to leave, I first noticed a man who had joined the company just before we had left for St. Mihiel. He was the darkest-skinned man I knew to go into the Marines—Edward Isham, an Indian, who had had several years in the service before war was declared. It was not long until Isham was recognized as a man of good sense and quick wit, who was ever cool under fire. His contagious optimism made him a favorite.

During the day we passed Negro soldiers working on the road. This was the closest I had seen Negroes to the front. However, the 92d Division, composed of Negroes, had fought at St. Mihiel, and we were told that they did some good work.

Due to the crookedness of what had been the line, our course, for a time, lay along country that showed little signs of war. Later, we came upon a waste of land that for four years had been the dumb victim of sweeping machine-gun bullets and bursting shells. In this barren scene of desolation we came upon a detail of men picking up unexploded shells and putting them in a wagon to carry away. As we marched we were surprised to meet General Pershing and staff, who seemed to be inspecting the field. A few minutes before our arrival, we were told, another group of men had been engaged picking up duds. A shell was accidentally dropped in a heap of others. A terrible explosion followed with fearful results. General Pershing could not have been far away when the explosion occurred.

We crossed the old front line a mile or two from where we had entered it some days before. The point of exit was at the village of Flirey. And this little village had undergone a siege. Never had I seen houses so shattered. Most of the walls had been leveled nearly to the ground, while a ragged, irregular mass of bricks, the remnant of a wall, rose here and there like the ruins of a past civilization.

Before sunset we were in the edge of habitable country again. The column turned from the road, to be given candy from an unknown organization. But those smiling *American girls* made a lasting impression. Did they catch the eye—and heart! It was like coming into Fairyland to receive candy—plus smiles—from honest-to-goodness American girls! From time to time in the past we had talked with YMCA workers, but most of them were older, and somehow it was just different. These girls seemed the embodiment of everything we had cherished back home. But a few fleeting moments, and we had marched on.

Several days following were spent in another French wood. It rained, and we had poor protection from the wet; but there weren't any shells falling. Several men who had received slight wounds got an antitetanus inoculation. Half for the novelty of the thing I took the "shot." For some reason the injection was made into the arm instead of the leg or hip, as was customary.

Hiking again brought us one moonlight night into Lay-Saint-Rémy. The towns and country about had unusual interest. And I did more than the usual exploring. Doubtless the thought uppermost in my mind was the securing of extra eats, and in this I was none too successful. In a vineyard, on a steep and rocky hillside, I ate some sour grapes, though I do not recall receiving permission to get them.

Back on the train en route to Paris Island, all had been surprised that the fellow with the sissy voice could be going to a training camp. Eddie Small, whom he had chided, was dead. During this stay behind the lines, the fellow with the girlish voice, Happy Summerlin, was commissioned. Summerlin was unpopular, and there was talk of his having followed a most unsavory occupation before coming into the Marines. If he was shrewd and scheming, at the front he was calm and courageous.

Notes

1 By Allies, Jackson meant the French divisions that were advancing with the more numerous American divisions.

2 Jackson missed on both. Mastin was KIA on 1 November 1918, not at St. Mihiel in September. Mayer was really Joseph Francis Maher, who DOW on 16 September.

9: Blanc Mont

SYNOPSIS

The battle for Blanc Mont Ridge and the taking of St. Étienne have been pretty much ignored by U.S. Army historians, mainly because the AEF ignored them. The 2d Division was, at the request of Pétain, assigned to the French army to be utilized in taking the ridge, which had been in the hands of the Germans for nearly four years. It was a position of great importance primarily because from its height the countryside was visible for many miles around. The French had been actively engaged in trying to regain it but, until October 1918, had failed in many bloody attempts and lost much manpower, which they could ill afford. The position threatened the important city of Rheims and protected the left flank of the Argonne Forest region. Pershing's planned attack upon the Argonne, at the behest of Marshal Foch, was possibly the deciding factor in loaning the ever-victorious 2d Division to the French.

This was the first important engagement that Maj. Gen. John A. Lejeune, as CG of the 2d Division, had a hand in planning. He and his staff decided that the 6th Marines would lead the brigade up the hill and take the heavily fortified ridge. Meanwhile the 3d Brigade would assault the ridge from the right flank. Supposedly the flanks would be protected by two French divisions. The division assigned to liaison with the 4th Brigade didn't make it up the hill. In fact, they barely made a few hundred yards the first day. Therefore, the 6th Marines and the following 5th were under constant German attack from the left flank.

The 6th managed to make and take most of the ridge that day, but the position was honeycombed with enemy machine-gun positions and it would re-

quire most of the week to dig them all out. After the 5th Marines were shat-
tered on 4 October, the 6th Marines were then assigned the task of taking the
important town of St. Étienne, which eventually was taken by them and mem-
bers of the newly arrived 36th "Cowboy" Division. It was a very badly run
battle, and once again a regiment of the 4th Brigade had to pay the price for
military mismanagement.

About 1 October we were carried some distance and detrucked in the night. A short hike brought us to a ditch, in which the outfit was to spend some days. We were back of the Champagne Front, and almost a stone's throw from what until recently had been French front-line trenches. In days following I was interested in wandering about, walking over what so long had been the disputed ground of No Man's Land. This front was another scene of interminable desolation. Washed-out trenches, pitted holes in the gray, sterile earth, fragments of shell that in places lay thick upon this scene of upheaval—it was a picture of war. In this former No Man's Land I came upon the bleached bones of a human skeleton. Could these bones speak, what stories might they not tell!

One day I visited a battery of French six-inch guns a mile or more from camp. As an American I seemed to be something of a curiosity to the Frenchmen. While I observed the firing of a gun, the French officer told me that the shells were falling about twelve miles away. And as I looked on, one of the crew told me to watch the next shell as it left the gun. Among the boys of the company there had been an oft-repeated joke of the green fellow who told of seeing a shell passing through the air; so when the Frenchman told me to watch the shell, I thought he meant to make fun at my expense. On getting directly behind the gun, I could see the shell as it passed through flecks of high clouds, far above.

One afternoon a blue object was spied high in the air, drifting in the wind from the direction of the lines ahead. In time a thousand glistening bits appeared, whipped here and there by currents of air. There was much speculation among the interested onlookers below as to what this meant. In a few minutes the specks grew larger, and we could discern sheets of paper falling here and yonder. The sin-

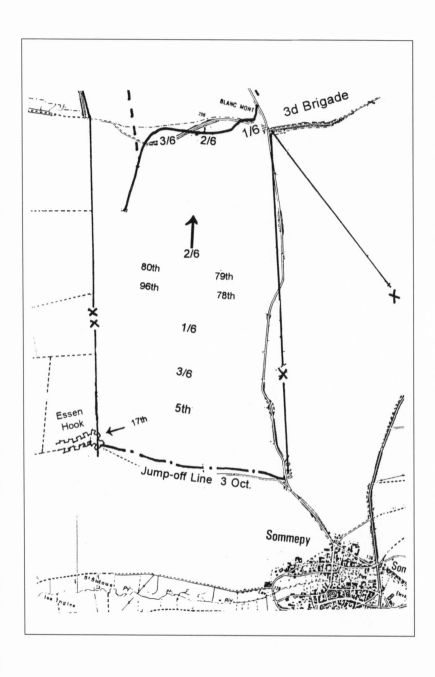

gle sheets contained German propaganda, printed in French on one side and English on the other. I picked up part of the paper parachute or balloon (I forget now which it was) that had brought over the sheets, and this bit of a souvenir I still have.

It was night and the company was hiking through an open country, toward the front. The night was not so dark but the column ahead could be seen strangely detouring from the road and back, forming a semicircle. In a moment we understood. At what had been the road was now a yawning crater that would have received an ordinary two-story house. The great hole was an awing sight, dark and ominous. And there lay another story.

We paused long enough to get some preattack "rations" at the side of the road, in the form of large entrenching shovels. French troops, coming out of the line, passed us and a few words were exchanged. We finally stopped and deployed along the embankment.

The next morning we were to go over, though again in support, as a first lieutenant commanded the company. The attack started at 5:30 on the morning of 3 October, with a barrage rolling. For some distance we hurried over a cloddy field, later to deploy and move forward more leisurely. Some French tanks pulled up. I feared they would only draw enemy fire with a repetition of the unforgettable disaster at Soissons. But due to a smoke screen or fog that blessed us, the advance of the tanks could not be seen from the enemy lines. The tanks smashed wire ahead of us; and one stubborn enemy machine gun I saw silenced by their activity was probably only one of many such instances.

And there were machine-gun bullets, shellfire, and prisoners. It seems that it was the middle of the morning that we were halted on a lone rocky ridge, with a sprinkling of scrubby trees about the trench into which we dropped. There followed what takes place a few hours after making an attack. Our own artillery was quiet, in that the guns and ammunition had to be moved forward to take up new positions. Meantime, the Germans had retreated into their ammunition dumps. The men on the front paid the bill.

A few hours on the ridge and we moved forward again. Up hill and down, through forests and across plains, we walked. The sun was getting low when we crossed a treeless incline to stop in a shallow

trench in the edge of the wood. As the setting sun sent its last few
feeble rays through the trees, our eyes fell upon several German bodies. It did not raise our spirits to know they were near the trench.

A few rather large shells fell about from time to time. The shells
of the larger variety did not have to fall fast or close to give a fellow
a creepy feeling. One dropped in the trench ten steps to the right
and there came an outcry from a wounded man. The little group I
was with felt considerable nervousness. One, however, among the
number seemed fearless and calm. Several of us huddled about Cpl.
Olin Larou, with an instinctive feeling that the mere proximity of a
man of his type afforded a degree of protection. Larou had been
twice slightly wounded, getting the "shots" at the time I got mine, after St. Mihiel. He was a big fellow—quiet, square jawed, and dauntless. We shall hear from him again.

Orders came to go forward again. We were halted in a deep ditch,
and the bunch started burrowing into the German side of it. Very good
protection, we felt, and easy on the nerves to sleep. But it was not for
us to spend the night there. It was rumored that we were to reinforce
the 5th Marines ahead, who were almost surrounded by the enemy.[1]

The night was dark and the guide lost his way. Shells struck
painfully close, sometimes emitting sparks that could be seen
through the brush. The column would move a short distance and
halt; move again and halt. Under those circumstances this kind of
thing was unnerving. The company was at last on a road, with many
shells (though many were duds) falling ahead and to the right, with
startling regularity. Would we have to go through that? The column
swung from the road to the left and halted for the nth time. In their
feverish desire to get to the destination—whatever and wherever it
might be—and dig in, the men in the rear jammed into the men
ahead. Scarcely more than an arm's length from me another shell
fell into the middle of the huddled group. An unforgettable "My
God" came from one of the men and he was dead. The shell had
passed through the man's body to strike the ground without exploding. So heavy was the impact on the hard, rocky ground that
rocks thrown up injured another man nearby. Falling on the hard
surface, had it detonated, the explosion would have made mincemeat out of all of us. It was said that the man who was killed had a

lone brother who was killed on the same front within twenty-four hours, and that the two of them were the sons of a widow. The one killed was among the little group who had sought protection from the shells the afternoon before.

As we went forward one of the new men asked some questions, as new men were wont to do. This particular fellow seemed unable to tell the fire of the enemy guns from our own, and it appeared that I had not made a good job of explaining. A gun belched forth almost directly to our rear and the questioner asked whose gun *that* was. Probably by this time I had become impatient. I told him that the gun was bound to be one of our own as it fired from behind. The words were hardly spoken when a shell from "our" gun fell among us! We were surrounded.

A little farther, and we finally stopped. As the front line was still ahead of us, it was not necessary to dig the holes in a line or in any certain order. Most of the holes were being dug pretty close together. Experience taught me that if the Germans the next day viewed so many holes close together they would draw fire. I dug my hole fifty yards from the main body of the company.

The company had gotten scattered during the night. Some were lost, and these straggled in the next day. Among them were Timmer and an old rum hound, who came in and dug a hole together near my own. Both they and I had found metal roofing to put on the holes, with the added protection of a layer of dirt. A large shell fell between their dugout and my own, dropping slightly nearer their hole and covering them up. Men in other holes about rushed to their rescue. The rummer—whose name I do not recall—was gotten out without much trouble, but Timmer was not in sight. For a time his labored breathing could be heard; then the sound of it ceased. We dug on to find him still alive, though severely shocked. He refused to go to the hospital, and later received a Croix de Guerre.

While we were trying to rescue the two men from the hole, a second very large shell fell twenty or thirty steps away. Ordinarily such a shell would have sent terror through me, but so intent were our minds upon rescuing the boys that we only half realized it had dropped. When we had moved to another position, a day or two later, a second man was covered by a shell.

In this new position Bob Robertson and I shared a hole together. One day as we sat in the hole, our backs to the German lines, the nose of a time shell tumbled heavily into the hole between us. There was no one behind to play a prank upon us. Men weren't thinking of that kind of thing then anyway. Planes were in the air toward the front line, and the nose of one of the shells used to try to bring down the plane happened to come in our direction. The shell nose must have spent its force by striking the ground before it fell into our uncovered dugout. Bob said that he was going to keep the piece of shell for a souvenir, but later concluded it was too heavy to carry.

There were frosty nights, and when exploring back of our position I found some blankets, which were mighty comfortable on those nights.

We moved up again, halting in the edge of an area tenanted with small and scattered trees. For half a mile beyond was an open stretch of country level as the floor, terminated by a low hill. Directly ahead of us, and at the foot of the hill, was the town of St. Étienne. Our front line and that of the Germans were in the neighborhood of the town. During the next day or two, as I learned afterward, the Americans drove the Germans from the town. As had been the case since the day of the attack, all that was expected of us was to stay in our holes and avoid exposing ourselves unnecessarily to enemy observation.

Bob and I again occupied a hole together. The hole was maybe two feet deep, with most of the dugout covered with a layer of sticks, and this in turn by a layer of dirt or some other convenient material. The protection thus afforded was more imaginary than real. This roof would stop only a shell fragment the force of which was near spent. It would be little more than tissue paper for a direct hit of even the smallest shell.

A line of observation balloons loomed up on the German side, and I do not think it could have been long after our arrival in St. Étienne that Fritz started throwing over some reminders that he was still there. And some of these shells were falling distressingly near. Maybe a hundred yards to our right front, half concealed in some shrubs, was an artillery piece the Germans had left behind. This seemed to be the object of much of their fire along that bit of front. It did not dawn upon me for some time that the Germans were just then more anxious to blow up that gun than they were to hit us. As the shells continued to burst that afternoon, Bob and I, like rats in a hole, lay on our sides in the dugout facing each other. Realizing how little the German gunners would have to adjust their range to bring those shells down on us, we had been worried, and I suppose that is putting it mildly. As stated, after a time I came to the conclusion that the enemy was bent on hitting that gun; I felt that our danger was not great. But Bob had apparently reached no such conclusion. I shall not soon forget the expression on his face as we lay there in that dusky hole, each with his back to a side of the dugout. With the belching of the gun in the distance, the hissing twirl of the oncoming shell, Bob's large, protruding eyes became larger, and in them was unconcealed terror. In thus watching Bob, my own fear was at such times considerably allayed.

I think it was 7 October that the 142d Infantry of the 36th Division came up and leapfrogged us. It was of one of these men, or some that passed us a day or two afterward, that two stories were told which were not flattering. Scattered trees to my immediate left prevented my witnessing the incidents, but other platoons of the company looked on and listened.

This was their first trip to the front, and they had just passed through our lines. A lieutenant of that division became so excited that he committed the most unparalleled blunder of advancing his men under fire in a column of squads or some other close formation. As they advanced, "Pop" Ansel, a 95th man who was a private by choice, hollered out to the looie:

"What the hell you pulling off there?"

The men who witnessed this swore that the lieutenant begged Ansel to come out and get the men in proper formation for making the attack, which request Pop ignored. It was thought that a great many of the 36th were killed because of their lack of training and due to the incompetence of many of their officers.

Another story was told at the expense of the 36th, which I am equally sure took place. Along with one of the advancing organizations of the 36th was a Frenchman, probably an officer. As the men moved forward, a falling shell brought the cry of "Gas! Gas!" The men were placing their masks with commendable haste, when the officer, attempting to correct the mistake, shouted, *"Pas gaz, pas gaz."* (No gas.)

By this time a 36th officer had come to a better appreciation of his grave responsibility in protecting the precious lives committed to his care and took up the saving cry, in frenzied tones.

"Put on your masks, men, put on your masks. That's the WORST gas there is."

Nor could I be content long to stay in my hole without scouting about in the rear. I saw an ammunition dump and some deep dugouts of a most strange construction. Only a few steps in the rear of my own hole, men of the 36th had fallen. Among their bodies I found eats that were gratifying to an ever yearning stomach. The hardtack we had always been issued became soggy after a time, if not musty, in the paper container. The men of the 36th Division carried hardtack packed in tin boxes. And did it taste like fruitcake.

From about the first time we went to the front, Charlie Slaughter had been away at hospitals with one operation after another. Before the company went to Champagne he rejoined it. Like most men who had little experience with German shellfire, Charlie found staying in his dugout and under cover hour after hour too irksome. When he was out of his hole one day a shell fell behind him and threw a large piece of shell with some force flat against his back. Charlie sent out a yipe that was a good advertisement of the lungs of a Texas football player and cowpuncher.

When the second contingent of 36th men came up, I was amused with one of their number who looked about him with petrified wonder. He asked many questions about the "battlefield."

On the morning of 8 October we moved into the open, toward St. Étienne. As the line of enemy observation balloons had an unobstructed view of us, we had advanced but a short distance when a heavy curtain of artillery fire was thrown in front of us. As we proceeded, the range was raised and soon we were in the midst of falling shells. Lieutenant Popham, commanding the company, was wounded in the leg.

It soon developed that the 76th Company, who were supposed to be advancing with us, were not in sight. The 95th Company halted its advance while I went over in the direction in which the 76th was supposed to be. As I went I saw my first Browning machine gun and was much interested in it. However, one or more bullets, which were probably strays, whizzed by and hurried me along. For a time I trailed along a shallow trench, failed to find the company I was looking for, and returned to the 95th. Orders were then given to return to the holes from which we had come. The boys afterward spoke of this shelling as one of the worst the outfit ever underwent.

A second contingent of the 36th came up to relieve us, which meant that the organization was to return to the rear that night. Being relieved from the front was always a glorious feeling. Then it developed that two of us—Sergeant Rheinheimer, I believe, and I— must stay with the new organization until the next morning. It was disappointing news. Having spent some days in the position, we were supposed to be able to give helpful information to those relieving us. During the night I spent some time back at Regimental Headquarters, though I do not now recall for what purpose.

Instead of our remaining with the 36th men until the next day, they allowed us to go before daylight. We lost no time in making our way to the rear and toward safety. The coming of day found us still hurrying on, grimly reminded of what might be our fate by shell-torn towns through which we passed. Then we came upon an endless stretch of desolation, even worse than we had found at St. Mihiel. As far as the eye could see was the thickly pitted earth, made sterile by multiplied thousands of shells falling and turning up the subsoil. In this barren waste we found the company getting ready to eat.

Miles farther on we pitched pup tents in a level open space. Only one incident of any consequence do I recall during our stay there, and I shall not forget it until I forget we had a war. One morning three of us hiked over to the town of Suippes, three-quarters of a mile away, where we visited a French canteen. It could not have been more than two hours from the time we left camp until we were back. While the three of us were away, there had been a company formation of some kind when a check of men was made. Several privates were absent. Also, Corporal Jackson.

The corporal went before the captain. Captain Clarence McClure had joined the company since we came out of Champagne, having only recently arrived from the States. He was hard boiled! When Corporal Jackson arrived, the honored captain inquired as to the recent whereabouts of the dishonored corporal (though I think he already knew). Yes, he had gone to the town and *without* permission. The captain was very solemn and stern. The corporal soon became infected with a new seriousness. And there was enough to make him think seriously—the captain was talking about "desertion in the face of the enemy" or something on that order and a general court-martial! Now, summary "courts" were usually not worse than a light cold; in a few days they might be forgotten. A "special" was only somewhat worse. But a GENERAL COURT-MARTIAL was worse than having the black plague, leprosy, and tuberculosis all at once with a bad toothache thrown in.

Yes, the corporal was under arrest. The captain began to dissect him, carefully and minutely. By that means death would be most prolonged and most painful. Had that captain only lived back in the Dark Ages, when torturing to death was all the rage, he would have left Bill Shakespeare and Julius Caesar in the shade when it came to getting fame. Unfortunately, he was born out of his time. I was sorry for it and would pay the penalty. I had been scared so many weeks and months before that it might seem by this time there would not be left in my system even one small scare. But compared to this all the others were small frights. I may not have gotten down on my knees before the old boy, but I felt like doing it then and there. Probably the captain had meant only to scare me in the first place. His effort was a one-hundred-percent success.[2]

From this position we went to Suippes. There I got my greatest thrill while in the war. Word was passed that the war had ended. Everybody was hilarious with joy. The staid French quartered in the town all but threw their guns away. The spirit of the occasion was greatly enhanced when that afternoon a program was given by a group composed for the most part, if not entirely, of American girls. The wild joy and exhilaration of peace still surged through our beings when those girls, scarcely less affected, sang a song we heard for the first time:

Keep your head down, Fritzy Boy,
Keep your head down, Fritzy Boy.

If you want to see your father in
    your fatherland,
Keep your head down, Fritzy Boy.

Keep your shade down, Mary Anne,
Keep your shade down, Mary Anne.
If you want to keep your secrets
    for your future man,
Keep your shade down, Mary Anne. . . .

Pervading the song was boundless enthusiasm, infused by the incomparable and almost unbelievably good news that the war at last was over. When that tune is played today by a good band, I can hardly keep my seat.

But the wonderful news was unconfirmed. Trucks of ammunition continued to pass through the town on their way to the front. The distant pounding of guns was not stilled. Gradually our hopes withered. Our souls were gripped by the terrible realization that the war was still on.

While we were in Suippes we watched with interest French troops going through the manual of arms and other exercises. It might have been for the benefit of onlookers, but those old Frenchmen did put pep into their movements.

After some days in the shell-swept town, the company was on the march. As usual the destination was unknown. The course seemed to parallel the front. A slight turn to the right or left would mean to the front again, or back. The road took a deep bend toward the front, and at least one soldier in that company was worried. But the road swerved again, and soon we were quartered in the little town of Bouy, safe behind the lines.

Although we had been in France a full year, it was while at Bouy that I got my first one-day leave. Several of us were carried in trucks to the historic Châlons-sur-Marne, a town of thirty-five thousand. The place had not escaped German bombs.

In camp was a Y we visited. Within walking distance of the barracks was an aviation field where some of the boys went AWOL. I was anxious to take my first plane ride, but I did not have the permission to leave camp. The narrow escape of a week or more before was fresh in my memory. I had come near being shot at sunrise as it was. More than usual was said at this time about the emergency rations. Every time we had gone to the front, hardtack and corned beef was issued, and sometimes bacon, with the injunction that the eating of these rations without an order from an officer was a court-martial offense. Each time at the front most of us, if not all, ate the rations. Before going to the front again there was another ration made, with the same caution, but with a seeming disregard of the fact that the past issue had disappeared without the order being given. There was to be pack inspection. There was nothing novel about this; but it was understood, if the positive statement had not been made, that trouble was in store for the man without emergency rations. My hardtack was lacking, or at least short the required number of packages. Again I was worried. But I got some hardtack somewhere—and my life was spared![3]

Notes

1 The 5th Marines were in bad shape. By the night of 3 October they were out in front and partly surrounded. The next day, on 4 October, they began their advance toward St. Étienne and they really took a shellacking, day and night.

2 McClure was an enlisted man promoted to captain in June 1917. No doubt he was still thinking as a first sergeant while handing out the usual hard time to enlisted Marines. I know just how Jackson felt.

3 As we have read, Jackson was constantly concerned about food, which we can sympathize with. Food supply to the fighting men was a complete disaster in the AEF. Or, at least, in the 4th Brigade. Possibly some, other than the troops in the rear, were getting regular servings, but the hunger cry was consistent among Marines at the front all during the period. He also implies that the kitchen people didn't always do their duty, at least for his company. Why the officers allowed that to happen can only be left to conjecture at this late date.

10: The Meuse Campaign

SYNOPSIS

At the urging of Marshal Foch, Pershing broke off his plan to continue his advance and take Metz and instead sent divisions northwest toward the Argonne Forest. This was done to take the pressure off the British and French armies in the north as they advanced against the Germans. The intervention of the AEF in September was decisive, but movement was slow and bloody. By mid-October the Americans had suffered, in comparison to ground gained, enormous casualties and the advance had stalled.

Catching their collective breaths, the remaining American divisions began collecting replacements and preparing for another strike. Meanwhile, after the success at Blanc Mont, the 2d Division had rejoined the AEF and was ordered to a position not far from the Meuse River. There, on 1 November, they and the [in line, left to right] *80th, 2d, 89th, and 90th U.S. Divisions jumped off at 5:30 that morning. The 2d and 89th were part of the U.S. V Corps, which by midafternoon had advanced at least five miles. The 4th Marine Brigade led the division with the 6th and 5th Marines in line, left to right. The 95th Company was assigned to the so-called "minor" battalion formed from one company from the 80th Division* [that division was part of I Corps, and consequently that liaison would be especially difficult] *and the 95th plus the 73d Machine Gun Company.*

The advance continued northeast toward the river for a week. By the night of 10 November the 6th Marines were preparing to go across the Meuse just above the town of Mouzon. Meanwhile the 5th Marines were assigned the task of crossing the river that night a few miles south of Mouzon. The 2d Engineers tried, but failed, to construct bridges for the 6th, but managed to partially succeed for the 5th Marines. They paid heavily for the engineers' success.

In rain and lightning flashes we returned to Suippes. A day or two later we took trucks and headed east, passed through St. Menehould, finally to detruck in the Argonne Forest. We hiked through a picturesque country of woods and hills and stopped at some frame barracks located on a slope covered by a forest of beautiful and towering trees. It was good to have a roof over our heads, as there followed some ugly weather. I suppose I remember as I do a payday at this time because we were impressed with the small likelihood of an opportunity to spend the money for some time to come.

The company was on the march again in the night. We thought that we would go into the line that night, but we were mistaken. The moon was trying to shine as we wound our way up a low hill through scattered bushes. Men lay asleep here and there in shallow holes, and in a little while we occupied like holes.

We were not so far from the German guns but occasional shells passed over us to fall in the valley a mile away. One night shells fell intermittently a quarter of a mile in the other direction, toward the front. The gas guard keeping watch (who was doubtless a new man) concluded that one or more of these shells must be gassers, and he decided to warn his comrades, lest death while they slept overtake them.

It happened I was awake before the alarm was given, and I well knew that if all the shells falling below were gas shells, which I was sure could not be the case, we could not, under the circumstances, be affected by them. The man with whom I shared a dugout at that time made haste to get on his mask when the first alarm was given. Possibly five minutes had passed when he discovered, to his horror, that the man beside him lay asleep, perhaps hopelessly gassed. He used no uncertain means to wake me and get my mask on.

While the company was in this position a tooth began giving me trouble. Not forgetting how the pain of an aching tooth was aggravated by staying day after day in a cold, damp hole at the front, I got permission to see a dentist a mile or two to the rear. Since I might have to leave for the front any time, the dentist thought it unwise to try to treat the tooth. He pulled it out.

When I was gone for dental work, Major General Summerall, corps commander, spoke to the men and told them they were going into it. He stated that within the German lines was an important railroad. If this main artery of travel were captured, the war would end! I suppose that sounded like myth and music to the listeners.

Again we headed toward the front. We passed through country that had only recently been laid waste by heavy shellfire. Here and yonder charred tree trunks pointed gloomily toward the skies like so many tombs. Night came and we continued on. We passed through the wreck of a town that stood ghostlike in the darkness. At times shells fell heartlessly near. Through another shell-torn town, and we cut to the right to stop in a deep ravine. The ravine was something like a mile from our front line.

A number of artillery pieces were little more than a stone's throw behind us. There was one or more machine guns that fired continually. All of this could not have been directed at planes; yet I do not see how the fire could have been effective if directed toward enemy lines. Shells from German guns bothered us little. However, one afternoon a gas shell fell upon the ground above and slightly to my left. The gas settled into a ditch, and the man who had dug into the embankment not six feet to my left had to go to the hospital.

It was the afternoon of 30 October and preparations were being made to go over the following morning. Before we went over at St. Mihiel I formed vivid pictures of the kind of thing we would experience in making the attack. I again conceived pictures of going over and how it would be. Sometime before night orders came for me and two privates to report to Major Stowell to act as runners. The major and those under his command were to have a function that was new to me. We were temporarily to be part of a "liaison" battalion. If for any reason a gap was formed in the advancing lines, the "liaison" men were to occupy that space.[1]

As night came, the 95th moved up to the position from which they were to "jump off" the next morning, while the three of us remained in the shattered village with the major.[2] Falling shells worried us and we looked for a safe space to spend the night. Nils "Nick" Haugen, a sturdy fellow from Minnesota, was one of the two I was detailed to work with. The other was a puny, consumptive-looking fellow from California, I think, and on his first front. I left the men to see the major, who was in a nice, snug dugout. When I started to leave, he told me to stay with him in the hole. Had he handed me a check for five hundred dollars instead, I might then have been little more gratified.

In the morning when the order for forward was given, all moved out but one man (as the story was told to me later). The man was a replacement and this was his first trip to the front. He was a big, angular fellow, about six foot two or three inches in height, and he was from the country. He was given a special order to come out of his hole, and he admitted that he couldn't stand the gaff. We heard later that he had been put in a labor battalion.

In contrast was the story of the captain of the 76th Company, Macon C. Overton, who had come up from the ranks. Back at Belleau Wood he had distinguished himself for bravery. In the course of the attack, on the morning of the first, a concealed machine gun was playing havoc with the American lines. While the men about the captain hugged the ground, this valiant officer stood boldly up, pointing out the destructive machine gun to his own gunners. As he stood he was killed by a bullet passing through his head.

Before we went to the Argonne, one of the 95th men told me of having his equipment struck while on him at no fewer than two or three fronts. It looked as though luck was with him, but he was among those killed on the morning of the first.

Events following are somewhat confused in my mind. It seems Major Stowell left the dugout rather suddenly, telling me to meet him at some place or other. I don't know whether I failed to get directions or the major changed his mind. As sometime later I neared the place I thought I was to go, I made out the end of a column just rounding a corner. Right or wrong, I concluded this was my bunch, and I hurried back to get the other two men that we might join the major. I found them gone. The result was I made two or three trips to the front line looking for and inquiring for the major. I even went to an outpost in my search for him. Failing to find him I felt the next best thing to do was to find the 95th and attach myself to it. I failed to locate it too. It was not exactly easy on a dark night to find anything or anybody in a place where one has never been before.

I was still making inquiries for the major and the company when, about 3:00 A.M. of 1 November, the American bombardment opened up. And such a roar no one until then had ever heard during that war. When the bombardment started, I was making my way along a line of dugouts, questioning men lying in them. The roar of guns and passing shells was such that it was almost impossible to make myself heard even when I shouted in their ears. At any moment the enemy might retaliate. Being in the open, exposed and away from my outfit, gave me most unpleasant sensations. I felt not unlike a man set adrift in a small boat on a stormy sea.

I was making my way back to the town again. I passed seventy-fives almost on the front lines. They were entirely too close to the enemy should they attack, I thought. But corporals weren't directing activities just then—thanks be. Since I had been unable to find the major, I would get the two runners and return to the front, major or no major. But in the village I was unable to find the runners either. Daylight had come, and since I had left the line a barrage had begun rolling and the bunch gone over.

As I returned to the front, once again I passed through a good many light artillery pieces in action. One of the guns was blown to pieces, either from the premature explosion of its own shell or from enemy fire. As I hurried along I decided to rid myself of some of my baggage and loosened the straps that held the blanket roll. The blanket, or blankets, I had received on Paris Island; and as in the case of the gun there was something of the same sentiment in parting with them. But I knew the discarded blankets would be picked up and that before I needed more there would be an ample opportunity to provide myself.

I came upon a wounded man unconscious and lying on his back. As his bulging pack was under his shoulders, his head had fallen back, causing the tight military collar to press hard against his throat. I loosed the collar and, without learning where the man was wounded, I moved on.

I passed through some engineers who were forming to go over as supports. Some distance ahead and to the right and front men were advancing. Shells fell among them. About a six-inch shell dropped in their midst, and I saw a man crumple into the hole made by the shell that hit him. I found my two men and we struck off obliquely to the left.

It was a rolling, treeless country, broken by an occasional valley. As we moved along, bullets sometimes whizzed by us. I remember several bullets in particular that did not go by. A number plunked into the ground, a few steps away, and sent into the air a geyserlike shower of dirt. I did not know whether this was to be accounted for by the nature of the ground into which the bullets fell or if they were of the explosive variety.[3] Whatever the cause of this phenomenon, whenever the bullets plunked into the ground they did not fail to quicken our steps. As we hurried along we passed what was left of the bit of a village of Landres-St.-Georges. I was surprised to find no dead Germans. The enemy must have evacuated their positions as soon as the bombardment started.

The three of us had advanced for two hours perhaps. A low ridge loomed ahead, a quarter of a mile or more away. The ridge was cut by a shallow ravine, which came toward us for two hundred yards, where it assumed larger proportions and turned to the left.

However, we had scarcely noticed the ravine when our eyes fell upon the unexpected. At the bend of the ravine, a hundred or more yards from us, with only part of their bodies exposed, stood several Germans, motionless and facing us. One of the men held a machine gun in his hands. How many more Germans there might be with them we could only guess.

Right there, three Marines held a council of war. On second thought, maybe I should call it a council of peace, for it was peace we were thinking of. Were those Germans waiting for us to get a little closer that they might shoot us down with more ease and greater satisfaction? Not another American was in sight. The three of us stood on the bald prairie, without a vestige of cover, while the Germans had their numbers—they only knew how many—and the ravine bank to protect them. We did not question the efficiency of the German machine gunner, not for a moment. And we had seen the Germans do the *"Kamerad"* stunt. I was in an unhappy state of mind because that machine gunner showed no disposition to part with his weapon. My thoughts were so intent upon him that I suppose I failed to take note what arms those beside him held.

As this was the first time one of the three had been to the front, the second time for another, and it was my seventh front, I was given credit for knowing a lot about dealing with the situation that, sadly, I did *not* know. There he was! As commander-in-chief I called for the expert opinion of each of the two next in rank. I think both felt pretty much like executing a to-the-rear-march but were just too cowardly to say so. Possibly I do them an injustice by judging them by my own feelings at the time. Anyway, after our little powwow we started ahead again. As well as I remember, our policy was almost one of peace at any price. None of us could speak German and *I* was declared spokesman! Nor was I at all disposed to minimize the precariousness of the situation.

When we were within fifty or seventy-five yards of the Germans we halted again, and I began motioning them to come out. It seems I even tried using on them my six-word stock of German words. While I was beckoning them, several Germans, bent far over, retreated up the ravine with all possible speed to disappear through the ridge. I didn't think it a good time to shoot. I think that none of those standing in the edge of the ravine had made a move when, back to the left, a German came in abandoned haste, an American following, firing at him with his rifle. Feeling that just then was not a good time for hostilities, I hollered out to the pursuer not to shoot the man. If he heard me he doubtless concluded that I had nothing to do with the case. The two passed over the ridge without our knowing the outcome.

Some of the Germans dropped back into the ravine. In a few moments about fifteen came out, unarmed, and wearing caps in place of their helmets. Others were still in doubt as to the wisdom of putting their lives in our hands. Finally the last of them surrendered. Allowing for my excitement at the time, with a consequent stretch of my imagination, there could hardly have been less than forty of them, and probably there were nearer seventy-five. The two other men took the prisoners to the rear, where they were to be turned over to the proper authorities.

The Germans being where they were when the lines had advanced ahead was doubtless due to some organization failing to follow the route it was supposed to take. The major and his liaison battalion were to take care of this kind of situation. However, during the day it seemed most of the men got lost from their own company, and the major, too, somehow lost most of his men.

Before going ahead I decided to look over what the Germans had left behind. Their toilet articles they had taken with them. In addition to equipment I found a lot of cigarettes, in bulk, sacks of hardtack, and sweetened butter. And the order not to eat food Germans had left behind because it might be poisoned was again disregarded. In a dugout were some empty bottles with a suggestive odor. I found a pair of the prized German field glasses. Then I came upon that souvenir of souvenirs, the Luger. As a souvenir this pistol had come to be more highly regarded than the German Black [Iron] Cross. I then added a Mauser to my trophies. Then I spied what appeared to be an old-fashioned money purse, though one side of it projected farther down than the other. Upon opening it I was astonished to find instead of money a third pistol, the smallest I ever saw.

I had just forgotten there was a war on, when troops came up. Their officer hollered out to me, and several more souvenir hunters who I think had come along, to move. These troops came up when I was examining the small pistol. To one of the group I sold it for fifty francs, something less than ten dollars American money. I was so tired out that I decided to leave behind the Mauser and the field glasses. Instead, I took with me the Luger, which was in a case, and by its strap I swung it from my shoulder. However, these few pounds were too much to carry. Three days later I sold the pistol to a motorcycle driver for 150 francs.

When I came upon the 95th it lay on a slope overlooking the town of Imécourt in a basinlike depression below. Shells from our guns were falling into the town. I was cautioned to get low because there were Germans in the town. I heard a friendly argument, I think between John Foley and one other, as to who was responsible for bringing down a German who had just fallen. I was told that earlier in the morning four prisoners had surrendered to the company. One of the Germans did something trivial that met with Captain McClure's displeasure and he told his orderly to shoot them. The orderly had spent four years before the war in German Alsace and hated Germans. He killed the harmless and unprotected Germans.

When I joined the company there were then on hand three or four prisoners, which for some reason the captain told me to take to the rear. One of them was an officer, who was an intelligent fellow who spoke English fluently. I wish I could now recall our conversation. Some distance back I found an American on his way to the rear and I got him to relieve me of the prisoners. He had hardly taken them when I saw that he was relieving the officer of his watch. I made him return it, but he probably got the watch later.

On my way back to the company I ran across a poor fellow who had been wounded in the stomach or intestines. His face was ashy and he suffered torture. He implored me to carry him to a first-aid station. I was so weak that I felt unequal to the task. But I did not have the heart to leave him alone. About this time a large number of prisoners appeared, coming in our general direction. I secured several of them to carry back the wounded man.

When I got back, the men had gone on ahead. As I have said, they were badly mixed: 95th men, 75th, those of the liaison battalion, and others all together. It seemed that in some of the companies there had been trouble on other fronts when men told their company officers that they had been lost. A number of men who did not know where their own company was reported to some officer of another company. I think I attached myself to the major [Stowell], who, because of the mixing of the men of various organizations, was virtually without a command.

Our advance was pretty much of a leisurely walk, and doubtless we were elated at the hurried retreat of the enemy, together with capturing so many. Our artillery continued to shell one town long after we passed it. I don't know whether we were beyond where we were supposed to be or not. Possibly some artillerymen were asleep on the job; on the other hand, Germans in the place may have fortified themselves to offer stubborn resistance. This was only another of those countless episodes for which we never got an adequate explanation. By late afternoon we had passed through some small patches of woods, as well as a town or two. About night we dug in. I believe it was that night that chow was brought up for men of one of the companies. Some men from other outfits took advantage of the dark to get into the chow line. Probably my keeping out of it was due to fear of being ungently thrown out.

A day or two here and the 95th got together to move to another position. For the nth time we dug in at the edge of a wood. I think it was Sergeant Rheinheimer who proposed digging in with me. But I had cold feet; in order to get as much protection as possible, I wanted a small, one-man hole. The front line was a couple of hundred yards ahead, so it was unnecessary for us to have open holes and stay on the alert. I dug a narrow hole and covered it with small limbs, dirt, and leaves, hoping to turn the dismal rain beginning to fall. The necessary rat hole was left in one end. By means of it one could go in headfirst and, in an awkward, wriggling fashion, get out feet first.

While digging in that hole I wished for something I never wished for before or since. For once in my life I longed for a nice little parcel of shells to fall close around. This for the special benefit of one Captain McClure. My desire for the special gifts may have been due in part to the bawling out I had received back of Champagne; but it seems now that I had been too scared to harbor any resentment toward him. To come to the point: The noble captain was having a thing done for him that I had never known an officer to ask before. While the captain amused himself doing nothing, a buck private dug his—the captain's—hole for him. Nor was it a volunteer job. The man had started to dig his own hole when he was called away to dig the other one. Had that officer had a sample of Belleau Wood, he would have forgotten there was anyone else in the world in his effort to find China.

Night was coming on. It was the second or third, and except for the German rations on the morning of the first, I had eaten nothing since the thirty-first. There followed one of the most wretched nights I ever spent. Although I had done all possible to put a good top on my dugout, in the night it began leaking. With my overcoat on I lay in the hole on the flat of my back on a thin layer of leaves. Down the water continued to come and I was soon soaked to the skin. When I attempted to shift my position in the narrow hole, mud from the clammy banks stuck to my coat. I now lay in a bed of mire and slush. And this was November in northern France. The night was inky dark. Had not the surrounding area been covered with trees that I would continually run into, I would have gotten out and walked about in the rain. This miserably long night was made longer by shells coming through the blank space. One or more men were entombed by the fall of a shell a few steps away to be dug out by those in the adjoining hole.

One afternoon, when we were on the eve of leaving, Major Stowell's canteen was missing. And the major's habitual geniality was much ruffled that a man could fall so low as to take his all-important canteen. The procession was held up while the major gave vent to his wrath. Then it was discovered that the canteen had been only misplaced.

It was the fourth and the day had been one move after another. Inexpressibly tired of hunger and exhaustion, I was nearing completion of the third or fourth hole I had dug that day; but ours was not to spend the night there. In a drizzling rain the column wound its way over hill and valley. Finally we came to a somewhat elevated position, bound by three intersecting roads. I think orders were given to dig in; I don't remember definitely. But that mattered little when the warble of shells could be heard. Although the shells fell a hundred yards short of our position, the simple raising of those gun muzzles a fraction of an inch would do the work. We began using the shovels—but, alas, the ground was too rocky and hard to dig a hole in. And the hardest rain began falling that I had seen during my year in France. Hungry, wet, and cold, shells falling suggestively near and sheets of water sweeping down in the darkness upon us, I sat down on the ground, my back to a scrub of a tree, my knees up against my chest. I pulled my overcoat over my head, blanket fashion, to turn back what rain I could.

The next morning the rain had ceased and that part of the front was quiet. There came the grand surprise of a breakfast. I remember well the canned meat, with prunes (probably two) and bread, and coffee that was real hot—when it was made.

We felt it in our bones that the war was going our way. (This, probably, after the refreshments.) Pieces of artillery passed us on the way up, the horses at a fast trot. We spent a part of the day on the ridge, with a wooded valley stretching many miles to the front of us. Our curiosity ran high just to know what lay in that vast expanse. Everything connected with the Germans was still shrouded with mystery.

There had not been entirely expelled from my thoughts that the German soldier was a sort of superman, a demigod. A fear still lurked in me that by some mysterious power they might at any time overwhelm and annihilate us with some new invention, some heinous engine of destruction.

On different fronts many hours I lay in my hole wondering just what things looked like on the German side. Many times I gazed into the distance to wonder just what the enemy was doing, the nature of their trenches, and whatnot. To have gone there we probably would have found nothing very new or strange; yet, years after the war my curiosity is little abated. During the day we saw a fallen German plane near the road. That Black Cross on each wing appeared far less formidable than it had on many occasions in previous months.

There were more days of hiking, with intermittent stops. One night when a few shells were falling about, I was told to leave the company in the wood and accompany one or more officers to an abandoned French house not far away. As it was not raining, I don't know why the officers should have wanted to go to the house. Nor did I ever understand the good of my going along. And when there were any shells, I much preferred being out in the open. During any kind of bombardment I ever had a fear of being in a house where a shell at any moment would bring tons of masonry crushing down. Before going to sleep that night I ate half a box of hardtack, the origin of which I do not remember. The thing about it, however, that does stick in my mind was that when I started to eat more of the hardtack, the next morning, I found the biscuits covered with a layer of mold. I thought mold was a deadly poison; so it appeared to me that the prospect was good of Jackson *checking out.* But the prospect of getting out of the mud, rain, and cold, interminable sleepless nights and hungry days—above all, the thought of getting away from the shells and bullets—these things gave little fear to the possibility, or probability, of a fatality of one redheaded Marine.

This position was not many miles from the war-famous town of Stenay. In my mind's eye I can see vividly the road marker *"Nach Stenay."* Always at or near the front, when men were not being hounded by enemy shells or bullets, there was unending talk about the war: what this organization was doing and that; of men killed and men wounded; where we might go next, and when; this, and ten thousand rumors.

While we lay in the wood, some miles back of the front line, I was granted permission to go back to the 6th Regimental Wagon Train to try to get a pair of shoes. My shoes were in bad shape for muddy weather. But I have something more than a hunch that I wanted to explore some, to see what I could find. I found the wagon train but could get no shoes to fit.

On my return, I found the company had moved, and it was doubtless with no little difficulty that I found them. On joining the bunch again, I was told that when making the move they had passed bodies in the road that had unmistakably been run over and crushed by wagons. The boys regarded this as cold-blooded carelessness. However, it may have been done without knowing it, in the night, or under the pressure of circumstances.

About a week had passed since the bunch had gone over. While the number of wounds and deaths had not been great, perhaps not more than a fourth of the company of a week before were still with it. Due to flu and dysentery most of them had been sent to hospitals. With the desire to get out of it all, some men managed to be sent out who had no disability other than greatly depleted vitality. A hospital corpsman or doctor told me he would "tag" me, but I could hardly allow myself to leave unless I was wounded or really sick. One morning I waked in my dugout soon after daylight with a strange itching on my face and hands. Upon examining my hands I found the backs of them covered with welts the size of a pea. Let the cause and result be what they might, I was sick and going to a hospital. "Finis" mud and shells. Between the sheets for me, with a pretty nurse to come around and hold a fellow's hand and ask him if he was dead! A benign Providence had descended and made me sick—it was a beautiful world after all. My dream had come true—not three minutes after I discovered the itching and welts, both had utterly disappeared! Before I could get out of that wet hole, sadly, sadly, I had recovered from the treasured malady. I was a well man.

When a man got hungry he was none too particular as to what he ate. Not far from the dugout was a road of mud and mire, over which

countless wagons and teams had recently passed. Sergeant Rheinheimer and I were crossing the road when in that muck and mud
there appeared a slice of bread. It was a case of first there, first served.
Rheinheimer picked up the bread out of the muck, cut as much of
the mud off as he could with his knife, and ate the bread—plus the
extras.

Another night we hiked along the road in a driving rain. We
turned off the road and stopped, presumably to spend the night. The
bottom of a hole would cover with water as fast as a fellow could dig.
Such a night! We were soon back on the road in a moving lake of
water.

Miles farther on the company halted in that favorite resort, at the
edge of a wood. There I dug my last hole during the war. Had someone whispered to me that I was digging my last, I probably would
have done more reflecting and praying than I was accustomed to. I
do not recall that anyone was wounded while the company was there,
though during the two or three days following a good many shells
went over our heads to fall on a road seventy-five yards away. About
this time some clothes were issued, and such clothes! As was frequently the case, the clothes had been picked over long before they
got to the men at the front, and the bulk of what was left consisted
of over- and undersizes. Among other things, in the issue proposed
at this time, were some leather coats. The smallest size I found was
a forty-four.

It was the night of 10 November. The company had fallen out with
packs and rifles, awaiting further orders to move up. An oppressive
seriousness pervaded the ranks. It was our understanding that the
German line lay just across the Meuse and we were to cross the river
(how, we were uncertain) and make an attack. While we crossed the
river the German machine guns would have a full sweep at us. One
town through which we passed reverberated with the hollow echoes
of falling shells. And there were gas shells, so we wore masks. Few
more unpleasant situations could be imagined than when shells were
falling about on a dark night, with the prospect ever present of having to try to dodge to some place of greater safety—then, in addition to the blinding darkness, to have to further obstruct the view
by sacking one's face in a gas mask. On the march the column drew

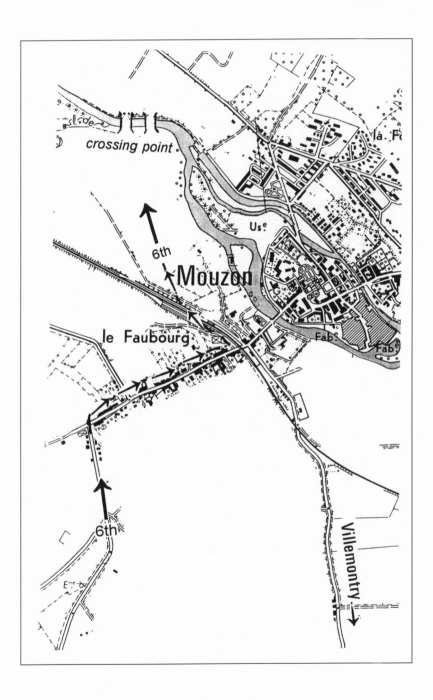

alongside some other organization upon the road and stopped. Shells fell some yards away, among men of the other outfit, and played havoc with them. Earlier in the war, experienced noncoms and officers who were then with us ever cautioned men to remain several paces apart when there was any danger of shells. When men were jammed together as they were on that road that night, one well-placed shell would wipe out several dozen men. It made a fellow want to move along.

There had been several hours of marching when we halted, on a railroad, presumably the one General Summerall had referred to. Not far off a building was ablaze. It had probably been fired by a shell. The River Meuse was supposedly only a few hundred yards away. We sat along the track for hours in the penetrating cold. When, at about four o'clock, orders came to move, there was frost upon the backs of our packs. And we were going back without attacking and wondered why. Not until after the war did I learn that our not crossing the river was due to German artillery destroying the pontoon bridge built by our engineers and on which the 6th Regiment was to have crossed. A little after daylight we crawled into the holes we had left some hours before.[4]

Back at St. Mihiel my pack had disappeared, and ten days before I had thrown my blankets away. [At this point there is a discontinuity in the text. It appears that on the march Jackson had jettisoned his rifle. He continues:] This act may seem the last thing in unsoldierness [sic]. For some time past that kind of thing had not been uncommon when near enough to the front for there to be no danger of inspections, yet far enough from the front line to be a minimum of danger of using a rifle on short notice. There was no trouble in picking up a rifle. But mine was a cherished rifle. It had been with me since those first days at Paris Island. I had come to have a sentimental feeling toward that rifle. I doubt that there were a dozen rifles in the regiment carried by the same man all through the war. The point is on that hike I was terribly tired or I would not have parted with that rifle.[5]

After being out all night, I had lost no time in falling into my hole. About nine in the morning someone waked me to say that an Armistice had been signed and the *war would be over at eleven o'clock.*

We of course knew that the war could not last always. In the days and months before, there had been talk among the bunch that the war might end anytime. However, when I was waked on that morning of 11 November 1918, to be told that the war would cease that day, the thought was inconceivable. To be told that someone was flying to the moon would have been easier to believe. Impossible. I spoke roughly to the fellow who waked me and went back to sleep—or tried to sleep.

Before eleven all were awake and talking, wondering. Was it a trick of the Germans? Could it be that the war was actually going to end? With baited breath we waited until eleven. Would the guns cease firing?

Eleven came. Officers assured us the war was over, but silence did not reign along the front. An explosion here and yonder in the distance—what could that be but that the war was still on! That uneasiness, that vague uncertainty!

I learned long afterward that at eleven o'clock there were Americans still advancing, due to the fact that the line of communication had been broken and word of the Armistice had not reached them.[6] Other disturbing noises that came to our ears that day were occasioned by the Germans in their preparation to evacuate. According to the terms of the Armistice the Germans were to leave behind them no mines. Some of the Germans were in too big a hurry and too thoughtless of destruction to remove the explosives. Instead, mines under railroad stations and bridges were touched off. We heard these explosions, and they sounded very like war to us.[7]

At the signing of the Armistice a pandemonium of joy swept over the nations who had been in the war. There were celebrations in grand style in expression of hilarious joy. When the eleventh had come and gone, some of the boys felt duty bound, I suppose, to celebrate. A few shouts were heard. But these were weak, unnatural expressions of joy. We just could not realize the war was over. How must it have been for those who had seen four years of that war!

First, last, and always there were rumors. The grand news now was of our early return to New York. Thanksgiving dinner in New York. But like the kaiser's belated Thanksgiving dinner in Paris, ours, too, was postponed till Christmas. Christmas in New York City. Hooray!

On the night of 11 November the flames of campfires leapt high. For months no kind of fire was to be thought of anywhere near the front; it would have advertised our whereabouts to the enemy artillery. And now the sight of flames had something uncanny in it, like committing an offense against man and God. Constantly something seemed to tell us that we were perpetrating an overt act against an insidious power, which in a moment would fall upon and strike us out of existence.

Those last six months and more of the war had seemed like years. Interminable days and nights had been prolonged into weeks that were age long. Now *all over at last.*

Our company of 250 men had been organized in Quantico, Virginia, in August 1917. When the Armistice came, I was one of the original four that had been with it all the time; this, of course, excepting the leave to Washington, the subsequent leave in France, and the two- or three-day stay at the dentist's, four miles away. In addition to the original 250, about 300 replacements had been added to the company roll from time to time. Some of the original number had gone to hospitals because of sickness or wound and had returned to the company. More than 80 had been killed and about 300 wounded.

Our company was about two miles from the line when the war ended. I should like to have had the experience of being on the front line when the war ceased. One hour men had tried to kill one another; the next they were no longer enemies but exchanged confidences. That must have seemed incongruous.

There were more rumors that blighted the rosy thoughts of our immediately leaving for home. There was more talk, too, of inspections. When the world had so long reeked with water, rifles were in bad shape, inside and out. Nor was there any oil left to remove rust. And these inspection warnings not only stimulated me to look for a rifle, but for one that had as little rust on it as possible. Regardless of circumstances, the offering of excuses for the bad condition of equipment was almost unheard of. Ashes and dirt were brought into operation in an almost futile effort to get that fuzee presentable.

Notes

1 This was unusual. Because the liaison unit to the west of the 2d Division would be the 80th Division, a relatively new unit and in another corps, it was decided to not take any chances on having a flank "in the air." Meaning, of course, to protect against any German infiltration on the division's left flank. Consequently, because the 4th Brigade was launching the attack and the 6th Marines were on the left, a unit was partly formed from that regiment to provide the "liaison," and it was of approximately battalion size. An old hand, Maj. George A. Stowell Jr., was given the task. He selected the 95th Company and was given a company from the 319th Infantry plus machine gun units for the task. Read *Devil Dogs*, p. 347.

2 The village was St. Georges. It, along with Landre, which was to its right and just a few hundred feet away, were listed as the joint "town" of Landres-St.-Georges.

3 Here he might mean the bullets used to ignite balloons or possibly the so-called "dum-dum" bullets then supposedly being used, according to widespread propaganda, by both sides.

4 The scenario: The 6th was to across just a few hundred yards above Mouzon, but every attempt by the 2d Engineers to complete a pontoon bridge was defeated by the Germans. The German position across the river would have created a complete disaster for the regiment had it crossed. They were on a hillside just opposite with a full, unhindered sweep of the terrain. The 6th was saved by the bell. Instead the 5th Marines went across a few miles south and were slaughtered. For some reason Allied command insisted that the forces should get across the river so that on the day following, 11 November, when an Armistice was to go into effect, they would be in a better position to enforce their will upon a defeated Germany.

5 Something is wrong. Previously he alludes to "losing his old rifle" now here he says the same thing again, months later.

6 Some of the remnants of the 5th did not get the word and were still shooting at the Germans late into the afternoon. The latter, mostly, ceased firing and even went so far as to tell the Marines the war was over.

7 Unfortunately, there were many incidents and destruction implemented by the departing Germans that led to even more severe penalties imposed at Versailles the following year.

11: Occupation of Germany

Some days after the Armistice several noncoms, including myself, went to Beaumont, about three kilometers distant, to see about temporary quarters for the bunch. On the way we carried only our rifles and light combat packs. Yet so weakened was our condition that we had to rest two or three times going this short distance. It is probable that for a period of not more than ten days I was not once thoroughly dry, and I know there was a period of several days when I was wet to the skin.

When the hope began to fade of an immediate departure for the French coast and embarkation for the States, the next most widely accepted rumor was that following our march to the Rhine we would take a boat for the U.S. When at last we became fairly certain that the war was really ended, it seemed that all earthly tribulation had ended with it. There were times to come when there was some cause to question this. In months to come, as in months before, we fairly subsisted on rumors.

While it was yet dark, on the morning of 17 November we began the long and unforgettable march to the Rhine. When we passed through the town of Beaumont, light streamed from the windows. While the war was on this kind of thing was not to be found anywhere in the war zone; it would have advertised the whereabouts to German bombers. Shutters were closed, with not a ray of light for enemy eyes. The lighted windows did seem strange, as of another age. In fact, so long had we been under unnatural conditions of life that they seemed natural, and vice versa.

Those first hours of marching carried us through a shell-torn, war-stricken country. We were sick, sick of looking at anything that suggested war. I remember well reflecting—though it seems somewhat strange now—that I would almost prefer not to return home, rather than again look upon those grim reminders of war. All day we trudged through desolate, forsaken country. Late in the afternoon of that cold, bleak day we stopped for a night at a barren bit of a gloomy village. We were quartered in a barn. I can picture myself, half submerged in the hay of the hayloft trying to keep warm, while I read letters I had just received. It was the first time for many weeks that mail had been delivered to us. Day after day there were to be long, hard marches, when shoulder straps of the packs cut heavily into our sore shoulders. With short and few periods of rest, little to eat, and at night a bed in a barn, we were glad to have the barn.

Nearly everything I had seen and experienced during the war had been a disappointment in a way. I had crossed the water with a storybook idea of things. Now I saw things as they were—stripped of their glamor. During days to come there would be notable exceptions. Our reception in southern Belgium seemed more like a fairy story than a reality. As we marched into a town we would go under an archway over the road with the inviting words, *"Vive les Americains."* The people of the towns turned out to line the road and give us the glad greetings. In a village where we stopped two days, the poor, war-stricken people went into their cellars, killed chickens—did everything possible to show their appreciation for what America had done for them. People in some towns prepared for the coming of the Americans, when the Americans went another way. Several of the boys took advantage of pauses in Belgium to visit these towns that had been passed up. And these fellows brought back stories of how there had been lavished upon them all the good things that had been meant for a young army.

I think that it was on our first day in Belgium that we came into the beautiful little city of Arlons. The place was decorated for our coming, and indeed we got an enthusiastic and heartfelt reception. While some of our bunch could swear that it was contrary to the policy of higher officials ever to let Marines stop in any but the meanest towns, we did actually spend the night in Arlons, twenty thousand people.

It had been a long while since there had been an opportunity to spend our money, and my own was threatening to burn a wide hole in my pocket. French money was exchanged for German. And what could be next for Number One but to look for something to eat. Among other friends was a bakery with hot rolls and butter. Oh, boy! In the course of my rambles I ran across a man who told me he had spent seventeen years in the state of Ohio. The fact that a man without uniform spoke the English language seemed wholly incongruous. The man sought to give me some idea of high prices by telling me that the shoes he then wore had cost him $40—or was it $60?—and his suit cost $240. He may have exaggerated.

From Belgium we crossed into Luxembourg, and there were unfailing indications of the industry of those people. One evening we halted for the night among several houses, nestled down in the valley, with picturesque hills rising above them. And the first thing was what did the place offer to eat? With the usual lightning speed the word spread that a newfound delicacy had been discovered. Presto! and I was waiting in a line to buy apples. It mattered little that they weren't large and red. A fellow got all he could handle in his overseas cap for about a half a mark.

As we marched, we saw the heavy helmets and other pieces of German equipment reposing in trees along the roadside. Other things, too, bore evidence that the German soldier was mighty glad to be out of the war. Back in the Argonne we had seen German horses that had starved to death. Here again, repeatedly, there were to be seen beside the road horses that had succumbed to exhaustion and starvation. Never did I see any other creatures so thin. There was hardly a semblance of flesh under the skin. These horses were veritably little more than skin and bones. One day I counted five of these in the course of a few hundred yards. Some people had evidently been hungry. There were carcasses with a hindquarter cut out.

Long, trying days we continued marching. The bugle blew long before day. There followed a feverish rush to be ready for the order to go forward. A scanty breakfast, and not uncommonly the order was given to line up before some of the bunch had gotten their breakfast. Then came the washing of a greasy mess kit in a pan of cold, greasier water where a hundred or more might have washed their utensils before. Frequently the would-be cleansed kit had more grease clinging to it after the immersion than it had before. I often wondered why we didn't all die of some plague. I should have known that no germ could have survived more than about three-quarters of a second in such abominable filth, and it would have taken a particularly vigorous germ to have stayed alive that long.

Then up hill and down, hour after hour we marched. Ten minutes of each hour were supposed to be for rest, but we felt that most of the time we did not get that. Major Barker led the battalion—the major and his horse. We knew that horse would take a prize for endurance. On slim rations we kept up, carrying a sixty-five-pound pack.

Before each rest period there was pretty sure to be a lot of talk about the pace being so fast and rest periods infrequent. Now that the war was over they were going to try to kill us by hiking us to death. Did they think we were a bunch of mules or cattle? Why did a fellow use so little sense ever to enlist anyway? In the next war, if they got a fellow into it, they would have to go to a cave way back in the mountains—or Mexico. "Join the Marines and see the world," the bright posters had read. This was sure a hell of a way to see it! The next time they would join the YMCA or home guards. . . . It was common for serious-to-bantering shouts to be directed to the leader of the column; particularly if he was mounted. These cries were not too loud, of course.

It seemed to be a part of a soldier's very existence to grumble about anything and everything under any and all circumstances. What other privilege did a fellow have! The weak characters of the bunch were not long in advertising their weakness. The star crabbers and "crepe hangers" at times sent forth an incessant stream of growls and murmurings. Even among the better men this complaining was not uncommon. The truth was the heavy packs were torturing. There had been no time for the men to recover their strength after the war before the march began. During the war we could sometimes see the necessity of forced marches. Now that hostilities had ceased, we could see no good reason for that kind of thing.

I think it was a town in northeastern Luxembourg into which we came one night. The barns the bunch was being assigned to looked particularly unattractive. My old friend Bobby Robertson induced me to look for something more promising. We came upon the railway station and there in the waiting room we unrolled our packs. I thought our flop was too good to last all night and that there would be some kind of trouble over our taking possession in this style. Bob maintained we had a right to the place, others joined us, and this was our quarters for the next two or three days in the town.

It fell my lot to go on guard. That night was rainy and sloppy, and I was thankful that I did not have to walk post. The next day I was standing over the open fire in front of the barn of a guardhouse. I had my mess gear in my hand, waiting for chow call. Chow call blew, and as it blew it dawned upon me that it was my birthday. Number twenty-two.

Thanksgiving Day came while we were in the same village. It was reported that we would have turkey for dinner. But dinner came and no turkey. Perhaps we would get it for supper. I was near the head of the line that night, but in place of turkey we got corned beef.

According to the terms of the Armistice, Allied troops were not to go into Germany until 1 December. And on that day, going from Luxembourg into Germany, we had the hardest march I experienced while in the Marine Corps. Several times in my life I have walked voluntarily between thirty-five and forty miles in a day. These walks were a day's play compared to the terrible twenty-eight or thirty miles we marched on that day. Weakened bodies, heavy packs, on almost empty stomachs, with few and short rests—that kind of thing was killing. I know only one word that expresses the feelings over such a torturous march. Since leaving France there had been so much dropping out on hikes that the men were told a court-martial would result for any man in the future who left the ranks without permission. But such a threat was idle when men were as tired as men got that day. Before the end of the hike two-thirds of 95th Company fell out along the way.[1]

Mile after mile we trudged on. Dark came on but we continued. Then, to cap it all, the last mile or more was up a hill. One man in my squad fell over unconscious. He told us months later that an old German woman picked him up and put him to bed and that he was later taken to a hospital. In the first platoon I was near the head of the 95th Company column, the 75th Company just ahead. A man in the 75th, and only a few steps ahead of me, fell dead of exhaustion. One time in my life did I feel that I might drop unconscious, or dead, and it was then. I thought I would be dead before we reached the top of the hill. Just then I didn't care. About ten o'clock that night we stopped to be quartered in barns.

I slept until twelve and was on guard the remainder of the night. The order had been given me at a designated hour to wake the men for breakfast, the first meal in twenty-four hours. After arousing the men I left for the kitchen half a mile away.

I had gone but a short distance when it occurred to me I was not armed, as we were to be at all times since our arrival in Germany. But terribly tired, hungry, and sleepy, I thought I would not go back for my gun to carry to breakfast. And the company was slow appearing. When the outfit did appear it was with packs and rifles. Orders had been changed, and when the bunch got their stuff together there was some extra equipment. Whose was it? The sad news was broken that it belonged to Corporal Jackson and, contrary to orders, he had gone off *unarmed*. During the days to come I thought Captain Wheeler had forgotten my crime. I was to learn later that I was mistaken.

The Armistice had hardly been signed when a cry went up that the enemy should have been driven into Germany and an unconditional surrender demanded. The condition of the Central Powers was such that this undoubtedly could have been accomplished in no great time, and to have carried this out would have avoided a lot of trouble on peace terms in months and years to come. This is one side of the matter. Those who hollered "on to Berlin" the loudest were five thousand miles from the sound of the German machine gun or falling shell. The "hip, hip, hooray" and bloodthirsty songs were conspicuous by the fact that they originated among those who had never spent a night in a muddy hole or heard the blood-curdling crash of an enemy shell. The deluded old fool that boasted of his willingness to lay down the lives of all his precious boys on his country's altar perhaps deserved a kind of credit. But had the same sacrificing father been mysteriously endowed with youth again and placed on the battlefield, in a few minutes he would have coined some fresh ideas about the whole thing.

Should the advance have continued without the Armistice, there were forested hills in western Germany where further advances would have been made at a bitter price. So well protected were many rugged spots that a handful of Germans would have been a formidable adversary for many men. With this in mind I recall looking upon one protected crag in particular. One machine gun could have played havoc with hundreds of men.

It was easy enough for high generals, unscrupulous politicians, and other swivel-chair fighters to cry "on to Berlin!"[2] At the time, it seems, I accepted passively this oratorical barrage at pseudopatriotism, but eight years later I became rancorous at the thought. That supposedly intelligent people back at home could have been permeated with such childishly foolish delusions in connection with the war has led me to wonder what other absurdities of equal monstrosity we may be worshiping today.

I have a good many times referred to our being quartered in barns. Under other circumstances the expectation of getting into the finest bed since Adam took the apple could not compare with our anticipation during those long, weary days of crawling into a barn, with hay for a bed, even though cattle might be under the same roof.

That all "should be in uniform," overcoats were worn by all, regardless of the weather. At the end of a hike we were frequently wet with perspiration. The rolling kitchens would not likely appear for hours to come, so there was the old fun of going to bed on an empty stomach. Though a man went to bed ravenously hungry, let him be waked at midnight for a meal off yonder somewhere, and most likely he would not get up to eat. By that time he was steaming under his blankets, and getting up in the cold for *anything* did not have a strong appeal. Even though my hunger had disappeared during the few hours of sleep, on such occasions I always got up and ate. Experience said never miss an opportunity to eat!

It seemed very strange to go peaceably among people who a few weeks before were our enemies. One of the first nights in Germany we quartered in a house—a regular *house*—where a recently discharged aviator lived. He seemed a very decent sort of fellow, showing us pictures of his service. A month before we would have tried to kill one another!

We passed through the most picturesque country I had ever seen. Even in the dead of winter the evergreen forests covering the lowlands and mountains, winding roads, well-kept villages, with many other new things, all helped to make less unpleasant otherwise unbearable days. For some miles we followed the Ahr River, which had been a summer resort before the war. A thing that struck my attention particularly was that mile after mile the continuous wall of rock bordering the stream had strata unvaryingly perpendicular to the ground. Certainly a great upheaval had been witnessed there in some past age.

At last we came in sight of the majestic Rhine. Several days after, in a drizzling rain, we crossed the stream on a ferry. For some days we spent a day or two each at several towns down the river.

One morning I was called up for office hours! Charge: going out without carrying arms on German soil. No, Freddie Wheeler had not forgotten. But Red [Joseph G.] Whalen pled my case and I got off without a court-martial. Whalen was perhaps as soldierly a looking man as the 95th ever had. At this time I think he had been busted to a private several times for drunkenness, though he was later commissioned. A princely fellow with a fine mind, but I don't know where booze may have led him.

On the march to the Rhine it had come to me from several sources that I was to receive my sergeancy. However, another man in the platoon got the stripes. It was my supposition that I was on my way to the raise until I failed to observe the keep-armed order, though I'm not sure that I was ever considered. While I had objected to being made a corporal, it is my recollection that I would have gladly accepted another raise.

And this afforded something to think about. Of the several times while in the service that I had gotten into trouble, or come near getting into it—from an injury in the mess hall on Paris Island to our march into Germany—every time it was in connection with a long liking to eat.

The towns along this part of the Rhine were strung out on the narrow, level strip between the river and the steep, rocky slope to the east. In one of these small villages about half of the company was quartered for the night in a large room, containing Rhinestein wine(?), famous for its superior quality. Bungholes served to admit straws, and many a gallon of treasured wine was drawn through the straws before day.

Several days after crossing the river we came into Bad Hönningen, a town of about thirty-five hundred people, on the east bank of the Rhine. Most of the business houses faced the one long, cobbled street that paralleled the river. This little city was to be 1st Battalion Headquarters during our stay in Germany.

Leaving the other three companies of the battalion there, the 95th left one afternoon to take up its position on an outpost. The thought of spending the remainder of the winter out in the open, in pup tents, on the cold, muddy ground—well, that lacked any appeal. The winding road that we followed disappeared in a depression in the wooded mountainside.

As we began the ascent, we passed immediately to the left of a pretentious German castle overlooking the Rhine. It was claimed that Napoleon had spent two months there. The man who had built the castle was said to have been worth about forty million marks before the war. The castle was in months to come to be a regimental headquarters. A few hundred yards farther, and higher, brought us to a level country covered by a most beautiful evergreen forest. It was part of the estate of the castle owner. A mile or more from Hönningen we came to a break in the forest with a large open space before us. In the nearer edge of the opening we saw our future abode. Nor was it a place to pitch pup tents. As a part of the estate there was a large quadrangle made of brick. The two-storied front was occupied by a keeper of the estate (our officers now added). Within the two high brick walls adjoining were lofts and stables, where most of the company were quartered.[3]

Most of the 1st Platoon was assigned to the hayloft to the right after entering. For some reason Bob and I left the bunch and went into a vacant stall below and beyond, where there was a rock or concrete floor. The entrance to our apartment was through a huge gate or door that would admit ample fresh air.

In subsequent months there was a routine of drills, maneuvers, guard duty, and inspections. These were less arduous than they had been during training days before we went to the front.

We arrived at this outpost of Hamborn about a week before Christmas. Rations were still very slim, which naturally gave zest to the talk of a turkey dinner Christmas Day. But Christmas dinner had not the faintest suggestion of turkey. Some excellent chocolates were issued, however, and we knew how to appreciate them.

Within the fourth wall of the quadrangle was some sort of room under which was a cellar that provided space for high crimes and misdemeanors. Under cover of night, meal was gotten from the company kitchen. There followed boiling of mush. Unfortunately the architect who designed that cellar failed to take our plans into account. Somehow that hole leading from the cellar through the outer wall just would not draw. Between stirrings of the mush the cooks would have to run up the cellar steps, at the opposite side of the room, to get air and give their eyes a chance to work out some smoke.

Rainy, sloppy weather lasted a good many days. Then frigid days when even the gloved hands got mighty cold at drill. There were games we played on the drill field to try to warm up. One game we entered into with zest was something on the order of drop-the-handkerchief, only a hard bayonet scabbard was substituted for the handkerchief and "dropped" unmercifully on the man who wasn't able to keep sufficiently far in the lead. Osterhout was the recognized leader in such sports. In addition to being tall, strong, and fast, he had a fine mind and courage. There were also maneuvers, though lacking in appeal. There was too much double time, with frequent advancing over difficult ground in fields and through woods.

For a period of possibly six weeks there was no cessation in the cold, with everything frozen up. This condition was made worse by short rations and no stoves. Bob and I doubled up in our stall in an effort to keep warm. Even then the snow and sleet drifted in on us at night. I stood one guard during the cold spell, and it was bitter cold for the man outside the walls walking post. I was glad that I missed that. The road leading up to Hamborn became frozen. I went once with a detail to dig through the frozen earth to get dirt and gravel to put upon the road, so mules drawing the supply wagons could get up the hill. The Germans sharp-shod their horses, but this would not do for American mules. No sooner did they get in their stalls than a kicking party began, and they would have cut one another to pieces.

In trying to get protection against the cold, some of the boys managed to rig up a makeshift stove. A gallon can was used for the stove; and smaller ones, with ends cut out, were joined for a pipe. Later, some of us of the 1st Platoon chipped in to buy a box stove. Then a good many of us moved into the warmer room to be a lot more comfortable. And there we fought the war all over again and talked of going back home. Old Man Rumor continued in with us and we were constantly going to do this and that—to return home in particular.

Of course, everybody was lousy when we came out of the Argonne. As bathing facilities were lacking at Hamborn, from time to time we marched to Hönningen for a scrubbing at a German bath.

As winter wore on and spring opened, the outlook brightened for us. Less suffering from the cold, more to eat, and welfare organizations were getting into the saddle. Instead of lining up for chow in the courtyard and eating wherever we could, a mess hall was built conveniently near.

I well recall being in a mess hall one day with one of the later replacements, perhaps telling him what a fearless warrior I had been. In the course of the conversation the new man asked me if I had ever eaten horsemeat. I told him I had not enjoyed that delicacy. The company cook, overhearing my remark, interrupted: "If you've been in *this* company all the time"—and he knew I had—"you've eaten horse meat a *couple* of times!" I didn't argue the point with him or ask any questions.

We played some basketball and enjoyed well-contested football games. I'm sorry that I did not play some company football. I may have felt that I was too light. I weighed 175 or 180 and was pretty solid. But I probably weighed considerably less than the average man on the team, which may have discouraged me. Pop Ansel was our star player. He was low, heavy, and extremely hard to tackle. Bob Robertson was probably next best, having played college football. The company played several games with the teams downtown, including one game with the machine-gun company of the famous Dan Daly. Sergeant Daly was an old-timer and was one of less than a half a dozen, I think, who in the history of the United States military forces received two Congressional Medals of Honor. It took a man to do that.[4]

I saw the 2d Division team play two games. In a group of nearly thirty thousand hardy men, there ought to be some football material. On the team were outstanding college stars. I think it was the 32d Division we were playing one day on frozen ground. Although our team was in the lead at the end of the first half, men of the 32d made the mistake of parading on the field between halves with band and colors. Our boys fell in and broke up the parade. Bob carried back to Hamborn a souvenir in the form of a part of the enemy flagstaff, colors, or something of the kind.

Bob was indeed a dynamic individual. He was impetuous, energetic, and undaunted. Of Scotch descent, he was hotheaded and loved justice. It seems that it could be said of him that "in his failings he leaned toward virtue's side." The fellows smiled at his childlike enthusiasm and hotheadedness and feared and loved him. While we were in Germany he was commissioned and, as was customary when men were commissioned from the ranks, he was transferred from the company.

Taking flu became all the rage over in Germany. When I returned from a divisional football game, I crawled into my bunk, feeling I was taking flu. But I couldn't take it.[5]

By this time I had moved from across the courtyard to a smaller billet where there were only eight of us. The first I recall in that little room was Joe Rhia, a company clerk and from Texas. Joe was no wizard but was known for his genial disposition and distinctive chuckle. Another company clerk in the billet was Pope, who was rather older than the rest of us. Pope was a level-headed man, even tempered, and seldom frowned or laughed. Among the number was Harry Washburn from "Chi." He was first sergeant at the time, and I regarded him as one of the strongest men the 95th ever had connected with it. He was fair minded and likable. He later received a commission. I think Bob must have been in the billet for a time. Moose Taylor was there, another able man. He and Bob had gone to college together. Taylor, who was tall and angular, and I put on the gloves one day. I think I was the challenger and got the worst of it.

A good many moons had gone by without our passing inspection before General Pershing. I quote from a letter I wrote home on 17 March 1919:

> We were reviewed several days ago by General Pershing. On the morning of the fourteenth reveille was at 2:30. At four we were in Hönningen on the trucks. It was about seven before we arrived at our destination across the Rhine from Coblenz. Soldiers, soldiers everywhere. There must have been at least fifteen or twenty thousand out of the division there. The inspection must have started about nine. General Pershing, accompanied by his staff, with General [Joseph T.] Dickman (Third Army Commander) and [John A.] Lejeune (2d Division). At first the inspectors rode, led by General Pershing, on a beautiful dappled gray horse. Later he and his staff were walking. He went up and down the endless lines with a pace that kept the staff blowing. He occasionally stopped and asked someone as to his welfare. The inspection was finished about one. We then "passed in review." It was certainly a fine spectacle as column after column and wave after wave passed along after the "review" was finished. Genl. Pershing made a fifteen or twenty minute talk to the officers and "Noncoms." He enumerated the most striking features in the history of the 2d Division, thanking the men for the services they had rendered.
>
> One of his statements that struck me most was that the 2d Division would remain with the Army of Occupation if it is kept here after peace is signed. So here's hoping the A of O will not be kept on the Rhine for more than about ten years more.

In my letter home I did not state that in the midst of Pershing's speech someone in the crowd had the audacity to interrupt with "When do we go home?" In reply we were told that the time of our departure was still uncertain, but when the forces on the Rhine did start leaving, the 2d Division would be among the first to go. In succeeding months there was a good deal of adverse comment that it did not work out that way.

About this time we went miles up the river, again to go on the rifle range. We slept in a large tent and went through much the same kind of thing we had on Paris Island, though with less care. On the Island I had been handicapped by sties on my eyes. Here I was more fortunate and, when shooting for record, made a score of 226 or 228. When shooting from the last distance I made the best score while in the service. With sandbag rest, prone, at six hundred yards, I hit the twenty-inch bull's-eye nine out of ten shots.

During off hours at the range I wrestled some with Nick Haugen, as I had done with Bill Piggott in days gone by. Nick was a droll, good-natured fellow from Minnesota. He was comparatively short, thick-set, and clumsy looking. But when I tussled with him it seemed he was made of iron. He usually got the best of me. It seems I had a habit of jumping on that kind.

One night while we were in the tent, a fellow came in particularly drunk. Drunkenness, however, was no novelty. "Payday night" the bunk room invariably resounded with noises of drunken men. Some fellow who had declared that he was going in for a "glorious" drunk payday, at midnight was wondering if his stomach would not come up next and thinking, if not swearing, *"Never again."* As I write I can hear the wails of some of the drunks.

Men not coming in all night, and others returning with bruises they could not account for, were the usual part of the payday celebration. Then would follow office hours with restriction to quarters for a time, or court-martial and a part of the pay taken away for weeks or months. Such punishments were not meted out for getting drunk but for failure to return to quarters at proper time or raising a disturbance when an appearance was made. And sergeants and corporals became privates again. I would venture to say that of the noncommissioned officers reduced during the war, ninety-five percent were "busted" because of getting drunk. Some of the finest soldier material in the 95th had repeatedly allowed drink to stand between them and promotion. Nor was drunkenness restricted to enlisted men.

In this connection, I remember in the early days of the company organization hearing men boast they could take their drink and stop. They knew *when.* Most of the men usually quit drinking before they got in such condition that it was necessary for someone to guide them home. But one fact in this regard I took careful note of. Of the men who went overseas with the company, there was not one I came in close contact with who did not drink at times. Without exception I saw every one of this number irresponsibly drunk at least once.

When the company was at Hamborn, leave could be obtained evenings to go down to Hönningen. There were times when at Hamborn large flakes of snow drifted downward and the earth was covered with snow. When one took the shortcut to Hönningen he could not keep from admiring the beauty of the evergreen trees, laden with snow. Then came the abrupt drop into the Rhine valley below, where a drizzling rain might be falling instead of snow. A few hours afterward came the return trip through the rain, up the mountain, and into the world of snow again.

These trips to Hönningen were a great source of recreation. The Y there was the place where most of the fellows went. The boys played games, sat around, and smoked and talked—maybe of the grand day when we would be on our way home again. Hot cocoa was sometimes served free. The richness of it would not have endangered the digestion. The Y sold cakes and candy, and men waited in line for their turn to buy a limited quantity of the much-desired sweets. And maybe a fellow who had bought once got in line to buy again. Or someone who was particularly anxious to satisfy a sweet tooth waited and waited for his turn, for the supply to be exhausted when his turn came to buy.

During the early weeks and months in Germany, when company rations were still very scanty, boys were unceasing in their efforts to supplement the company chow. Food of all kinds was scarce on the Rhine and there were stringent German regulations limiting, or forbidding, the sale to Americans of various articles of food.[6] One night two of us made a strenuous effort to buy some bread from a baker. But the selling of bread was "verboten." Some unpalatable cookies could be had at very high prices, but the rank German flavoring was foreign to my taste. There were pieces of candy that were sold for chocolate bars, which lacked any kind of cream or milk in the making and contained little sugar. These pieces of candy were no larger than a five-cent chocolate bar sold in America. The price was three and a half marks, which at that time was about eighty cents.

Among other places visited when the bunch was flush was a café. Not infrequently, as the drinks went down, a fellow's estimate of his own prowess went up. Then he would imagine that the war was on again and that the barkeeper was carrying a gun instead of a tray— and glasses flew.

Before the final peace terms were signed, we were theoretically at war with the Germans. Not until we had been in Germany some time could we go about without being armed. Even then the strict order against fraternizing was in effect. But it goes without saying that rigid enforcement of the regulation was practically impossible. And in the bunkhouse boys talked about their escapades with German girls and made unsavory comparisons of German and French girls. Before the time came for return home there were those who bitterly rued the day they entered France or Germany.

In France the people were very slow to learn English. They insisted that the Americans learn French instead. In Germany the attitude toward learning English was quite different. The German boys on the street were soon picking up English. Nor were the words they learned first taken from a prayer book.

Altercations were not uncommon between Americans and Germans. The Americans were probably the aggressors most of the time, as the Germans could hardly afford to make trouble when the Americans were in authority. While we were in Germany the burgermeister of Hönningen was locked up by the American officials. I do not recall the charges against him, but it was easy to imagine trouble arising when there was an autocratic, egotistical, domineering German official in the town, as the burgermeister was credited with being. In America there is no office that is comparable in importance and dignity with that of the *"Bürgermeister."*

The leave to Washington and the one-day leave in France were all I had had while in the service. Sometime in the spring I obtained a three-day pass to Neuwid, a town of about ten thousand between Hönningen and Coblenz. A place to sleep and meals were provided to Americans on leave there. While on leave there we were given our choice of a trip on the Rhine or a visit to one of the ex-kaiser's castles on the west bank of the river. I chose the boat trip, though we did pass the castle.

A 2d Division school was to be established and several of us made application to attend it. As weeks passed and nothing more was heard of the school, I concluded the plan had fallen through. One morning I decided that the next morning I would go to see Captain Wheeler in regard to a leave to Paris. Since I was one of the "old men" of the company, and had not had such a leave, I felt my chances were good for being granted the coveted leave. Not two hours after these reflections, a runner came with the word that all who had applied for entrance to the Divisional School would leave the next morning. Accordingly, the next morning we went down to Hönningen, where we were transported to Neuwid to await further orders. This was 1 May 1919.

The 95th Company had been organized about 15 August 1917. The company had lost a few men as a result of our month at the Verdun Front. At Belleau the company casualties ran about fifty percent, at Soissons between eighty and ninety percent, at St. Mihiel thirty or thirty-five percent, and at Champagne a somewhat fewer number. At Argonne the casualties were possibly not heavy, but with the flu eighty percent or more died or went to hospitals. As I have said before, twice in Germany flu cut the company down to about forty men. During this time five or six hundred men had been on the company rolls.

When the Armistice was signed there were four of us who had been with the company all the time. About eighty had been killed, about three hundred wounded, and others left the company because of sickness and for other reasons. Some of this number in time returned to the company. On 1 May 1919, I was the only one of this number who had been in the company throughout that period. Not a few of the bunch seemed frankly to wonder if I carried a charm. And, too, there was a decided change of attitude among fellows who in the early days of the organization had been disposed to kid me because I did not always think and do as they did.

But to return to Neuwid where we were waiting and wondering where the school was to be. During the day I recall looking a dozen kilometers to the east, far up on the crest of the slope overlooking the spacious Rhine valley. A town was there, and about it still remained traces of snow—the only place in the whole country where snow was still to be seen. Little did I suspect that this was to be our destination.

That afternoon we entrucked and left the Rhine to follow that winding road, gradually up, up. It would be difficult to imagine more beautiful country than that through which we were passing. There were picturesque forests of evergreen to the right and left, broken here and there by a well-kept field. On the way we passed one or two towns, and at the top of the ascent, on a ridge overlooking a great basinlike valley along the Rhine, we arrived at Rengsdorf, our destination. It was an attractive little city and, before the war, had been an attractive little resort. The first billet to which I was assigned for some reason I did not like. In a few days a change was made, which was quite satisfactory. I was now the sole occupant of a snug room, overlooking a beautiful garden.

There were about five hundred men attending the school. The classrooms were scattered about the town, and there was no pretense of special equipment. Among other subjects I studied German. Not having any text for about two weeks was regretted, but when the books did come there was certainly a fine opportunity to learn the language when in a country where little else was spoken. In the English class there was the necessity of trying to adapt the work to men, some of whom had not finished grammar school and others who had had some college.

There was not more than two hours of drill each day, which came before noon, and I think the boys really enjoyed it. We also did a little maneuvering. One day when a column had stopped on a road for a short rest, a fellow in my squad asked me a question that for a time I was unable to fathom. He had lived in France until he was nearly grown, and for ten years before the war had been in the States. Something in that English class was giving him trouble and he had decided that I might be able to help him out.

"What is that *chekspur?*" he asked. I didn't know.

"*Chekspur, chekspur,*" he requested again and again.

Finally I made a guess. "Do you mean Shakespeare?" His face lighted up.

"Yes, yes; *Shakespeare.*"

• • •

A platoon was being selected for competitive drill with other organizations on the Rhine. Men were being selected, and *I* wasn't. I wanted to get with that bunch and I know I put out the best I had, whatever that may have been. I got into that platoon, but school coming to an end unexpectedly soon prevented my competitions.

Discipline was not strict, and men did things they wouldn't have been allowed to do back in the 95th. In fact, a fellow would have difficulty finding anything to complain of beyond the fact that he had not been sent home. Had it not been that so long a time had elapsed since most of us had left home, we would have been content to remain on the Rhine for some time to come.

In Rengsdorf was a large recreation hall where we spent pleasant afternoons and evenings. At the stores a fellow could purchase most of the little things he wanted. The surrounding country was ideal for strolls. Trees were just beginning to bud the first of May, when we went to school, but in two weeks the whole universe was green. Back of the house where several of us stayed there were most beautiful wooded hills, intersected by tumbling rivulets that had seen little of the fisherman since the war began. Paths had been made here and there for the tourist, and if a fellow had trouble in popping the fatal question, I could not think of a more ideal spot to summon the courage than along some of these walks about Rengsdorf, Germany!

One fine day school was dismissed for a very enjoyable boat trip on the Rhine. It was either on this or a previous trip when scarcely had the thousand men boarded the boat than the band began playing. A dozen Red Cross nurses came on deck and dancing began. There was a great time. But with so few nurses and so many men, each fellow had short and few dances. A ring was formed, a dance was on, while others anxiously waited for a turn. Not more than two minutes and the whistle blew, when the men dancing were to retire for others to take their turn. With the blowing of the whistle there was almost a stampede. Half a dozen men rushed to be first at the side of each nurse. In the desire to be ready and in an advantageous position when the whistle blew, the ring of soldiers constantly crowded in. It was a job for the man in charge to keep that ring large enough for the few couples to dance in. Unofficial whistles were blown, which complicated things somewhat for a time. A Y man aboard pointed out historic scenes along the Rhine, but the dancing went on. At noon we went below to eat.

The boat stopped at Bonn, though for only an hour. Going back up the river, we passed Coblenz and the Lorelei, where the steep slopes rise abruptly from the water's edge. The sight of occasional castles came up to the expectations of the observer. Three ancient landmarks in particular come to mind. Down the stream from Hönningen, on a towering cliff that dominated the country round, were the remains of a castle that many centuries before had been the stronghold of some lord. Farther up the stream, on the opposite bank, were scarcely less ancient remains of a great castle built on the hillside. Far down in front of the castle proper there was a honeycomb of tunnels, which presumably led back to the castle. Still farther up the stream, I believe it was, covering a rock that projected from the middle of the rolling waters, was a castle still in good repair. It was located at a bend in the river, from which there was said to be an unobstructed view for thirty miles in each direction. It must have been a formidable stronghold.

In the house in Rengsdorf where I stayed was a very attractive German girl, quiet and refined. In some manner I learned that she had studied Latin, and on the common ground of Latin we sought to converse. I am sure that the exchange of ideas was extremely limited. If she knew much Latin, I registered a very black spot beside the name of one eminent Latin teacher I had left back in the States. I might have been able to dig from the narrow and dusty brain cells the appropriate forms of *amo,* only the bug did not attack me.

A soldier on the floor where I was had been awarded a Distinguished Service Cross and he doubtless had my envy and admiration. In those days little things often looked big. I remember about this time that I would have given a small fortune—had I had the fortune to give—for even a Croix de Guerre, and to know that I deserved it. But the thought of such a thing was as remote as the ancients' thought of flying to the moon.[7]

When I had been at Rengsdorf a few weeks I obtained one day's leave to visit the company. About a mile or two down the road was a village where one could take an electric car to Neuwid. Two Germans operated each car, a motorman and conductor, who went through the car taking up fares. And the conductor had a job, as the American soldiers were about as likely to ride on the top of the car as in it. From Neuwid I probably caught a ride in a truck to Hönningen. I quote from a letter written some days after the trip to the company:

You can imagine my surprise when several days ago I learned that I was to get a Croix de Guerre. Last Saturday a week ago, when visiting the company, one of the first fellows I met offered his congratulations. Seeing my surprise, he said, "For the Croix de Guerre!" After questioning him I couldn't decide whether he was "kidding" me or had been misinformed. I soon met the "Top," who told me that on May 1, the day I left the company, I was supposed to have been decorated, for services at Champagne.

I felt certain that I had never done anything to be cited for, and was as sure I hadn't been recommended for anything. I addled my brain trying to figure out what it was for.

Friday morning I got orders to go down to the parade ground between Hönningen and Rheinbrohl, to get decorated. Here the regiment was assembled, and twelve of us, including four officers, marched up to get our decorations. As each man's citation was read, Major General Lejeune presented the medal, shaking each man's hand and congratulating him. Whether all received the Croix de Guerre, I don't know. My brain wasn't in very good working order at the time. My citation read, "For maintaining the liaison while under heavy bombardment at Champagne," or something to that effect. But as well as I remember, I didn't "maintain" it. At the time I was a runner for about fifteen minutes. We had advanced into an unpleasant barrage that the Germans had thrown over to impede our progress. Fearing that we had lost touch with the company on our right, I was sent to reconnoiter. I don't remember whether I was ordered to go or whether I volunteered, but we had been under fire ten times as heavy in Belleau Wood. A few machine gun bullets spat-

tered around, but only a few, and I don't think they were
meant for me. . . . The Croix de Guerre is the least that can
be given a soldier, but with my sparse supply of nerve, I did
well if I deserved it.

If I had been offered the Croix the day I first learned of it, I would
have turned it down flat, as not deserving it. Before the day came
for receiving it, however, I weakened. I had had numerous oppor-
tunities to stick my head out of a hole and race about heroically, but
I knew that I wasn't that kind of a girl.

The citation coming with the Croix was signed, supposedly, by the
French general Pétain. There was a typewritten translation accompanying it. On parade, some weeks after, I received an American citation with a signature that was supposed to be Pershing's. Scattered
over a period of several years after the war I received several more
papers and citations in connection with my little trip. Five years after the Champagne engagement I learned that I had been originally
recommended for the Distinguished Service Cross, but the decision
was made that what I had done did not justify such an award.

The school had been running for something over six weeks. But
for the fact that we weren't on our way home, everything was lovely.
Then one evening after supper there came the unexpected order to
roll packs and be ready to leave in "ten minutes." What did this
mean—the Germans on the warpath again? All the suffering and
dangers of the war passed before my eyes. After some delay trucks
came for us and returned us to our companies.

While it was probably midnight or past when we got to Hamborn,
all was astir with preparations to move out. And what did all this
mean? Additional ammunition and even hand grenades were issued.
We knew these weren't for a picnic. We were marching down the
river. The heavier rolls were left behind, and now we marched east,
toward Rengsdorf, with the neutral zone and heart of Germany beyond. That night we spent at Rengsdorf.[8]

The next day we resumed the march, and that night we pitched
shelter halves no great distance from a cherry orchard. The cherries
were being gathered by the Germans, and I went over to buy some.
While I was there, a German asked me a good many questions (in

German) about "A-mer-i-kaw." I had difficulty understanding some of his questions, and I understood him to say something to one of his companions about my being *"Viel dumm."* I wanted to punch him one, but I was not sure of his meaning and I gave him the benefit of the doubt.

At the end of the third day's march we pitched tents again. And I shan't forget how sore my feet were before we finished that hike. As I had been fortunate with bullets and flu, so had I been with my feet. So far as I know, all the men who had taken many long hikes had suffered with blistered feet. Since we had gone to the first front I had escaped this. However, that night I was veritably afraid to remove my socks—I feared all the skin on the bottom of my feet would come off with them. Again, I had no blister. What must have been the suffering of the fellow who did?

Our being where we then were was, as I understood it, an effort to force the Germans to sign the final peace terms. In case they did not sign, the Allied armies were to cross the neutral zone into Germany. While there, we maneuvered some and enjoyed sweets passed out by the Knights of Columbus, I believe. The company picture was taken there too.

At a tank, or pond, near camp we would go swimming. I had been out but a few minutes, on one occasion, when a man was reported to have gone down. Various means were used to get him out of the deep, funnel-like hole, but it was almost an hour before the efforts were successful. Efforts to revive the man were futile. I think it was the same afternoon, and only a few minutes after hope of resuscitation had been given up, that a plane swept low and dropped papers with glaring headlines. It was wonderful news: Peace had been signed. Not half an hour after the plane had come over until it fell and the flier was killed.

We returned to Hamborn. During the hard winter the bunch had greatly envied the rest of the battalion, who were quartered in houses down in Hönningen. But now they would doubtless have been very glad to change places with us. They continued to have rigid inspections and were annoyed with various regulations in connection with army life. The 95th, isolated as it was, came to the point where the bunch did not fall out at reveille, and drill was not such as to worry anyone particularly. All would have been well if we hadn't wanted to go home!

After we had become fairly well settled on the Rhine, some of the noncoms began to assert themselves as they had not done for a long time. (The war discouraged that kind of thing.) For instance, there was the big Paris Island prizefighter and drill sergeant. He had joined us before St. Mihiel, but the front was too much for him. He had been hard boiled until shells started flying, when he sought comfort in a dugout, even at times when he was supposed to be above. Now that we were in Germany and the war was over, his big voice and hard-boiled ways were returning to him. The bugle would blow for a formation and Sergeant Bell was at hand to cry:

"OUT-side, third platoon! OUT-side, third platoon."

But some too imaginative private brought the fall of Bell. Far away in a dark room or hayloft a well-concealed fellow would shout in reply to the sergeant's summons, so everybody in the company could hear:

"Get in your DUGOUT!"

Maybe the lusty-voiced sergeant would belch forth again, and a chorus came from every nook and corner of quarters around:

"Get in your DUGOUT!"

Sergeant Bell's voice became weaker.

From the time we arrived in France, all our letters had been censored by some officer of the company. No letters were to contain any information as to position, name, and activities of organizations, as it was felt that such information would be used to good advantage by the enemy should such mail fall into his hands. These restrictions frequently kept a fellow from having anything worth writing, it seemed. Nor did a soldier get a thrill out of writing matters at all personal with the knowledge that these things would be read, or at least might be read, by one of his own company. And of course, a fellow wanted to write something pleasant, which was not always easy to think of. This combination kept the average man from having much inclination to write home. However, in July 1919 the censorship was lifted, when one could write what he wanted to and as much as he cared to write.

As I have indicated, payday in the service was an epochal event. The whole scheme of things revolved around payday. From a week after the paymaster had visited us one time, there was talk of his coming again. Many the time were the glad tidings spread that this much-heralded day was upon us, for the paymaster to fail to put in his appearance.

When that welcomed gentleman did come, there was no more having to bum seconds or thirds on cigarette butts. Then came hilarious nights spending the money. Sometimes, however, the money did not last until the first night. And that was hard on the fellow who had anticipated the good time he would have when the great day came. No sooner would the paymaster start paying than the cards and dice came out. Imaginations had been kindled by almost fabulous tales that were told of how some boy in some organization or other (always indefinite) had cleaned up big and had won several thousand marks or francs.

Certain men of the company nearly always won, and others were as sure to lose, never to learn that they were going to lose. I've spoken of Isham, the Indian who joined the 95th. Not until after the first payday in Germany did the bunch learn that he had the gift of shooting dice. He could roll them against the wall to bounce back and still win. And when he had won he was as free with his money as fresh air in Australia. But it took some of the boys several paydays to learn not to roll the bones with Isham. It was of common occurrence for some to lose all their money before buying even a sack of tobacco. One payday a boy in the billet had lost his whole pay thirty minutes after he had received it. If a fellow stayed in the game until he lost all, he was sometimes spoken of as a good sport; more often, he was regarded as a fool. If he won some and left the game, the others did not like it. Some fellows would clean up and then send the money home.

I've spoken of the castle between Hamborn and Hönningen serving as regimental headquarters. For a time the 95th sent men there for guard duty. I drew this guard once, I and three privates going there for a three-day guard. During our stay there we were billeted in servants' quarters connected with the castle. The boys decided to make the watch four on and eight off, rather than two on and four off. Even this soon got irksome. As corporal of the guard, my duties were virtually nil, and I began to feel like a thief and a robber.

So I decided to do a watch, though I knew it would never do for Captain Wheeler to know of any such arrangement. As the beat while on guard was along the regularly traveled path between Hamborn and Hönningen, I would be seen if I was on guard during the day. I took the midnight-until-four watch.

In the billet there were electric lights, and their unaccustomed brightness caused me to get little or no sleep before going on. The result was I got sleepier on post than I ever did anywhere except the six on and six off in the Verdun trenches. I walked fast and even pinched myself to stay awake, and still I was afraid I would drop off to sleep. The beat was beside a wall about a foot from the narrow path where I walked, but there was a drop of eight or ten feet on the other side of the wall. When I began to get very sleepy I feared I would wake up on the other side of the wall—if I waked up! But even the fear did not serve to keep me awake.

During our eight months in Germany I think there was not a time I looked on the Rhine without seeing one or more boats ploughing up or down the river. Often there were five or six barges, piled high with coal, strung behind the riverboat.

I suppose it was to keep contraband from going up and down the river that Marines, in motorboats, were placed on the Rhine. Among other men from the company who were taken for this patrol was Larou. While assigned to this duty, Larou won two medals for saving drowning persons from the river. Not many men could or would have rescued a person, especially a stranger, from those whirling waters.

I believe I've spoken of Larou getting an inoculation with me after St. Mihiel. This was for his second slight wound. I referred also to his coolness at Champagne, when things seemed pretty squally. The very nearness to him at this time gave a fellow confidence. That night, when we moved forward in the darkness, a good many men got separated from the company, Larou among them. What happened in Larou's case, I don't know, he may have gotten lost, or he may have lost his nerve and gone back. I never learned the particulars. I have an indistinct recollection of hearing him at an earlier time express his dissatisfaction at not being raised from corporal's rank. Men inferior to him in many respects were to be commissioned. It was my surmise that his disappearance that night was due more to disgust than anything else.

Following his disappearance, the next I knew he was under guard and up for a general court-martial. This was early in October, and even after he got to Hamborn he was under guard. I've often reflected on what happened. Two of us as corporals had gone to Champagne together. Whatever else may be said, it seemed a strange trick of fate that the weaker one should receive a medal—though to be sure the medal did not mean much—while the stronger man, big physically and mentally, should come near being disgraced. It was some time after the charges were dismissed against him that he proved again what was in him by risking his life in the swirling, treacherous waters of the Rhine.

On 4 July we had a big time, finishing the day by shooting off flares and other leftovers from the war. And before the Dempsey-Willard fight perhaps the boys on the Rhine talked more about it than men did back in the States. There wasn't a lot else to think about. Our former captain, who had been seriously wounded at Belleau and was now *Major* Cauldwell, visited us at this time. By now there were about 40 of the original 250 in the company, and most of this number had been wounded one or more times.

Ninety-fifth Company had not been able to keep commanding officers very long at a time. A few days after going to Belleau Wood, Cauldwell received his wound. A capable and brave first lieutenant took charge of the company, only to be killed by a shell a week later.[9] Another lieutenant assumed command, to be wounded and die on the way to the hospital. A second lieutenant then took command, shortly to be evacuated to a hospital.[10] At the next front, Soissons, Captain Kearns headed the company. He was mortally wounded and only one officer of the company, I believe, came out of the battle unscathed. At St. Mihiel Captain Black was killed by a shell. At Champagne the lieutenant commanding received a shell wound. At Argonne my friend Captain McClure went through without an accident.

Before we went to the first front there had been dark talk about how English and French took advantage of circumstances to shoot unpopular officers at the front. And there was Sergeant Hickey. So many had received punishment at his hands that a number of times I heard a man say that he would "get" him at the first front. While I had no particular love for Hickey, I began to feel sorry for him. My sympathy was wasted. Hickey was on several fronts, and the only wound he received was in the foot, at Soissons, when machine-gun bullets flew thicker than on any of the other six fronts. Even though a man had a deep-seated grudge for another, at the front that man was less likely to think of shooting one of his fellows than he was of taking care of Number One.

Notes

1 I have searched through every 6th Regiment unit history and no others make mention of the "terrible first of December." Of course that doesn't mean a thing. Most people would avoid mentioning it or their memory would drop the very unpleasant aspects of a postwar hike.

2 Pershing in particular was one of those dissatisfied with the armistice—preferring to go "on to Berlin" instead. Most of the foreign military leaders were just as happy with the war ending as it did. In hindsight, giving Germany an armistice instead of driving into Germany was the real mistake. It allowed the concept of an "unbeaten army" to fester in Germany for years. Naturally, even the enlisted German soldier grabbed that theory as one that would uphold his honor before his women, children, and countrymen. Officers weren't far behind.

3 According to the official history of the 6th Regiment, the 95th Company was stationed at "Honborn Farm" on 16 December 1918. Jackson uses Hamborn continually, so perhaps he was right and the official history was wrong.

4 Dan Daly was one of two Marines earning that highest award twice, the other being Smedley D. Butler. Daly was also awarded a number of other medals for his services in France, the DSC being the most outstanding.

5 The "flu" meaning, of course, the deadly Spanish influenza disease then devastating the entire earth.

6 Even though the Allies were then occupying a portion of western Germany, the British navy maintained their stranglehold by its blockade of all imports into Germany. This was effective because it forced the reluctant Germans to accept the despicable terms France and Britain were imposing on their defeated foe. The Germans had already been starving for several years, and this additional imposition was more than they could take.

7 Jackson was awarded a 2d Division Silver Star citation and another from the AEF. In addition he was awarded a French Croix de Guerre, all for his heroic actions at Blanc Mont on 8 October 1918, for his "courage in voluntarily establishing liaison." Perhaps his writ-

ing was directed toward that period in 1919 when he had not yet been made aware he was recommended for the awards?

8 This movement was initiated because the German government was slow in accepting Allied peace terms. The 2d Division led the "parade" eastward into unoccupied Germany and the 4th Brigade led everyone else. Soon, the Germans backed down and the scare was over.

9 First Lieutenant Clarence W. Smith, KIA 13 June.

10 I cannot identify either officer but have to assume the first was a U.S. Army officer, since I have no record of any Marine officer of the 95th dying at the time mentioned. I have few records of either sick or wounded, consequently cannot identify the second lieutenant.

12: Going Home!

Finally—FINALLY—at a formation of the company one afternoon, the order was read for us to go home! This must have been only less difficult to realize than the news that the war had ended. About 17 July we entrained and were on our way down the Rhine. Almost wildly happy were those men, going home at last!

The position was pointed out to us of Caesar's famous bridge across the Rhine. Perhaps that dear old general thought the job was complete when the bridge was finished. The real work didn't begin until boys and girls tried to learn from his own account how he did the thing.

As we came in sight of the Cologne Cathedral, we swung leftward toward northern Belgium. During the night the train passed through Antwerp and other war-famous cities. As we approached the French border, more and more did the country bear the marks of war. We saw what had been great factories, now blasted shells with every piece of machinery gone.

Then came the most widespread and complete destruction we have ever gazed upon. There were ghostly remnants of forests, with naked and charred limbs stretching spectrally upward. In those trenches full of water—what had life not been for men in those holes in freezing winter, men hungry and hounded by bullet, gas, and shell! Boundless wastes, every inch of ground pitted. And there were millions of poppies, much as we had imagined, and the silent crosses "row on row." There remained leftovers of battles, when men fought and fell. There was mile upon mile where villages had been in sight of one another, and now not a house stood. In a stretch that I estimated to be not less than fifty miles across, which before the war had been thickly settled, there was now *not one wall standing as high as a man's waist!* It was not hard to imagine the thousand heartbreaking stories back of that scene.

As the train neared Arras, the destruction was not so complete, but yet miserably torn was Arras. German prisoners were at work removing debris. The train stopped for a while at Amiens. The disfigured Amiens Cathedral was not more than about two blocks away, but we did not have the opportunity of a nearer view.

We came into Brest after more than a year's absence. A year before, the Napoleon Barracks, in which we had been quartered, had been surrounded by wide fields. This space was now covered with frame barracks that would house multiplied thousands. During the week in Brest there were boxing matches and other diversions. While there we again went through a delouser.

About 25 July we boarded the *Rijndam*, which was said to have been a Dutch cattle boat. (It has since had quite an interesting history.) Where the *Henderson* had brought over only a battalion, and these all Marines, the *Rijndam* carried several times that number, including army men, white and black. Instead of sleeping in hammocks, or on the deck, as we did on the first voyage, there were bunks about five tiers high.

I went on that boat with the perfectly good intention of refraining from all seasickness. But most of the joys of the trip on the *Henderson* were repeated on the *Rijndam*. To be sure, we were denied the pleasure of doing the manual of arms several hours a day on a rocking deck, nor were there any of the delightful abandon-ship calls. But it was the same old Atlantic, with lots of ginger in her spine. How many times I would have gladly parted with my Adam's apple—and every other internal organ. Several times I thought the happy separation was going to take place.

And getting sick was even humiliating. It seems that I was sick enough to lose ambition and pride; but there was something that made me feel worse, if possible. On board was a 95th boy eighteen or nineteen: yellow, weak kneed, lying, and brainless. Every time we had started to the front he had been taken suddenly and violently ill, with toe ache, or his health was endangered in some other manner. Nobody had any use for him. There on that boat were men limp as a rag, and this bird as unperturbed as if he didn't know he was on the water. That disgusted me with the Atlantic, though they say a fellow ought to respect age.

Among those on the boat were French "war brides." So far as I knew, no Marine brought back himself a wife. Not so with some of the men who had not seen the front, but had fought the Battle of Paree. During off hours at sea the brides and grooms sought seclusion on deck, though the seclusion was not to be had. The fellow who had won both a war and a wife was not envied by any of our bunch. Uncomplimentary remarks were made, though doubtless some of the brides were true blue and made good wives.

There were boxing and wrestling on the boat. While the bunch idled about, some fellows hit upon a novel idea of fun at others' expense. I don't remember whether or not it was with the aid of some mechanical device, but a sudden whirring, whistling was made, remarkably like the distant approach of a shell. Although more than eight months had passed since the sound of a shell had been heard, the feeling had not gotten out of our bones. For a fraction of a second there was an unguarded moment and a fellow *would dodge*.

When we were a few days out of New York a storm blew up and the boat was steered about a hundred miles out of its course to avoid the worst of the blow. Even then, the hatches were closed and heavy spray broke over the deck. Some men were sick for the first time on the trip. During the storm chicken was served. Those who could eat should have had their fill.

On the afternoon of 4 August 1919, after an absence of twenty-two and a half months, I saw land. A glad hour it was when we pulled into the docks and touched Old U.S. again! How strange, yet how wonderfully good, everything seemed. A short hike and we boarded an honest-to-goodness passenger train. And there were folks on the train to pass out the eats.

We were quartered in Camp Mills. Before the next morning everybody went through the delouser again. The precaution was taken to preclude the possibility of foreign cooties starting a war with American lice.

During the next few days I twice got leave into New York City to visit relatives. Before we had arrived in New York, General Lejeune had the men vote on whether or not to parade in that city. The boys wanted to go home as quickly as possible, so there was an overwhelming no-parade vote. But the decision got *twisted* before it reached the commanding general. (Doesn't that sound a bit suspicious?)

Early in the afternoon of 8 August we were passing through the East Side. Before the parade started we saw former members of the company. Among others was Sgt. William Conroy, who had been wounded at Soissons. A glove covered an artificial hand—he had lost an arm in the battle. The men had been urged to wear any decorations they had. I seemed to be in doubt, but I did not take the Croix de Guerre out of the snuffbox where it reclined in my pocket. I had never worn the corporal's chevrons either—except for a day or two back on the Rhine when I was ordered to put them on. It was a misplaced self-consciousness.

With fixed bayonets, helmets, combat packs, and probably gas masks slung, the column was formed at Fourth Street, and the march began up Fifth Avenue. Thousands lined the streets and looked out from windows. Along the way soldiers would be greeted by friends, or flowers would be thrown upon us, and the spectators probably did not understand that those in ranks could show no recognition, but must keep head and eyes ahead. From Fourth Street through the business and residential district we paraded to 116th Street, where the parade ended. We had looked forward to a terrible siege of it, marching so long at attention. But common sense was used and there were rest periods along the way.

We boarded a ferry to Jersey City, and there we entrained for Quantico. And Quantico we found to be a very different place from what some of us had left two years before. The place was in fine shape, with everything attractive and spic and span. The Marines there were in their spotless khaki; there were amusements and lots of good chow. If a fellow was meant for a soldier, he couldn't resist shipping over then.

From the time we had gone to Quantico the first time until after the parade in New York we were a part of the army and under army regulations. For nearly two years we had worn the olive-drab army uniforms. Now we were issued new outfits, with Marine uniforms. We were to parade again.

On the morning of 12 August we waited under the shadow of the Capitol for the parade to start. While we waited, my former platoon leader, Lieutenant Mills, walked up with his characteristic sprightly step to greet the boys. Some were not enthusiastic about seeing him. They thought he had left Belleau for no good cause. The United States Marine Band leading, regimental bands following, we paraded along Pennsylvania Avenue, by President Wilson and other officials.

It was 13 August. The day had come that we had long, long hoped for. But for me, at least, the day lacked the exhilaration expected. Parting with the fellows in the most intimate association, during storm and sunshine—this could not be without a touch of sadness. I wrote my home address in some of the boys' notebooks and I now have thirty or more names and addresses of 95th boys in a little book of my own. We said good-bye, and about ten in the morning, twenty-six months and three days after I was sworn into service on Paris Island, my little sojourn as a soldier came to an end—for all time, I hope. There were fellows who were going to "clean up" on a sergeant or corporal when that discharge was in hand, but the grudge was forgotten then.

I stopped two or three days in Huntsville to visit Lucy and family and to see old friends. It was a pleasant surprise to be greeted on the street by people who I thought did not even know me.

Then to Houston, over the Sap, and LaVernia! Papa and Mama had not known when I would arrive and someone told me they were visiting "across the creek." Before they returned, how I did look over every object of furniture—the old bookcase and books, the dresser, bed, the old dining table, the piano. How strange to gaze on these old familiar objects again. And how good.

Home at last!